A Suburban Mom:
Notes from the Asylum

Meredith O'Brien

Wyatt-MacKenzie Publishing, Inc.
DEADWOOD, OREGON

A Suburban Mom: Notes from the Asylum
Meredith O'Brien

ISBN: 1-932279-51-2
ISBN-13: 978-1-932279-51-1

Library of Congress Control Number: 2006935780

See appendix for complete list of previously published articles.

Wyatt-MacKenzie Publishing, Inc., Deadwood, OR
www.WyMacPublishing.com (541) 964-3314

Requests for permission or further information should be addressed to:
Wyatt-MacKenzie Publishing, 15115 Highway 36,
Deadwood, Oregon 97430

Printed in the United States of America

To Abbey, Jonah and Casey who give me
laughter, love and meaning every day.

To Scott who gives me courage.

Table of Contents

Motherhood, etc.

Pregnancy, Birth & Other Bloody Things

Growing Pains

On the Home Front

Random Ramblings

Introduction

Honest. Flawed. Oftentimes idiotic. Sleep-deprived. Messy.

That's how I'd describe the real story of suburban parenthood, not the fuzzy greeting card vision of motherhood filled with smiling babies and rainbow days that we see in diaper advertisements. Not the here's-the-moral-of-the-story, simplistic TV sitcoms with canned laughter where Type-A moms know best and the well meaning dads are dunderheads. Not the adoringly gazing moms who peek out from the pages of parenting magazines with pitch-perfect craft projects to complete in the cozy confines of a well organized kitchen, right next to the freshly picked flowers – from a home garden no less – in an unsmeared glass vase.

Parenting circa *now*, in the 21st century American suburbs, can be wonderful and stressful, in a comedic, over-caffeinated kind of way. And, in reality, it doesn't look the way it does in parenting periodicals.

When I first became a parent, I was sucked into the parenting culture, a culture that fed me all the wrong messages about motherhood. As I struggled to care for my premature boy-girl twins, I got it into my head that my life parenting infants was supposed to resemble that of some wryly humorous script carved out by Hollywood writers on a back lot somewhere in Fantasyland. I thought I had to be a model mom who at least appeared as though she had it all together. I thought that if my kids weren't a close facsimile of the best that they could be, then I had failed. I thought that only if I routinely got up early, exercised, showered, dolled myself up, kept my house clean, made my own organic baby food, made wholesome meals, organized great kids' play dates and birthday parties, kept my children away from TV and only did educational activities with my cherished offspring with what remained of my waking hours, *then* I'd be considered a good mom.

Sadly, my life didn't adhere to the script I'd created in my head after having submerged myself in women's and parenting magazines. I desperately needed sleep for so very much of my first parenting years and was incredibly cranky through a lot of them. My daughter ate a half dozen diaper wipes when she was a baby, but, ironically, not the homemade baby food I slaved over. My youngest son ate cat vomit when he was a toddler while I was busy making a meal he too wouldn't eat. He was the child who wouldn't sleep through the night until he was nearly 3 years old despite trying literally everything to try to accomplish that feat. The second time I gave birth, the blessed event nearly occurred in the parking lot of the wrong hospital (i.e. – not the one in which I planned to labor) despite the birth plan I'd concocted after reading articles urging pregnant moms to come up with one and bring along the necessary supplies, like the all-important hard candies and back massager. My post-baby sex life . . . well, despite all those keep-the-home-fires-burning articles I read, I found that trying to actually find a time when my husband and I were simultaneously awake, in the mood *and* ALONE was not quite as simple as the magazines made it out to be.

"Is something wrong with me?" I wondered. "Am I just an atrocious maternal specimen?"

My response to the disparity between my real life and the faux lives portrayed in the glossy pages was to chronicle modern parenting in the American suburbs in essays, pointing out how and where my life differed from the life I *thought* I was supposed to be experiencing with my kids. This book contains the fruits of that effort, 76 essays dating back to my early days of parenting my twins, who were born in 1998, through today when those twins are in grade school and the youngest is going to kindergarten. These columns – most of which were previously published in a Boston parenting publication *Parents & Kids* and posted on the web sites BabyZone.com and FamilyMan.com — trace the evolution of my life as a laid-back yet stressed-out, insecure, sleep-starved, TV-obsessed, news-junkie, Generation X parent navigating the labyrinth of modern parenthood.

The *Suburban Mom* essays are organized in five categories: Motherhood, etc.; Pregnancy, Birth & Other Bloody Things; Growing Pains; On the Home Front, and Random Ramblings. Topics run the gamut from social criticism (like the one on fashionistas trying to convince the pregnant public to buy maternity thongs and low-rise maternity jeans despite the teeny tiny inconvenient fact that pregnant women get hemorrhoids, and the piece on whether at-home moms have sold out their feminist sisters by not taking paying gigs), to commentary on the inane (like the essay on figuring out how to have that aforementioned sex life while three kids pound on the outside of a locked bedroom door, and the column about coping with school drop-off and pick-up car line rage).

This warts-and-all portrait of mommydom is for all the parents — and for those to whom they are related — who feel as though they're the only ones who routinely forget that it's school picture day and inadvertently send their kids to school with toothpaste and jelly stained shirts, who fret over their daughter's growing interest in transforming herself from an innocent girl to a pop tart who looks like a streetwalker, and who aren't sure if the nicknames they give their kids (like "The Thug") will become self-fulfilling prophesies. Or it's just for those who just need a good laugh.

And, while reading this, you can laugh.

I won't mind.

It's at my expense after all.

It's okay.

I can take it.

Motherhood, etc.

A Suburban Mom: Notes from the Asylum

The young mothers were telling each other how tired they were. This was one of their favorite topics, along with the eating, sleeping and defecating habits of their offspring, the merits of certain local nursery schools, and the difficulty of sticking to an exercise routine. Smiling politely to mask a familiar feeling of desperation, Sarah reminded herself to think like an anthropologist. I'm a researcher studying the behavior of boring suburban women. I am not a boring suburban woman myself.

"Oh my God," I gasped as I read the opening lines of Tom Perrotta's bestselling novel, <u>Little Children</u>. "That's me."

For years, I've been struggling with the stereotype of suburban motherhood. Since becoming a mother, moving to a house in the 'burbs and then surrendering to the fact that I couldn't fit my kids' three car seats into a sedan and was forced to buy a minivan, I've felt compelled to rebel against the images conjured up when the terms "suburban mom" or "stay-at-home mom" are uttered.

Those images, I have protested, aren't me.

Really.

Only a few days after I graduated from college, I began working as a daily newspaper reporter. In the years that followed, I strove to forge a career and develop an assortment of skills to help me advance in the journalism field. Then, in the late 90s, my husband (my college sweetheart) and I decided we wanted to start a family. The short version: We then had trouble but eventually wound up with three kids, including a set of twins (with an assist by fertility doctors).

Following the premature birth of my twins, I left full-time, out-side-of-the-house employment and spent the next 365 days barricaded in my house half-naked, trying to master nursing them simultaneously, keeping them clean and, frankly, alive, never mind remembering to feed and bathe myself on occasion. When the twins were about 1 year old, I felt confident enough to dip my toes into the professional world again and started working as a freelance writer from home, later adding part-time university teaching to the mix. And, although I do most of my professional work from my home, I still consider myself an at-home mom. I thought I had struck a good balance between family and career. Then I started interacting with the rest of the non-at-home parent world and found that many people viewed me and my stay-at-home brethren in the leafy suburbs with pity or even disdain. I discovered that people whose current careers can be summed up with the moniker "stay-at-home parent" are rarely taken all that seriously. Anywhere. Even at cocktail parties, I found that some would ask my husband what he does for a living and never ask me anything because, of course, I had three kids, therefore I must be at home, ergo, I must have nothing worthy to discuss.

By staying home with my kiddos, some believe that all of my education and professional experience has been seemingly wiped clean from my slate with the swooshy sound made by one of those handy disposable wipes that clean and sanitize at the same time. (Gotta love those convenient wipes.) Doesn't matter what college degrees hang in my office, I'm "at home" so, apparently, my experience and knowledge are no longer relevant. If I actually do get a chance to enter into a conversation outside of the school or at-home parent realm, there are many who are apt to ask, "Yes, but what *else* do you do?" as if parenting small people isn't job enough.

On TV, on the radio and in print, I hear and see people like myself referred to as merely brainless "housewives." We suburban moms are thought to while away our time watching Oprah and Lifetime TV, flipping through *Better Homes and Gardens* looking at ads for granite countertops while stuffing our faces with highbrow snacks bought from overpriced organic whole food stores. The image is that we all buy huge lattes at Starbucks, drive enormous vehicles and leisurely hang out all day with our friends, while donning our brand-name shades and funky slide sandals that would make Carrie Bradshaw proud. (Okay, so I do like lattes and have slide sandals, but they're not funky.)

We "at-home" parents obviously have no idea of what's transpiring in the outer world; we "just play" with the kids all day, you see, and have little interest in anything else, if you go by the stereotype. Ask suburban mommies about diaper disposal mechanisms, the argument goes, and you'll likely be given chapter and verse on why the Diaper Genie bests the Diaper Champ or vice versa. Ask us our opinions on Barney vs. the Wiggles and you'll find that we're veritable fonts of opinion on the subject. But some think that's all we know. For some reason, this shallow image of Stepford Wives-ish suburban moms in *Consumer Reports* approved minivans and the requisite mommy hair (short or modestly ponytailed), persists.

Don't get me wrong. I loved the book that got me thinking about all this, <u>Little Children</u>, whose main character is a highly educated mother of a toddler who has suddenly found herself marooned in stay-at-home-parent-land in a fictional Boston suburb, who hates the fact that people think she needs to be a "perfect mommy" whose children are always clean and fed well (on organic fare), but also has the kids' toys (only educational) organized in neat little wicker baskets lined with cheery gingham prints.

Perrotta did a great job of portraying the conflict between the love an at-home suburban mom has for her offspring and her yearning for an identity apart from that of a mother, something much more than a "housewife."

As someone who graduated from a liberal university where declaring oneself a "feminist" was as natural as breathing, the idea that in the 21st century, a woman (who never exchanged marriage vows with a house, thus making her wife of said house) would be referred to as a "housewife" made my skin crawl.

So when "Desperate Housewives" suddenly became a television phenomenon, I was skeptical, afraid it would only further erode the opinions people held about women who were at home with their kids. I hoped that the show would be a spoof, a satire on how suddenly bewildering it is for a new generation of women who were encouraged to graduate college and build careers, to suddenly find themselves sitting in suburban living rooms across from a drooling creature while the Wiggles gratingly sing on, wondering whatever happened to that hard charging career woman. Is she gone or just on hold for the moment?

The show surprised me. It didn't make at-home moms seem vacuous. Of that small miracle I was thankful. But as for the rest of the world's take on suburban moms, well, I think too many still cling to the "housewife" moniker. And judge.

Hide and seek

I was in the middle of extricating cold, congealed maple syrup from the insidious nooks and crannies of my son's booster seat in the kitchen when my stomach started doing "Mambo Number Five." It had to be fed. I had to eat, no matter what it took, even if it meant hiding from my children so I could sustain myself.

Almost two hours beforehand, I had been jolted out of bed by a loud, insistent "Mama!" holler from my toddler son Jonah's room alerting me that my day as his personal servant had begun. A half-hour later, his twin sister Abbey awoke and the two of them demanded that "bwe-fis" ("breakfast") magically appear before them *right now*. After sucking the juice out of their sippy cups in a mere 90 seconds, they quickly grabbed my ankles – clearly irritated that I was moving too slowly for their taste – and requested, "Moor duce." When I replied, "No more juice right now, you'll spoil your breakfast," two sets of feet began stomping on the crumb-covered linoleum in a fine exhibit of toddler rage.

An eternity later, from a toddler's perspective, I finally put their gourmet meal of toaster-heated frozen waffles, maple syrup and sliced bananas on their booster seat trays. While they devoured their food, I made some coffee, my personal drug of choice.

No sooner had I poured myself a cup and settled in to drink it, then Abbey and Jonah decided they were done and had to be set loose, *immediately*.

"Why don't you try to eat a little more banana?" I pleaded.

"No! All dun!" they yelled.

"Fine," I grumbled, getting terribly fatigued surveying the mess they'd made, feeling like I needed to start a caffeine IV just to keep up with them. I really needed that coffee. I did a cursory kid clean-up (a fire hose would have done the job best) and then flouted the warnings of the clueless, so-called child experts who say kids under two years old shouldn't watch TV (bet they all have nannies), and put on a "Teletubbies" video.

I went back into the kitchen, got on my hands and knees to

commence with the clean up, but then decided my growling stomach took precedence. I popped my cup of coffee into the microwave and started slathering a bagel with cream cheese. But then, I heard it … that distinctive sound of tiny, bare feet slapping the ground coming at me. If they saw me, they'd demand my bagel. If I had the temerity to say no, they'd torment me until I made them one. If I shared it with them, they'd sit there until all the cream cheese was gone and my bagel was covered with toddler spit. Despite their insistence that they were stuffed beyond all reasonable measure by my exquisitely prepared breakfast, if something better came along, like, say, anything Mommy was eating, my bagel didn't have a prayer.

So I did what any hungry parent who didn't feel like engaging in a life lesson about sharing and boundaries and appropriate eating habits at that very moment.

I hid.

That's right, I'm not ashamed to admit it, I hid from the little buggers to stuff my face.

I dove behind the divider wall in the kitchen clutching my bagel protectively. I wasn't going to cough it up to "The Vultures," as I'd come to nickname them. Listening with the attentive ears of prey being stalked, I heard their little footfalls hesitate and eventually retreat. Slowly, I poked my head above the wall and surveyed the room. No kids. But, not wanting to risk the sanctity of my meager breakfast, I hunkered down on the cold, hard floor and ate in peace.

Yes, I hide from my kids, quite often actually. And all of you who are shaking your heads saying, "This poor woman, she's obviously lost her mind," have obviously never been stalked by the two toddlers. You probably have never had eagle-eyed children watching your every move, waiting to pounce when you make the slightest mistake, like leaving a cup of anything unattended, even on the highest surface in the house, only to turn around and find that your toddler is drinking your coffee and will likely be awake for the next 18 straight hours bouncing off the walls. A pen mistakenly left on a coffee table results in a new kind of television test pattern.

Before I had kids, I never really understood parents who said they never had a moment's peace. Where ever they went, they'd tell me, their kids would be there. No place and no item, particularly their food, is safe. "Who runs their household, the kids or the grown-ups?" I'd muse silently to myself, when I had the luxury to ponder such esoteric things.

That was before I realized that trying to fold clothes when the kids were awake was a ridiculously futile undertaking. (Who knew how much fun it could be to roll around with freshly laundered towels and Daddy's boxer shorts?) That was before I witnessed Abbey and Jonah unmake a bed and empty a closet in under a minute, before I realized that reading a newspaper within 20 yards of Jonah was interpreted as an invitation to wrestle and before I learned that, to a toddler, every grown-up's unattended cup must contain an irresistible elixir that must be sipped.

I jealously guard the few creature comforts I'm unwilling to part with – like reading the newspaper and actually eating something that isn't a soggy, pre-chewed Abbey/Jonah reject. And, when the situation calls for it, I hide.

I have shamelessly bolted down the hallway upon hearing the pounding of four feet behind me in furious pursuit, and then quickly shut my bedroom door behind me in order to get dressed without having someone pointing at my butt and saying, "Mama bum-bum." Or worse.

When I've wanted to munch on something I didn't want them to have, I've hid around the corner or out of sight. I'm not above diving to the ground in instances when I'm having a barbecue chip craving and don't want to fill the kids with junk food, or deal with the laborious clean up afterwards.

As a result, I've gained a whole new understanding of why my father seemed to spend an inordinate amount of time in the bath-room when my brother and I were kids. It was the only room in the house with a lock on the door, the only room where he could go and be left relatively undisturbed. He'd go in there with the whole Sunday paper and be in there for what seemed liked hours.

Now, I get it.

So I've adopted it as my own refuge. A mommy's locked bathroom is her castle, now go watch the "Teletubbies."

My kid's better than your kid

It starts out innocently. You see a colleague at work or a friend in the drug store. You inquire about his little tot at home, the one who's about the same age as your little darling.

"So, how's Junior been doin'?" you casually ask about your friend's six-month-old son. "Has he started sleeping through the night yet? God, we still fight with Charlie every night trying to get him to go to sleep in his crib and stay there. But it never fails. He's back in bed with us by 3 a.m., like clockwork."

"Oh that's too bad," your soon-to-be-former-friend says as he audibly tsks. You can see it coming. Think of that steamroller that routinely runs down Wile E. Coyote in the Warner Brothers cartoons. Even though Wile E. saw the steamroller coming, he couldn't seem to get away fast enough. "Junior has been sleeping through the night ever since we brought him home from the hospital. Not a peep from him. My wife and I get to enjoy a quiet, gourmet meal each night, you know, just for us grown-ups, because he's in bed promptly at 6:30."

You paste a plastic smile on your face and secretly wish you could kick this person in the shins without fear of incarceration or a nasty civil suit. "Wow, that's great. That's pretty unusual isn't it," you stammer defensively, "sleeping through the night right off the bat? Gourmet dinners? Hmm, wow, uh, good for you guys."

"Well it's not that unusual really," your now-despised colleague says as he relentlessly continues. "There have been several studies done which found that if parents use a little discipline and structure, even in the early days of a child's life, your baby can and will sleep through the night."

As you pick at a crusty spot of spit-up, snot or some unknown baby substance off your shirt, you try in vain to think of some sort of witty comeback. But your mind is blank. In fact, you're still in a fuzzy haze, courtesy of Charlie who likes to kick you in the ribs while he sleeps and you lie awake all night. For the life of you, you can't even remember why you started this conversation in the first place.

"Wait? Is that my cell phone ringing?" you lie as you pretend your cell phone is vibrating and head in the opposite direction. "Sorry, gotta go."

No matter how you try to avoid it, how you try to be an adult, to stay above the fray, there is no escape. You find it at work, at family gatherings, at play dates and on the playground. It's a parent's silent mantra: My kid's better than your kid. Not only that, but I made her better because I'm the world's greatest parent.

You see the same sentiment expressed in those ubiquitous bumper stickers about how the fruit of the vehicle driver's loins is an honor student and has already been accepted to Harvard on a full scholarship at the tender age of 10. Parents either brag or are unwittingly drawn into comparisons between their kids in others all the time.

You start a conversation with a parent whose kid is around your kid's age and start talking about the little crumb crunchers. You have the best intentions, or so you think. You would never tell your friend, for example, that her kid is the clumsiest child you've ever seen and that your little sweetheart can balance the complete set of Encyclopedia Britannicas on her head while twirling a baton. And you'd never mention how your 2-year-old made you breakfast in bed for Mother's Day complete with a sun dried tomato and spinach omelet, while your boss's toddler just scrawled some crayon on a mysteriously soggy piece of paper. Of course you'd never brag like that. That would be too, well, too gauche.

But let another parent talk about things their kids are doing that yours aren't and you feel that vein start to throb in your forehead. First, you feel that pang of fear. (Should Mary be reading <u>War and Peace</u>? Elizabeth's kid has already read that. Sure, they're only seven, but what if Elizabeth's kid gets an edge in private school admissions?) Then you feel jealous that you didn't think of pushing your kid into doing it first. (You jot yourself a note to enroll your preschooler in Calculus Summer Camp. That'll show 'em.)

Parental guilt inevitably creeps in. (Sure, Marcy can't crawl yet. She's only three months old, but I just wish she could move like

Paul's kid. He's been crawling since he was six weeks old. Is something wrong with Marcy, or with me? Or is Paul just a stinking liar?)

Speaking of lying, let's get to brass tacks shall we? I'm sorry, but no one really believes that Junior was sleeping through the night when he came home from the hospital, no matter what his dad says. Okay, so maybe Junior does sleep through most nights just not *every* night. So maybe his father is exaggerating, but that's a sin that can be excused. Exaggerating is expected. What self-respecting person could even call themselves a parent if he or she didn't brag just a little?

But there's a big difference between patting your child on the back and making the other guy feel like a schmo, like a failure as a parent, like his kid is a no talent imbecile. I'll take those obnoxiously perky bumper stickers proclaiming a child's intellectual prowess over a parenting lecture from Junior's dad any day.

I just can't let them get to me, all those parents out there who cite studies and their parenting techniques as the reason why *their* kids are excelling or reached developmental milestones before mine.

All I have to remember is that one little phrase: My kid's better than your kid.

Buh-bye

I was certain I'd have the urge to weep.

I thought that the twin tiny, chirpy little voices saying, "Bye-bye Mama" as I closed the door behind me and I traveled hundreds of miles away from my babies, would set me off for sure. How could I possibly leave them overnight?

But the tears didn't come. Their father — a person who'd been a veritable stranger during the 18 months my kids had been around – sat across from me in a restaurant hours later smiling. We enjoyed the quiet. And, shockingly, it wasn't the angelic faces of my little twins that sprang to my mind as we settled into our seats to figure out what to order.

"Excuse me, waiter, can I get another gin and tonic please?"

My husband Scott and I hadn't gone out much when we finally mustered the courage to make our first overnight trip away from the kids. As with most parents of young children, we stayed in. A lot. In fact, our local video rental store named Scott and I their most valuable customers for renting the most videos so far this century. They made so much money off of us – and that's not even counting the late charges for failing to return videos on time because, just before the store's closing time, a naked child elude our grasp pees all over the house – that they named an honorary recliner in the store after us.

Going out for the evening — never mind overnight – used to be a major event in our household, particularly when Abbey and Jonah were little. They were my first children, born fragile and pre-mature, thus making me wildly, fiercely overprotective of them. (You know the adage, you hover over your first kid and let subsequent ones play in traffic as long as they don't play chicken with Mac trucks?) I followed my twins around with an invisible protective bubble desperately trying to keep anything dangerous or anything on the parenting magazines' list of top five choking items at bay.

And for this, friends and family roundly mocked me.

For example, just after Abbey and Jonah turned 1 year old, Scott and my sister-in-law Judy let them feed straw to goats at petting zoo at a local apple orchard. Convinced that the kids would yank the animals' tongues, catch some bizarre disease or lose a few fingers, maybe a wrist, I had to turn away in horror while Scott and Judy laughed at my paranoia.

As for my parents, they were known for offering the kids everything I wasn't allowed as a young kid. Whereas my main after-school snacks were fruit and Nilla wafers, Abbey and Jonah are offered hot fudge sundaes, cookies and candy by the gross when I'm not around. My parents have made no bones about the fact that their intention is to spoil them so they'll be little monsters when they discover that Mommy won't let them eat cotton candy while sitting on the couch at 9 a.m.

My mother once gave my barely 1-year-old son Diet Coke because she said he was thirsty. "Are you high?" I yelled when I saw her trying to covertly wipe the offending dark, bubbling substance from his chin. Parenting magazines and the pediatric associations all say that soda — never mind the diet kind — is bad for young children, I sternly lectured with all the verve of a first-time parent.

It's not as if I didn't think our relatives wouldn't protect the kids, it's that I was an insufferable nitpicker. The first time I left little Abbey and Jonah in someone's care, I typically printed out a customized, multi-page set of instructions detailing how snack time, dinner time and bedtime were to be handled, as well as how much TV was allowed and what programs or videos were acceptable. (Now I just leave a list of phone numbers and probably way too many verbal instructions. Old habits die hard.)

I once made my younger brother sit at my kitchen table while I watched him read the directions. I then gave him a pop quiz and had him sign a binding agreement because I feared he'd laugh the instructions off and feed them beef jerky while they all watched MTV's "Cribs" together. When I handed sister-in-law Judy the child care instructions for the first time, she gave me a look that said, "This girl needs to get out more often." My mother thought that the whole directions business was so entertaining that she put the list of instructions in her photo album. "You and your brother never came with instructions," she laughed sarcastically.

Sure, it was easy to make fun of the neurotic, first-time mommy. But I couldn't help myself. In the days leading up to my first overnight trip with my husband since we became parents, I was wracked with guilt and worry. Would the kids be okay? Did my parents know how to work the car seats? Did they know that Abbey and Jonah would eat trash (a la George Costanza in "Seinfeld") if given the opportunity? If they give the kids grapes, do they know to cut them in half so the kids won't choke? That they need to slice hot dogs into really tiny pieces? Would they let them imprudently invest their piggy bank savings in a risky Internet start-up?

This is why Scott and I, by the time the kids were 18 months old, had only gone away for one overnight. Once. It was too much stress. The planning, the list making, it all made me too anxious.

I must admit, though, that a few minutes after we pulled out of the driveway and embarked on our first overnight, I finally allowed myself to get excited about an adults-only 24 hours in New York City. And by the time we were sitting in a swank restaurant, partaking of a late dinner in a Cuban restaurant after a Broadway show, I didn't feel wracked with guilt. I was able to leisurely eat hot food (we're usually allotted five minutes of cold food dining at home) and greedily eat my dessert without having someone beating on my knees whining, "I wanna have some. Piece please!"

We didn't have our second overnight trip until many months later. I spent too much time editing the 16th edition of the Abbey and Jonah instruction manual, reflecting their new skills and propensity to get into mischief. Precooked meals, stocked the house with diapers, wipes, children's Tylenol (with accompanying dosage instructions) and Cheerios. Washed the kids' clothes.

And as Scott and I pulled out of the driveway, I swear I could hear my mother laughing.

Don't tell Daddy

It was 12:30 p.m.

If I pressed on and did that last errand without feeding my toddlers lunch, I was just asking for trouble. But I really needed to get that errand done and didn't have a lot of time. The kids' naptime was around 1:30. Whatever decision I made, it had to be quick.

Desperate, I went to a drive-thru, fast food joint.

It's one of those things that when I was pregnant and naive, I swore I'd never do, like when my husband Scott and I vowed we'd only feed the kids healthy food, no hot dogs, chicken nuggets, cookies or candy.

Morons.

We had decided that we wouldn't go to the golden arches — at least until the kids were older — and that we'd make sure their meals were always well balanced. We weren't going to be slaves to fast food.

Then I broke The Vow.

I ordered them two chicken nugget Happy Meals that they happily ate while still securely strapped in their car seats. (An advantage of drive-thrus: You don't have to go through the hassle of getting the kids out of their seats, dragging them into the restaurant, having them stand there and whine while waiting for the food and then fighting to try to get them to sit in their seats while eating.)

It was quick. They were happy. And I got all my errands done.

Later that day, I carefully inspected their seats to make sure there was no evidence of my indiscretion, like stray fries wedged between the seats somewhere. I even opened the windows to air out the car so the incriminating fried food odors wouldn't linger.

I smiled, thinking myself so clever, that I'd gotten away with my parental misdeed. Until a few days later. All four of us – Scott, myself and the kids — got up early to drive to my parents' house on the other side of the state. On the way, we stopped at a doughnut shop drive-thru for coffee for Mommy. (Mama needed her fix.)

As we neared the pick-up window, my son Jonah shouted, "Hey, chicken nuggets! I want my chicken nuggets."

I was exposed as the fraud that I was.

The no fast food vow wasn't the only one I flouted after coming face-to-face with the reality of parenting. I frequently shattered agreements Scott and I foolishly made before our children entered our lives. It's one thing to sit around a kitchen table and talk in platitudes about the best way to raise kids, the best things to have them eat, how we'll spend X amount of time reading to them, this amount of time coloring and virtually no time in front of the TV.

Then there's life.

Then there's the morning when you realize that you haven't showered in three days and that powder and deodorant will no longer camouflage the smell any longer. You decide that you will go mad if you don't plop kids in front of the tube while you finally shower. If you don't put them in front of the TV, you rationalize, they'll wreck the house or hurt themselves or call someone long distance. And if you don't shower, you fear you will soon turn into a smelly barnyard animal and your husband will start putting on a gas mask before climbing into bed with you.

That's one of the biggest agreements I busted wide open in the early days of parenting: TV time. It was easy for Scott — who got to leave the house and go out to business dinners where people didn't spit or hurl food, where the people struggled in a civilized way with how they could possibly eat one more bite of lobster or prime rib — to tell me that the kids shouldn't watch "a lot" of TV. He didn't have to try to go to the bathroom or shower in nanoseconds, all the while keeping an ear out to hear if the toddler twins knocked over something heavy or bashed each other unconscious. While I didn't put them in front of the TV for hours at a time, there were moments when I absolutely needed to get something done and they were being impossible. But with the magic words, "Who wants to watch 'Blue's Clues'?" I suddenly got a half-hour to finish what I was doing.

Then there was the ketchup thing. For a while, Scott maintained this bizarre belief that if I let the kids eat food with ketchup on it, that they'd never eat anything but ketchup. He likened it to a juvenile narcotic and insisted I was enabling an inevitable addition. (He used to have nightmares of having to bring ketchup with us wherever we went, of having to serve a bowl of it to Abbey for lunch, to the shock and dismay of the onlookers.) Whenever I used to take the ketchup bottle out of the refrigerator at dinnertime, he would demand that I put it back. "They don't need that," he'd say, desperately trying to keep the drug away from his children. But when he wasn't not around and the kids weren't eating, that ketchup bottle, boy did it do the trick.

Now I'm not alone in conducting this secret life with my kids. I know plenty of other at-home parents who let their kids do things that the at-work parents would go nuts over if they knew. There was one mother who would give her kid Oreo cookies on the sly, but the kid ratted her out one day when he told his more health conscious father that he wanted "the cookies in there" pointing to the telltale blue bag in the cupboard hidden behind the more wholesome Fig Newtons. Another mom – who, as far as I know, was never found out – used to let her kid have handfuls of chocolate chips when chocolate was expressly verboten in the father's point of view. Yet another mother let her kid run around her husband's office and bang on his computer keyboard, an explicit no-no in that house, at least when Dad was home. She argued that sometimes you just get sick of saying, "No," all day.

All I needed – longed for – was for the kiddos to understand what I mean when I said, "Shhh! Don't tell Daddy," and to not rat me out to The Man. And it'd all be good.

Play it again Sam

I can still remember the blissful sounds emanating from my hard plastic, turquoise Fisher Price record player when I was 5 years old. To my kindergarten ears, listening to my two very favorite 45's was the auditory equivalent of being served an overflowing bowl of peppermint stick ice cream, drowning in chocolate sprinkles and hot fudge while watching, "Sesame Street."

I could let the strains of Andy Kim crooning, "Rock Me Gently," wash over me for hours. And when Dave Loggins pleaded for me to, "Please come to Boston for the springtime," I was ready to pack my bags . . . okay, just my Raggedy Ann doll, my Barbies, some animal crackers, my fold-up Fisher Price record player and my two prized 45's to meet up with him.

The grooves in those vinyl singles were worn deep. Nearly 30 years later, whenever I think of that pair of 1974 hits, I can recall every detail, every "ahh," every heartfelt guitar stroke.

And so can my parents.

In fact, the very thought of rocking gently, or fast, or in any discernable rhythmic pattern, or, for that matter, coming or going to Boston, still makes them involuntarily shudder. I asked them recently if they remembered those songs that, in my mind, are symbols of my youthful introduction to the world of popular music, and my mother pretended to put a gun to her head and pull the trigger.

Now, I get it.

If you're a parent and your child gets access to audio/visual equipment and is empowered with any decision-making ability, you too will find yourself aiming a pretend, index finger gun to your head. And pulling the trigger.

Thirty years later, when my twins were almost the same age, it wasn't the hazy, groovy 1970s tunes that were running through my head. They were replaced by songs on the "Toy Story 2" CD. And when I wasn't hearing those Disney ditties, I was visually bombarded by so many repetitive images from the "Toy Story 2" movie that I thought the silhouette of Buzz Lightyear had been burned into my retina.

This juvenile obsession began at my kids' fourth birthday party when Abbey and Jonah got their first taste of what I've come to believe should now be a controlled substance: Animated figures who come equipped with musical audio tracks and accompanying orchestral arrangements.

Not only did my kids fall instantly in love with Buzz Lightyear the toy spaceman, Woody the 1950s toy cowboy, and Jessie the effervescent toy cowgirl, they wanted to inhale, digest and live "Toy Story 2," so that from every pore, from every orifice, the phrase, "To infinity and beyond" would be a way of life.

The video became an insistent staple in our humble abode. Over and over it played. The kids dressed up as Buzz and Jessie for Halloween. For Christmas, they got more "Toy Story 2" stuff, including a CD and a cassette. (My fault, I bought the stuff. For my offense, I should've been convicted and sentenced to community service to warn other unsuspecting parents about the dangers of serving as your child's auditory dealer).

Since that fourth birthday party, all I heard for a year was the over-earnest vocals of a woman pretending to be Jessie, lamenting the fact that her owner had grown up and discarded the cowgirl doll. Abbey loved to grab the red, hard plastic tape recorder with karaoke microphone (a step up from my turquoise turntable), and demand that everyone hush and listen to her Whitney Houston-esque rendition of the tune, "When Somebody Loved Me."

For Jonah, it was the Buzz Lightyear's anthem, "I Will Go Sailing No More," the melancholy tune where Buzz realizes that he, sadly, isn't a real spaceman, but merely a toy without the ability to rocket across the horizon and save the universe. While Jonah didn't make a major theatrical production out of the airing of the song, a command for silence was usually issued, so that his Buzz action figure could pretend to sail through the living room. At the appropriate dramatic apex of the song, I was summoned to put Jonah and Buzz aloft in my arms and fly them through the air.

As I grew tired of having the "Toy Story" CD repeatedly take over the airspace in the living room and most of the kitchen, I started to demand that the kids revert to their portable red tape recorder with a cassette tape bearing the same "Toy Story" music, and go to the far end of the house, certainly out of earshot.

But it was no use. By resorting to the tape recorder, Buzz and Jessie tunes became mobile and could follow me into the bathroom. Into the kitchen. Into the hallway. Near the door jam to my office.

Sure, maybe I could've hidden the "Toy Story" tape for a while, play dumb as to where the CD went. But, like a nasty viral bug that you can't shake no matter how much vitamin C capsules you down and how much orange juice you gulp, the music and my kids were persistent.

Buzz, Jessie and, for that matter, Andy Kim and the Please Come to Boston guy were the focus of juvenile obsessions that, as adults, send us screaming into the hinter lands, places without CD players or TVs.

The only cure for this juvenile auditory/visual media fixation, I thought, was to try to seduce the kids into latching onto another fix, luring them away from the "Toy Story 2" music and onto something else, while simultaneously trying to get them to watch videos other than "Toy Story."

It only resulted in feeding their addiction. While they'd initially become enraptured by something new, they inevitably picked one new thing to obsess about in tandem with the old standbys, the "Toy Story 2" CD and video. (Kind of like how my first obsession was solely with Mr. Kim, and then the Boston guy entered the picture.) So instead of being beset by "Toy Story 2" songs and videos, our VCR began to threaten to wage a work stoppage if one more Rescue Heroes video tape was played (featuring absurdly buff fire fighters with great teeth), while the CD player was filled with kids' music that had to be played to the near exclusion of every other kind of tune.

At least I could handle a mix of kids' songs better than the same set of six ditties over and over again. Maybe if my parents had thrown some other groovy 45's into the mix, they wouldn't feel like flogging themselves at the very thought of Andy Kim.

But, just between you and me, I think my mom really liked being rocked gently . . .

Kid rock

Some women have Oprah. Others have novels, play dates, meet up with others at coffee shops or long telephone calls. I have radio. Without being able to listen to the radio – my personal coping mechanism to remind me that I am a full grown, thinking adult and not a Nick Jr. disciple – I think I'd go mad.

But, by the time my twins grew into preschoolers and my youngest son became a toddler, I started to worry about whether my daily radio habit would turn them into potty mouthed butt-shakers movin' to the groove, or kids who'd ask a few too many questions about reports about insurgent attacks in Iraq.

On any given weekday, I can be found listening to an interchangeable mix of contemporary music, news reports or talk radio. When I'm not tuned to a pop station, I typically have news or talk radio on, something I think can be a good substitute for TV news, which beams graphic carnage from throughout the globe into my living room and in front of little, impressionable eyeballs.

At first, I didn't think my kids paid any attention to the babble of the talk radio or to the music which didn't remotely resemble the vocal orchestrations of Barney or Elmo being played in the kitchen or in the minivan. Then I painfully learned that indeed, they were listening.

When my son Jonah was 2, he started marching around indiscriminately uttering, "You chump!" at people, potted plants and the cat. He picked this phrase up from a particular Boston radio talk show to which I am a regular listener. Surely that interjection would go over really well in play groups and preschool.

When the Sheryl Crow and Kid Rock duet "Picture" was a popular staple of contemporary music stations a few years ago, my then-4-year-old daughter Abbey asked, "Mommy, what does it mean when the man says, 'I was off to drink you away'?"

"Uh," I stammered. Should I explain the concept of drowning one's sorrows while we were sitting in a book store parking lot? "He, ah, he was just very sad, and went, uh, to drink a lot of juice to forget about being sad." After an agonizing moment of silence, she buoyantly nodded her head and that moment passed . . . only to be followed days later with an inquiry about her favorite female singer, Jennifer Lopez, and what J.Lo. meant when she seductively sang, "I'm glad when I'm makin' love to you."

When rapper Eminem had a popular song that was played exhaustively on even the tamest of pop stations – the multiplicity of expletives barely excised, if excised at all – Jonah became fixated on it, mostly I think because he envisioned an energetic, color-coated chocolate candy, running around singing, "Lose Yourself." When I'd lean over to flip the song off the radio, Jonah would shout, "No, that's an M&M! I want to hear it."

The jig was up when my husband Scott was in the car with us and that song came on the radio. The Good Daddy immediately reached over to turn off this terrible, corrupting influence when Jonah proudly announced, "Hey Daddy, this is M&M!" Scott's eyes sent lasers through my obviously addled brain, "You *let* him listen to Eminem?" I had no real response other than to shrug and to say that at least I turned down the volume well in advance of the hardly omitted swear words and that I didn't let him watch any music videos or TV commercials. Then I smiled weakly.

It was no better when I tried to wean myself totally off contemporary music and replace it with talk and news radio. I was barraged with questions about words like "killed," "child molestation," "raging fire" and "Iraqi ambush."

I was in a tight spot. As a news junkie, I craved the political and pop culture discussions. Debates about things other than whether Goldfish crackers should supplant graham crackers as today's snack, why it is necessary to wear underpants, or why it's not a good idea to wear a tank top and pink flowered flip-flops when it's sleeting outside just weren't enough to get my intellectual juices flowing.

But how could I listen to news or popular music if it had become unsuitable for my curious kids' ears? "Will I be forced to listen to Barney tapes? Sit in silence?" I desperately asked myself. It was unthinkable. As someone who used to work in bustling news rooms but was now around small children all the time, I needed something for me, something to keep my brain functioning above the level of explaining that one needs to blow one's nose into a tissue and not into a Barbie's hair or your brother's back. The children got to use the CD player and their cassette tapes for their music, certainly I could listen to my talk radio or music elsewhere.

And, unlike some of my selfless friends, my kids had no idea that when we were in our minivan that I *could* play kid's music but chose not to do so. (One time they inquired about bringing a tape into the car and I lied and told them that for some inexplicable reason, their music couldn't play in our vehicle.)

But, being a guilt-ridden mom whose stomach sinks every time Jonah wrinkles his brow upon hearing a news broadcast that anyone has died anywhere, I had to become a lightning quick censor. Once I realized that little people were listening – even if it looks like they're searching their armpits for rogue dragons – if I want to listen to news or pop music, I had to have a quick hand, ready to censor in a seconds' notice.

When I'm out of arm's reach and something unexpected occurs on the radio when the kids are within ear shot, I've taken to shouting various insanities unnecessarily loudly to drown out the radio: "Hey! Guys! Look out the window! Is that Frosty cooking brownies on the front lawn?" or "Hey, is that Daddy doing the Hokey Pokey in the driveway in his underpants?" As the kids dash to the window, I lunge for the "off" or "mute" button.

That way, not only will I shield their delicate ears, I'll get a little exercise darting around to hit the "off" button. Just don't ask me anymore questions about lyrics, particularly what Justin Timberlake meant when, in "Rock Your Body," he pleaded for "that a*&-shakin' thing you do" or promised, "I'm gonna have ya nakid by the end of this song." I have no *&-@#@ idea.

Passing down the pain

(Written in 2003, BEFORE the Boston Red Sox won the World Series in 2004)

I am a very bad mommy.

I have knowingly and cruelly passed my Boston Red Sox fandom down to my children, my 5-year-old twins, Abbey and Jonah, my 2-year-old son Casey.

Why would I do something so heartless as to introduce them to the cult known as the Red Sox Nation which hasn't seen its team win a World Series since the dawn of time, a team that has repeatedly come tantalizingly close to winning it all, only to repeatedly blow it, sending its cult followers into fits of self-flagellation?

I don't really have an answer for ya.

Maybe I can blame it on bad genes, I was, after all, raised by a Red Sox fan.

As a kid, I could often be seen sporting a four-inch-wide button bearing the dashing mug of my favorite Sox player, the unheralded right fielder Dwight Evans, to whom I penned a loving tribute when I was in grade school. The platter sized button big enough to have its own zip code was a staple on my navy Red Sox jacket, the one with the cherry colored racing stripes down the arms and the team name in red cursive writing on the back. When the Sox won, I'd be happy. When they lost, I'd cry.

I hold my father Jack responsible for all of this, this Red Sox Nation business, although he's as much a victim as I was. In fact, my family is filled with people plagued by this disease. My dad was unwittingly infected by the Red Sox baseball bug by his father, who was infected by his father before him.

My dad has vivid memories of spending summer nights during his childhood family vacations in New Hampshire having the tranquility of the lakeside cottage punctured by the static rasp of the ballgame broadcasts emanating from the radio inside the screened-in porch. His father would avidly follow each play, banging on the arm rests of the green wooden rocking chair at errors or blown opportunities.

Though Boston never came close to winning the pennant during my father's youth, he still bears the wounds from Red Sox-almost wins throughout his career as an adult fan. Just don't talk to him about the 1986 World Series when the Red Sox were one out away from winning the whole she-bang. It could get ugly. Profanity will be used.

The fifth generation of O'Brien Red Sox fans evolved in the spring of 2003, when my older kids, Jonah and Abbey, were sick one weekend. Yes, sick. And then I made them sicker, infecting them with a lifelong ailment by introducing them to the sport of baseball and, more importantly, to the Sox.

I probably should've given them a warning in advance before flipping on the Sox games that weekend. Maybe I could've said something like, "Watch at your own risk kids. Getting emotionally invested could cause a heart condition, heart ache and an irrational hatred of the New York Yankees. Maybe you should just go read a book instead."

But I didn't. I marched the sport, the team and the bug directly into their hearts.

Abbey took an instant liking to Boston's star shortstop at the time, Nomar Garciaparra. Jonah didn't settle right in on a favorite player. It took him a few weeks before he decided that Sox centerfielder Johnny Damon was his personal idol.

Their interests kindled, the kids and I would wake up each morning, grab the newspapers off the driveway and search the sports section for the previous night's scores to find out if the Sox won (the games usually ended well after their bedtime). They'd scan the paper for the words, "Red Sox" and then check if Boston's number of runs was bigger than the other teams'. At Abbey's request, we'd also look at the box score to see if Nomar had gotten any hits.

If games were on TV during the weekend days, my husband Scott and I would watch with the kids, patiently explaining terms like "bases loaded" and "full count."

During the season, when Jonah would wake up from a bad dream, watching a few innings of a Sox game while he was nestled in the crook of Mommy's arm was just the trick.

Then there was Casey.

By mid-August, Casey had renamed himself. He was Nomar. Ask anyone who had any interaction with this toddler during that summer and they'll tell you it's true. From the playground and play dates, to birthday parties, this kid refused to answer to his own name. This proved particularly embarrassing when he'd force me to call him by the shortstop's whole name while we were in a public place, as in, "Nomar Garciaparra, stop hitting Jonah in the head with that shovel! Stop eating sand . . . It's time to go Nomar Garciaparra."

Casey would frequently retreat into our hall for batting practice – especially during Nomar's end-of-the-season batting slump – and wildly swing at anything in his path with any object that was long and thin, like a wiffle ball bat, plastic golf clubs, legs from plastic kid chairs, broomsticks, whatever he could get his hands on at a moment's notice.

As the Red Sox season progressed and the team made the play-offs, the kids soaked up the excitement that so captivated New Englanders. All they'd talk about was when the Sox were going to become, as Jonah put it, "the best team in the whole world." During night games, the kids would fall asleep to the sounds of Scott and me either cheering or screaming, not just from bad plays, but once from me actually scraping my knuckles across the ceiling after I leapt from the couch to celebrate a homerun.

As a family, we watched as much of the Red Sox-Yankees 2003 pennant series as we could, including that very sad game where we had to explain to our kids the on-field fracas involving then-star Sox pitcher Pedro Martinez. And we had to concur with Abbey and Jonah's conclusion that everyone on the field was in desperate need of a time out.

However the most heart wrenching moment in their budding careers as Red Sox fans came the morning after the Red Sox lost Game 7 of the American League Championship Series to the Yankees. Jonah woke up, suddenly remembered the game and raced down the hall. "Did the Red Sox win Mommy?"

"No honey, they didn't. They played really well, but they lost."

He bit his upper lip. "Does that mean that they're not the best team in the whole world?" Jonah asked.

"Not this year," I said. Then I decided to level with him. "This is what it means to be a Red Sox fan buddy. But that's okay. They still played great."

He didn't understand what I meant and just walked away, disappointed, to share the bad news with his sister.

"Welcome, kiddos, to Red Sox Nation," I thought, "Lord give you strength."

Passing down the pain: Revisited
(Written AFTER the Red Sox finally won the World Series in 2004)

I owe the Boston Red Sox an apology.

A little over a year ago, I — a lifelong member of the motley group known as Red Sox Nation (RSN) — wrote an essay eviscerating myself for passing down my Sox fandom to my three children, likening that fandom to a form of child abuse.

"Why would I do something so heartless as to introduce them to the cult known as the Red Sox Nation, which hasn't seen its team win a World Series since the dawn of time, a team that has repeatedly come tantalizingly close to winning it all, only to repeatedly blow it, sending cult members into fits of self-flagellation?" I wrote.

Yeah, yeah. I know.

I was wrong.

And, let's be honest here, so were many of you Red Sox fans.

For those of us who put signs and stickers in our car windows (the ones that said, "Why Not Us?" and "Believe"), for all of us who stayed up way past our bedtimes last fall in absolute disbelief to watch the Sox win the World Series for the first time in 86 years, we were one big group of Faithless slugs.

Although I — and I'd venture to say all New England Sox fans — have always wanted the team to win, although our hopes rose every spring and fell every fall, most of us never thought that the Sox would ever pull it off. Ever.

I thought that by introducing my kids to the Sox, they'd learn valuable life lessons, like the value of perseverance through heart break. I wanted them to learn that you can still love something even if you have no shot at changing it or being repaid for your devotion (kind of like having a cat). By loving the Sox, they'd learn to love for the sake of loving, for the sake of tradition, of regional pride. They'd learn a lesson in good sportsmanship, as in how to lose.

Maybe the skills my children would acquire through their inevitable years of disappointment as Sox fans, I reasoned, would be good training for coping with the disappointments of career turns, of potential marital discord, of family difficulties, of nearly every human conflict. Ya work through. Ya stick with it, through it all, even through Bill Buckner's legs in the 1986 World Series.

And then the 2004 Red Sox, the group of guys who nicknamed themselves "The Idiots," taught me a lesson, a lesson my three kiddos (ages 6, 6 and 3) seemed to comprehend long before the grown-ups. I learned a thing or two about Faith.

My belief in the Sox was the conviction that, despite the devotion of the RSN, the team would always lose. They'd put up a good fight, send adrenaline pulsing through our veins at an alarmingly dangerous velocity, but would always lose.

But they didn't lose this time.

And on the way to victory (I still have a hard time grasping this victory concept), they marched right through the hearts of their nemesis, the evil New York Yankees. Not only did the Sox slay the fabled curse of the Boston-turned-New York-player Babe Ruth, they went into the World Series and took every game.

I was in shock.

My kids, however, never showed a moment's doubt. "They're the best team in the world," my kindergarten son Jonah announced matter-of-factly, weeks before October 27, 2004, that crisp night when New England had a lunar eclipse and pigs flew.

My 6-year-old daughter Abbey's Faith was challenged earlier in the year, after the mid-summer trade of her beloved Nomar Garciaparra to another storied, cursed team, the Chicago Cubs. After initially vowing to give up the Sox for a lifetime as the penalty for trading Nomie – she requested a Garciaparra Cubs' shirt for her birthday – by early fall, she was dividing her loyalties, keeping up with both clubs in the sports pages. By October, she was shouting, "Man-nee" (as in Manny Ramirez) with the best of 'em.

Then there was Casey, who had to stop calling referring to himself in the third person as "Nomar" after the trade and then assumed the name "Pedro" (as in Martinez, who was traded to the New York Mets this winter, there's another lesson there, but, why complicate things at this juncture?). The preschooler saw no reality other than the Sox winning the World Series. True, we're talking about a kid who still finds it fun to chew on crayons and eat flavored ChapStick, but his Faith in his team was unshakeable.

As the Sox entered the divisional baseball playoffs, my husband Scott and I tried to gird the threesome for what we saw as an unavoidable let-down. But they wouldn't hear of it. When we reminded them of the heartbreak of 2003 at the hands of the Yankees, of how they had sobbed, they just waved us away.

They had Faith.

We, of course, did not. We had Experience. Experience in losing.

After the American League playoff series rendered us sleep deprived with five-plus hour long games that ran late into the night – kind of like the days when we had newborns in the house – Scott and I were certain that the Sox collapse would occur during the World Series and would bring many dark days to our doorstep.

When that didn't happen, when we woke up the kids (who had fallen asleep in front of the TV wearing their Sox jerseys and hats) so they could see that momentous last out, when we popped open a celebratory bottle of champagne, when we made and received stunned phone calls in the midnight hour after the RED SOX WON THE WORLD SERIES, the kids just smiled, like they just knew it would happen.

Like how you know the sun will rise tomorrow.

Like they had Faith, the naïve Faith of children, the Faith I once had as a kid in the days when I sported a gigantic Dwight Evans pin on my navy blue Sox jacket and wore rainbow shoelaces in my hard white leather Nikes while rooting for the Old Towne Team.

Each day, I learn a great deal from my children. Love. Trust. Patience. Humility (oh, the humility). And last fall, I added another: Unrelenting Faith.

"Faith is believing in something when common sense tells you not to," the formerly cynical mother Doris Walker told her daughter Susan in the 1947 flick "Miracle on 34th Street," where the adult characters grapple with the question of whether the Macy's Santa

Claus is the real deal.

In the film, grade schooler Susan had Faith, despite her mother's entreaties that there wasn't a Santa. In the end, it was Susan's Faith that helped turn her mother around, open her mom's heart to possibilities she couldn't even fathom.

So, as the new baseball season commenced in April 2005, as the World Series Championship rings were distributed to the RED SOX in front of the Yankees during the Boston home opener, I was thanking my children and the team for renewing my sense of Faith.

Parental sex lives: An oxymoron?

Is it possible to have small children in the house and still have a sex life?

I know that other parents still have them, sex lives that is. Evidence of the existence of their sex lives is running around and ransacking homes in suburbs near you, eating all the breakfast cereal and stuffing whole rolls of toilet paper into the potty just for yucks.

But how? How do they maintain these sex lives? Is there a way to do it and not get caught, thereby searing torrid images of Mom and Dad into their kids' brains? How do they manage to overcome fatigue and get in the mood?

My husband and I have no idea. These remain open questions whose answers we're still trying to locate somewhere amidst the mountains of unfolded laundry and the unwashed dishes.

To say that having three young kids puts a crimp on our interpersonal relations is an understatement. It's not that I have delusions of steamy erotic "Sex in the City" exploits had by single gals on the prowl. But every once and awhile, I find myself wistfully remembering times filled with candlelight, soft music and uninterrupted moments.

The transition between having those uninterrupted moments with one's spouse and having to hire armed guards and install security gates which require fingerprint authentication to open in order to keep the kids away, crept up on us, slowly.

When we first had twins, we had neither the time nor the interest in sex. It seemed like a luxury we couldn't afford. And, to be perfectly honest, the luggage-sized bags under our eyes and the omnipresent odor of sour breastmilk just weren't big turn-ons. But eventually, the twins started to sleep through the night. We got more rest and, consequently, became more interested in one another (or maybe we just got used to the smell of baby spit-up by then).

"This won't be so bad," I remember thinking when the twins were about 9 months old.

But when they hit 18 months, they started nose diving out of their cribs. After their foreheads began to resemble relief maps, we decided it was safer to move them into their own beds on the floor so the high flying acrobatics would end. An unexpected side effect of the new "big boy" and "big girl" beds was freedom, the freedom to get out of bed, the freedom to surreptitiously creep into Mommy and Daddy's boudoir in the middle of the night only to find an appalling, sweaty knot of parental limbs on the bed.

When our third child was born (we actually got a chance to conceive our third child . . . but we were on a child-free getaway), he didn't start to sleep through the night until he was almost 3 years old.

We have realized that our pre-kid cavorting was definitely over. In order to find opportunities to have sex these days requires Stratego-like planning, to find time when: a) We can be alone for at least, say, 20 minutes, b) We both aren't completely drained of energy, c) We are both in the mood, and d) We are unlikely to be interrupted (thus having any budding mood snuffed out by the sounds of a scuffle over who got to hold the stretchy green alien guy the longest).

Not an easy feat, my friend.

For our four-point plan to work, we decided we needed two things: A door lock and a veritable library of kids' videos (or an always available "On Demand" cable option).

Though nighttime is when most spouses wind down and relax with one another, by the end of most of our weekdays, we feel as though we've been peeled like an orange. My husband spends a lot of his time running around to meetings, sometimes late into the night. I spend my time doing work at home and dealing with three small, irrational people, trying to get them to keep their clothes on, to not stuff pieces of bread in their ears, to eat their food instead of flinging it and, once they finally go to bed, cleaning up the war zone at the end of the day. Shifting gears and mustering the umph to psyche ourselves up to feel jazzy, sexy, in the mood *and* be clean shaven ("Did I shave today? Yesterday? Have I even showered recently?") can be an enormous uphill struggle.

We sometimes dabble in late night antics, maybe after a glass of wine, but there's always that fear that our littlest will suddenly appear at our door at an inopportune moment. It sometimes seems like we endure less pressure if we wait until a weekend day, put on a long kid's video (making sure to check the exact running time) and remember to lock the bedroom door.

But daytime encounters are fraught with their own unique set of obstacles. One weekend morning a few years ago after a video of unanimous pediatric consent was put on TV and we thought all three children were under the hypnotic spell of the soft glow of the television, my husband and I decided that, while we were both awake and willing, we'd be daring. Quickly retreating to our bedroom, we turned on the radio, lit a scented candle and tried to pretend that there weren't little people in the same building. We tried to focus on us.

But when Mommy and Daddy are alone together somewhere, sometimes even videos can become of secondary interest. Curiosity piqued ("What could they be doin' in there?"), the trio made their way to the hallway outside our bedroom. We could hear them approaching, followed by our toddler's irregular knock on our door. "WhaddaRyadoin'?"

On this particular, ill-fated occasion, their shadows loomed under the bedroom door. We heard them discussing what they could see if they crouched down and looked under the door. The kids then began shoving random objects under the door — paper dolls, Lego pieces, books — and demanded their immediate return.

After about two minutes of this, I began to think that maybe engaging in daytime relations wasn't such a good idea after all. Would we have to wait until they went to college to ever reclaim our sex life?

"This ain't happenin'," I groused to my disappointed spouse who was trying really hard to make it happen.

As we made ourselves decent, our toddler began to literally slam his body into the door, like a cartoon character trying to knock it down. My husband dramatically opened the door. "*What* do you want?"

"Nuffin. I jus wan-ned to say helwo."

"Well . . . so . . . did . . . I."

Bowing to the overachievers

Okay, I'm jealous.

Let's get that out of the way up front here. I'm an unpleasant shade of green courtesy of my being plagued by one of the seven deadly sins.

I'm envious of all you overachieving Super Moms. I've decided that there's just no way I can compete with you. I throw myself on the mercy of the court of public opinion and ask for leniency lest ye judge my slacker self too harshly.

It doesn't matter if you're at home full-time with your kids, if you're at home full-time and do part-time work (that's me) or if you're plugging away outside the home full-time only to return to your abode and parent until you fall down from exhaustion. Any mom can be a potential Super Mom. And you if you fall in the Super Mom category (definition of which will follow), I'm begging you to please take it down a few pegs. Or how 'bout a hundred pegs? A thousand for the love of Mike?

To whom am I referring? Who's a Super Mom? The well meaning moms at the playgrounds, play groups, PTOs, Little League, Brownies, your neighborhood. I'm talking about the women who are making my life a living hell because they appear as though they have got it all together, that they can do everything with aplomb, never forget due dates for anything (No mad dashes one minute before the kids have to leave for school, "You have to bring WHAT to school?"), perpetually look well coiffed, seem to volunteer for everything and prodigiously produce Marthaonian-perfect baked goods for every national holiday. Being an overachieving Super Mom is a state of mind, as well as a state of being.

And I hate them for it. Well "hate" may be too strong of a word. How about: I am wretchedly jealous of them? (Sounds nicer.) So, for all that is good and holy in this world I have this plea: Please stop.

I — along with my never-good-enough, laid back mommy brethren — strive to be good mothers. We try to make sure our kids don't watch too much TV. We read to them, give them arts and crafts supplies to use at the kitchen table. We try to keep our children's extra curricular activities to a moderate level. We patronize the public libraries and book stores. We sing our kids to bed at night and tell them that we love them.

So what's my beef?

Well, if you compare what I (a mom who has serious issues with the fact that I am always falling behind with my kids' school and extra curricular stuff) do for my kids – in between writing and teaching a journalism course at a university – to what Super Moms manage to do, my contributions pale in comparison. Makes me look like a slug.

I know, I know. I'm not in high school any more. I should be confident enough in myself and my mothering to not care what other moms do. I shouldn't try to keep up with them. But it kills me that, with all that I do for my kids, I still feel like a loafer, particularly when my kids comment on what Johnny's mom did for their class and then ask why I haven't baked anything or read to the class in a long time.

This is what I'm up against:

Never forget. The mothers of which I speak rarely if ever appear to flake out and accidentally blow off dental appointments or forget permission slips, order forms or that it's school picture day and let their preschoolers dress themselves and "comb" their own hair. (My twins' 4-year-old preschool photos are a testament to my forgetfulness.) They never forget that their school library books were due four weeks ago, never forget that their preschooler DOES have school today (It's not Friday, it's Thursday!) and have to frantically shove everyone into the van and drive to school while still wearing plaid pajama bottoms with a baseball cap pulled down over unkempt hair.

Tireless school volunteers. By the time my two older kids were in preschool, I had a newborn baby. And, seeing as though the preschool didn't want me to bring my baby to the preschool, I couldn't volunteer to help out in the classroom. When the twins were in kindergarten and the youngest was in preschool, I did volunteer to read to my kindergarteners' class, but couldn't volunteer as frequently as the other moms for math day, Valentine's store duty, to serve as a literacy tutor, a computer room helper, craft helper, etc. I also couldn't volunteer at the preschool for my youngest because of scheduling conflicts.

But if you're an overachieving mom, not only do you find a way to volunteer during the school day, but you make time on the weekends – when louses like me finally get a break from 24/7 parenting and need to chill with my family – to do things like volunteer to spruce up the school grounds, run bake sales and do PTO activities. By the time the weekends roll around, after my kids have sapped the life out of me for five days when my husband had meetings every night of the week, the last thing I want to think about is organizing another school activity. (Which is why, of course, both Scott and I volunteered to coach our kids' sports teams. Go figure. Guilt got to us.)

Non-stop gift givers. I don't know what my problem is. I can never remember that, in the 21st century, many parents dole out special gift bags for everyone their child knows for nearly every holiday. I cannot seem to remember that, in addition to sitting my kindergarteners and my preschooler down to write dozens of Valentines for everyone in their class, in their play group and in their immediate family, as well as a special one for Daddy, that overachieving moms (of which I am not) get (better yet make) Valentine goodies and candies for their friends to be put inside decorated goodie bags. A few years ago, I was one of the only parents whose daughter didn't give everyone in her dance class a Valentine and candy. Schmuck.

My gifts for my children's teachers at Christmas time, excuse me, during the Winter Solstice observation? Handmade picture frames? Gift certificates for teaching materials? A laminator? Serving platters? Nope, a handwritten letter thanking them for their individual contributions to my children's education along with a packet of gift certificates to the local coffee shop, which has a drive-thru window and peddles the non-controlled substance known as caffeine. (Go ahead, call me cheap.)

Energetic craft proctors. I never cease to be amazed by the great lengths some mothers go to in creating unbelievable craft projects with their children, particularly to hand in as school assignments. There are some moms who oversee projects in every medium for their kids to master – not just the finger paint, crayons, markers, construction paper, kid scissors, chalk, glue and Play Dough I have at my house. These are ladies who dabble in complicated, and very messy projects, where their kids make wooden objects, grow their own gardens, decoupage . . . the list is exhausting. I just put the craft supplies on the table and, in my laissez faire manner, let them go to it after some cursory directions.

Perfect children's birthday parties. Here's a summary of my kids' birthday parties: A kiddie pool in the back yard. Cake. Pizza. Tacky decorations in the form of the cartoon character du jour with accompanying balloons. A flat cake from the local grocery store with the character's likeness and my kids' names in colored frosting. A goodie bag of a few token gifts. (Full disclosure: One time, my daughter and six friends went to Ben & Jerry's for her birthday where the big activity, other than eating ice cream, was tie-dying T-shirts.)

This, my friends, is a mere blip on the party radar compared to some of the other blockbuster extravaganzas some people throw for their kids. (Not that I'm being competitive . . .) I'm talking about inviting everyone the child knows (20-30 kids), making unbelievably generous goodie bags that include hard cover books, hiring children's entertainers (sometimes for a *toddler's* birthday), hosting events in exotic locales, organizing themed games and activities, hanging pitch perfect decorations and having homemade cakes fashioned and frosted in unique shapes, any shape other than flat.

One good friend of mine, who had a Dora the Explorer themed party for her then-toddler daughter, actually handmade backpacks out of a beautiful fabric for each child. Inside of the backpacks, she put homemade maps – for the kiddos to follow to find the piñata – and other assorted "explorer" items. (Sorry Kerry, but I wouldn't put you in the Super Mom category; you're a mere mortal like me, but on this particular occasion, we hated you.)

I don't dislike these overachieving moms mind you, though I must confess that I do silently curse when I see some of them break out unexpected goodie bags to celebrate Bastille Day and bring the teachers tree saplings bearing exquisite fabric bows (that they learned to tie in their bow-tying class at the local craft store) on Arbor Day. I would love to be them, if only I had the talent, the patience, the wallet, the energy and the memory.

Frankly, and I'm a terribly selfish mommy in saying this, but by the time I get my trio of crumb crunchers to bed at night and try to put the house in some sort of order, I'd rather read a newspaper, book or magazine, or kick back in front of one of my favorite TV shows than bake or fuss over 100 goodie bags for kids who have too many things already and who won't even appreciate the work that people put into the bags.

I'm throwing in the white towel to the overachieving Super Moms. Well, it's not really white anymore. It's kind of a dingy eggshell, kind of like the "before" examples in those bleach commercials. I'm just gonna watch my "Alias" and "Once and Again" DVDs, ignore the not-so-white tone of that towel, and call it a day.

Desperate for real desperation

Amid the skimpy outfits and ample bouncing bosoms displayed on ABC's mega-hit "Desperate Housewives," I've discovered something surprising: A glimpse of reality.

It's not everyday that the real life desperation of women who stay at home to care for their kids is portrayed on television in a way that doesn't challenge a mother's love and devotion to her children, or her competency to care for them. Or that doesn't assert in a patronizing backhand, that staying at home with one's children is a pampered luxury.

An early episode in the first season of "Desperate Housewives" — meant to be cotton candy for my mind — actually brought tears to my eyes instead of sugar to my system.

A character who is a former executive turned stay-at-home mom for four little hellions was portrayed as having a full-blown meltdown as her offspring marauded through her home, willfully disregarding her pleas for calm. Left to parent alone on one too many nights because her husband is off working and traveling everywhere but through his front door (hmm, sounds familiar), the mom fantasized about chucking several pieces of dishware to the floor and a tub of peanut butter through the kitchen window, then putting a handgun to her temple. Horrified by the wanderings of her mind, she gathered her kids together, safely dropped them off at a friend's house and left saying she just couldn't do it any longer.

Her friends (all perfectly attired mind you, sexy to boot) later found the emotionally broken woman staring at an empty soccer field. They admitted to her that they'd lost their cool numerous times when their kids drove them to the brink and that they often felt as though they had no idea what they're doing as parents. "Why didn't you ever tell me?" the mom sobbed.

No matter how many times or in how many ways parents are told that raising kids on a full-time basis is hard, the notion never really seems to sink in until they experience it first-hand, until they've been worn down by day after day of incessant demands, floor scrubbing to get rid of various repulsive spills and unspeakable substances (both organic and inorganic), fruitless cooking (since no one ever eats the food), refereeing between siblings (I could use a striped shirt and whistle), prying sobbing children off their legs at preschool drop-offs, providing educationally oriented entertainment (The "ABC" song is the soundtrack of my dreams), potty-training (don't get me started) and sleep deprivation from a nightmare plagued grade schooler, all the while enduring a household decibel level that rivals a space shuttle launch.

It's a rarity for today's parents to feel comfortable enough to openly share their frustrations, their fears or parental miscues without worrying about being perceived as bad parents. Too many think that every other parent is a paragon of rational perfection and peacefulness while they themselves must be the ones with no clue who shout like bears behind closed doors.

In an era when parents fear legal and social retribution for any form of punishment they may utilize to discipline their kids, when parents are pressured to plan every moment of their children's days with enrichment activities in order to prepare them for an Ivy future and to present a perfectionist front to the world, for an at-home parent to admit that she sometimes feels like she's drowning seems in poor taste, after all, the reasoning goes, she should be grateful she has this "luxury" to be with her kids.

Honesty about parenting is hard to find, particularly amid magazine covers dotted with perpetually smiling children with the headlines promise the answers to how to stop your children from whining (bet ear plugs aren't among the suggestions) and how to potty-train in one day.

To be honest myself, there are times when I've felt that gut level pang of despair, particularly when I've had no break from caring for my three young kiddos for days. Granted, I've never dropped them off at a neighbor's house or dreamt of putting a gun to my head, but I've been tempted to send some of my dishware crashing to the floor.

To see those feelings validated, dramatized on network television where we're typically treated to an onslaught of goofy family sitcoms which inevitably have some subtle-as-a-brick moral lesson to bestow upon its audience, was a revelation to me, a signal, perhaps that it will someday become socially acceptable to talk about the frustrations of parenthood without having one's love and devotion for one's family called into question.

Being an at-home parent to small people is exhausting work which takes an emotional toll on its practitioners. Yes, the job has tremendous value and offers emotional gratification, but make no mistake about it, there are days when even those of us who may seem like we've got it together fantasize about chucking a tub of peanut butter through the kitchen window and playing hooky for an afternoon.

Hot mommies

I tried not to take it personally. But I couldn't help myself.

"Why can't moms just dress like moms?" whined a radio talk show host following the publication of a *USA Today* article (and later a "Today Show" segment) about mothers in their 20s-40s who still desire to be (*stop the presses!*) attractive.

I felt like they were, in some respects, talking about me.

After listening to callers to the talk show opine that today's mothers don't know their place, I came to the conclusion that far too many people must be nostalgic for the days when housecoats were the rage and when moms submitted the keys to their sexuality to their ob/gyn in the delivery room.

But wait. We need the back story:

In a piece provocatively entitled, "Mommy hottest," *USA Today* published an article about mothers who have dared to remain fashionable and, in some cases, sexy.

Here's a little sample: "Mom has come a long way, baby. Of course, she's far beyond the ironed and buttoned-up June Cleaver archetype . . . She pays attention to trends, assiduously avoiding anything pleated, tapered or high-waisted (the blueprint for the mom jeans memorably lampooned in a "Saturday Night Live" sketch)."

A color photo of a 28-year-old Virginia mom wearing a lower cut blouse, form fitting jeans and heels while playing with her infant, accompanied the article. Svelte celebrity moms — from the fictional "Desperate Housewives" to thirtysomething actress Uma Thurman, mom of two, who is frequently photographed in midriff bearing attire — were mentioned as new mommy fashion icons.

On the day the article was printed, I listened to callers on a Boston radio show complain that women who wear not just sexy, but simply fashion-conscious clothing are selfish, are trying to "beat the clock" and are trying to tell the world that they're "on the market."

USA Today later ran two letters to the editor from readers responding to the article, including one that lambasted a 36-year-old mom who had told the reporter who wrote "Mommy Hottest" that she once dropped her preschool son off in an alley adjacent to his school so she wouldn't be publicly seen in an un-coifed state. That mother, the letter writer seethed, "doesn't deserve to have a child." "As a 45-year-old mother," the letter writer continued, "my son's well-being and education are my top priorities – not my cleavage or the color of my hair. Of course I care about my appearance, but not at my son's expense."

Ouch.

The alley dropping-off incident notwithstanding (I would push a baseball cap over my un-coifed hair, never unload my preschooler off in an alley), I started making a mental inventory of my own wardrobe. Though I mostly own cotton and various L.L. Bean/Land's End duds, I do own some form fitting pieces, even two tops that would be described as in the "halter variety." My clothing choices migrate back and forth between comfortable and wanting to have a little bit of edge amid the child-induced food stains (like, for example, a form fitting white tee with a cartoon called "Margarita Girl" on it, which completely covers my stretch-marked belly, FYI). It depends on the day. And my mood. And whether I've had time to shower before trucking my three kids all over creation.

If any of the letter writers or talk radio callers saw me out in public with my small people on one of my spry days, like on a Margarita Girl T-shirt day, I'm left to wonder if they'd be silently making assumptions that I'm self absorbed, that I'm trying to act like a teenager, that I'm trying to send out signals to others that I'm "available."

I thought we'd outgrown all of this, all of this judging other women based on how we look and how we dress. I felt, after reading the articles and hearing the talk show callers (mostly female), like I was back in high school and that I everything about me – most egregiously, my fitness as a mother – was being assessed based on my wardrobe choices. I never realized that being a mother, in the minds of many, meant giving up my own sense of self, when, of course, I have the energy and time to dress like some semblance of my inner-wannabe-fashionable-self.

A sociologist/author summed up this recent phenomenon quite nicely in an interview with *The Chicago Tribune*. "Just as you can't be a working mother and be a 'good' mother, you can't be a sexy mother and be a 'good mother,' because in both cases you're being too narcissistic," Sharon Hays, author of <u>The Cultural Contradictions of Motherhood</u> told the paper.

Well, much to the chagrin of the *USA Today* letter writer and talk show folks, I waste my time coloring my hair, putting on make-up and occasionally going shopping for fashionable clothing. These things don't make me a "hot mommy" or a "bad mommy," they just make me *me*. And they don't come at the expense of my three kids… although perhaps those chemical odors from the hair dye do kill off a few of my own brain cells every six weeks or so when those gray hairs start to reappear, but no more brain cells than one would lose on a true "Margarita Girl" day.

Family drama

I'm what some may call, irrationally attached to certain, fictional, TV characters who just so happen to reflect my life, my thinking, my parenting angst.

I derive some degree of comfort from watching these characters struggle to live normal lives, from seeing that they don't exist in polished, Pottery Barn bliss, and whose storylines rarely end with everything wrapped in a tidy bow.

These characters populate shows that have no laugh tracks. No sight gags. No cardboard, one-dimensional mother-in-law characters. No dad-is-a-dunce let's-watch-while-he-duct-tapes-the-kids'-diapers scenes.

After my three kids are in bed and I'm seeking some TV-oriented relaxation (provided it's not the night for my escapism in the form of the spy drama "Alias," or the anti-terrorism thriller "24") I seek out family dramas (melodramas as some may derisively call them), ones that don't trivialize life on the home front, that don't mock parents like some of those nanny reality shows which use other parents' miscues as a form of entertainment.

Quality family dramas are a rare breed on TV these days, now that HBO's "Six Feet Under" has ended, and shows like "Judging Amy," "Joan of Arcadia" and "Once and Again" exist now only in DVD land. The only drama left on television which portrays suburban parenthood with any degree of insight and that isn't a sitcom, is "Desperate Housewives."

Though I was initially skeptical of "Housewives'" premise, I was surprised to find moments of incisive clarity about American parenting in the Lynette Scavo character (played by Felicity Huffman). She's the one who relinquished a high-powered job to be an at-home parent, secretly hated it and never felt like she measured up to the uber-moms who seemed all-confident. At the end of "Housewives'" freshman season, Lynette's always-on-a-business-trip husband quit his job and declared that he was going to be the at-home parent. An at-home daddy character offers potential grist for a meaty examination of modern suburbia, but unfortunately it's wedged between plots about cheating spouses and murderous neighbors.

"Six Feet Under," which centered on a Los Angeles family-run funeral home, ended in 2005. It dealt with very real, not always pretty parenting issues: Miscarriage, a spouse's ambivalent feelings toward a pregnancy when the baby might have unseen serious medical conditions and how a marriage can survive the domesticity of everyday life amid lunch boxes, Pull-Ups and Wiggles CDs. Its characters – which now live only on DVDs – wrestled with their decisions. And they didn't always make the best choices, like many of us, non-Stepford types.

People who know me are all too familiar with my obsession with "Once and Again" which ran for three seasons (1999-2002) on ABC (two of the seasons are out on DVD). Not as dark as "Six Feet," this show's two main characters — Lily Manning and Rick Sammler — are divorced parents of adolescents (Lily also has a grade schooler) who try to navigate a new romantic relationship and create a blended family. And unlike the corny sitcoms about step-families, this blending is awkward, tense and difficult for their children, as the parents try to be parents *and* adults trying to live their own lives.

Why I'm so attached to this particular program – I'm not divorced; my kids aren't teenagers (yet!) – I can't say, except that it is breathtakingly honest in the face of so much parental happy-faced posturing we see reflected back at us on goofy TV family sitcoms. Or maybe I adore shows like this as my own, personal response to what Judith Warner so eloquently depicted in her best seller, <u>Perfect Madness</u>: A preponderance of suburban, middle class moms who feel enormous pressure (from one another, from parenting literature, from children's "experts") to achieve parental flawlessness and be ever vigilant about every aspect of their offspring's existence.

I'm far from an ideal parent. In fact, I blog daily on a parenting web site about my mishaps. Watching family dramas such as these helps me keep me focused on an alternative message, an antidote to rampant, Type-A parenting: We're all flawed parents and there's nothing we can do about it.

While watching season two of "Once and Again" on DVD recently, I listened to writers Marshall Herskovitz and Edward Zwick (creators of "thirtysomething," tragically unavailable on DVD) as they commented on an episode about a 14-year-old character's anorexia. In the episode, the daughter's mom was beginning to understand, as Zwick put it, "the ways in which she has screwed up her daughter."

As I listened to their commentary — their labeling the mom as complicit in her child's anorexia — I didn't judge or fault the character. I could see from that particular episode, as well as previous ones, that she was trying, that she loved her daughter and that she too was struggling. From the vantage point of the omniscient viewer, she was humanized as just a person, muddling through life, doing the best she could.

When you watch a good family drama, you can sometimes find a character who leads a life like yours: Untidy. Uncertain. Mistake-ridden. And when I'm feeling like less-than-the-perfect mom, like I have no idea what I'm doing, I can take solace from these shows that I'm not the only flawed parent on the planet.

Selling my feminist soul for Legos?

I've been stewing in a bubbling, acidic pot of frustration over a debate sparked by an article in the December 2005 issue of *The American Prospect*. The article — by retired Brandeis professor Linda Hirshman — labeled people like me retro-1950s, Stepfordesque women with no ambition who are stabbing feminism in its beating heart and killing it for future generations.

Why?

Because I decided to be a work-at-home mom. Because I decided to leave full-time, paid employment to cobble together writing gigs and part-time teaching so I could be at home with my three kiddos (when I'm not in the classroom). In Hirshman's view, college-educated women who willing leave the paid work force entirely, reduce work schedules or work from home are feminist sell-outs who are not working seriously.

Here, I'll let you sample these choice Hirshmanian chestnuts of wisdom that sent me into a frenzy:

In discussing "high achieving" women whose marriage announcements were printed in *The New York Times* in the mid-1990s and opted to stay home after having children, Hirshman wrote: "We care [about work choices] because what they do is bad for them, is certainly bad for society and is widely imitated, even by people who never get their weddings in the *Times*."

"Worse, the behavior tarnishes every female with the knowledge that she is almost never going to be a ruler."

"Finally, these choices are bad for women individually. A good life for humans includes the classical standard of using one's capacities for speech and reason in a prudent way, the liberal requirement of having enough autonomy to direct one's own life, and the utilitarian test of doing more good than harm in the world. Measured against these time-tested standards, the expensively educated upper-class moms will be leading lesser lives."

As I make lunches for my preschooler, drive my daughter to gymnastics, help my son with his reading homework and do work-related reading of my own at night when the house is quiet, my life is considered "lesser?"

Weeks after the Hirshman piece first appeared, a woman who'd been thrust into the national spotlight some 25 years ago after she wrote an op-ed for *The New York Times* extolling the virtues of being an at-home parent revisited the topic in the same newspaper, only this time saying that perhaps she made a mistake. On her 40th wedding anniversary, she was handed divorce papers, found herself on shaky financial footing and questioning her life decisions.

"I read about the young mothers of today – educated, employed, self-sufficient – who drop out of the work force when they have children, and I worry and wonder," Terry Martin Hekker wrote. "Perhaps it is the right choice for them. Maybe they'll be fine. But the fragility of modern marriage suggests that at least half of them may not be."

"If I had it to do over again, I'd still marry the man I married and have my children: they are my treasure and a powerful support system for me and for one another," she continued. "But I would have used the years after my youngest started school to further my education. I could have amassed two doctorates using the time and energy I gave to charitable and community causes and been better able to support myself."

Good points. You need to be able to be self-sufficient. Taking time to do paid work when your kids are in school isn't a bad idea. Unfortunately Martin Hekker's public self-examination was interpreted by some to be one more piece of evidence that anyone who stays at home with kids is making a grievous error.

To add more fuel to the fire, syndicated columnist and host of the PBS show, "To the Contrary," Bonnie Erbe chimed in:

"Full-time homemakers of the female and male persuasion need to get over ranting against being looked down upon. They're not. But neither is full-time homemaking something you do for anyone other than yourself, your spouse and your children. It's simply not an ambitious or competitive pursuit and will never hold the same allure as pursuits in which ambitious people compete and succeed."

Parents who've made an at-home choice – whether on a long-term basis, or for a short-term stint – feel rightly angry to be swept to what's considered the ambitionless margins and told that their days caring for the future of the world are beneath them.

An advertising executive turned stay-at-home mom and part-time business owner voiced her anxiousness about being labeled in this way. "Why do I feel I have to justify my decision to leave the work force and take care of my kids?" Celia De Benedetti asked in an article in the premiere issue of the magazine, *total 180*, for professional women turned at-home parents. "Every time I talk to someone who works, or worse, works and has kids, I feel as though I don't measure up. My anger is a response to the suggestion that I am not pulling my weight in society. Is devoting most of my waking hours (and some half-awake hours) to raising children a waste of time?"

Apparently to Hirshman and Erbe, it is. De Benedetti should just be quiet, they'd argue, get a real, paying job and stop messing around with Legos and Barbies to be considered thoughtful and successful.

But by that measure, the first female U.S. Supreme Court justice's five years out of paid employment when she was at home full-time with her kids would be considered unsuccessful. Although Sandra Day O'Connor did volunteer work in the legal arena to keep her current in the field while she was at home with her children, she wasn't working for pay. What a slacker. The same would apply to the first female U.S. Secretary of State, Madeline Albright, who juggled graduate studies at Columbia University with caring for her three very young children and entered the paid work force for the first time when she was 39.

Authors Carol Fishman Cohen and Vivian Steir Rabin, who have written a book on "relaunching" your career after being an at-home parent, disagree with this mindset. "Indeed, there's been an implicit assumption that high-powered women who choose to spend time with their little ones will return to the work force in inferior roles, at best and, more likely, will disappear from the professional landscape forever," they wrote in *The Boston Globe*. "As Sandra Day O'Connor's story illustrates, women who opt out can relaunch their careers and, yes, their relaunch might even overshadow their initial professional accomplishments."

There's not a single, catch-all way to live one's life that will establish you as a serious person, as an intellectual person, as a person who is contributing to the good of society. And deciding to spend time at home with your kids doesn't nullify your worth or your seriousness. Or make you a "lesser" anything.

A Suburban Mom | *Meredith O'Brien*

Pregnancy, Birth & Other Bloody Things

Pregnancy jail

I just wanted to swim, to get the pressure of my seventh-month twin pregnancy off my back in some nice salty water. It was hot. Humid. I was cranky and desperately wanted to cool off. But I couldn't.

I was in jail.

Pregnancy jail.

When I was pregnant with my twins during a particularly hot New England summer, my husband abandoned me while I was on vacation on Cape Cod. Trying to save his time off from work for when the babies were born, Scott left me with my parents at the Cape Cod cottage my family rented each summer. Scott spent four days out of seven there. During the days when he was there, I was able to go swimming, watch 4th of July fireworks up close, walk around and do some window-shopping.

But the moment he walked out the door to return to work, my father sternly stuck out his right index finger and admonished his unborn grandchildren, "Now you don't come out of there. Your daddy is going home and you wait for him." My dad was absolutely terrified that I'd go into labor while at the cottage and that he'd somehow be forced to perform the gruesome task of helping deliver twins. We're talking about a guy who faints when he gets a cut on his finger and trembles at the thought of even conversing with a doctor over the telephone.

What pregnant ladies (like myself at the time) tend to forget is that the world around them – except for the losers on the subways who refuse to give up their seats for you (heathens!) – thinks that you're a walking, overfilled water balloon ready to blow at any minute with just the slightest little jostle. Everyone who's around a woman "great with child," as my dad likes to say, lives in constant fear of being on the 6 o'clock news as someone who had to put his rusty Swiss Army knife to use and use his shoelaces to tie off the umbilical cord after making a grisly, bloody delivery in the back seat of a car or in the middle of a subway car.

That's why, come the end of a pregnancy when all a woman feels like she's doing is waddling around and peeing (when she gets to a bathroom of course), people would much rather see her sit down. All the time. "Don't get up," they beg, fearing that any motion will trigger labor right there in their presence, as if the strength of her water breaking would surge from her womb with the force of a fire hose and pin them against a wall and cause permanent, disfiguring damage.

Worse yet, would be to have her water break while she's at some-one else's house and ruin their leather furniture. (Watch the looks a pregnant woman gets when she sits on nice furniture. "Just don't move," people shout in their heads. "Don't go into labor now.")

In my father's defense, he had good reason to be worried about me going into premature labor. Women carrying twins statistically go into labor about a month or so early. In fact, I delivered my twins when I was 34 weeks (out of 40) along. I was put on a moderate form of bed rest a month after getting home from the Cape. I had those so-called "fake" contractions – Braxton-Hicks – for weeks before the twins were born.

However during the time I was on the Cape, I wasn't having any contractions. I wasn't dilated or effaced. I wasn't exhibiting any signs of premature labor. But my dad was so paralyzed by the mere possi-bility of it that for the remainder of my vacation I was thrust into a veritable jail as he sat in bed awake each night with his fingers crossed and his lips moving in silent prayer.

I felt like a teenager who'd just been grounded. The beach was deemed off limits. I could hear the teasing of the surf from the cottage deck. And it took only five minutes to walk there (slightly longer if you're a puffy chick with two rug rats growing in your belly who gets out of breath easily). I couldn't convince him or my mother to accompany me. True, there were some pretty steep sand dunes to tackle to get there, but I was able to climb them as long as I had a strong arm to help me. Even the beaches that you could drive to, where there was no dune climbing involved, were off limits.

They were too afraid.

I wasn't allowed to go shopping or to walk more than 10 feet without being asked, "Are you sure you're okay? Why don't you have a cool drink and go lie down." Suggestions ran from eating something to napping. And believe me, I didn't need to eat anything. The photos of that vacation, particularly the nice shot of my shorts wedged so far up my rear end that I'm surprised they didn't stick out my nose, remind me of how much I didn't need to eat more.

My parents' idea of vacation fun for their preggo daughter was to put my sorry butt into the back of their car and drive me around pointing out things I've been seeing every year since I was 5.

"Oh look Mere, there's the town pier," they'd say with fake enthusiasm.

"Ah, yeah, didn't we just eat there a few days ago, when my husband was here and I wasn't shackled to the back seat?" I'd reply.

They'd take me on drives around Cape Cod to look at the scenery like I was 80 and feeble. They'd suggest that I sleep in the middle of the day when I wasn't tired. Or eat something like I was somehow emaciated. Those were my choices. At one point, I grabbed my cell phone and secretly called Scott, begging him to come back so I could get into the early release program.

Weeks later, when Scott went to a friend's wedding some 100 miles away from our house (I couldn't attend for obvious reasons), my brother Sean "pregnancy sat" me. We ate pizza. We watched videos. The most I was let out of the house was to help select the videos at the rental store and to briefly walk into a furniture store so he could pick out a bed frame. The entire time he was at my house, I swore he was sweating as though he'd swallowed a gallon of Tabasco, even with my A/C blasting. Any time I got up or moved, he looked at me in abject horror as if he was thinking, "Oh God, it's time."

He's his father's son after all.

The stork patrol

They descended upon us like a swarm of locusts.

First, there were the coupons.

Then the department store portrait deals.

The cases of formula.

And the capper, the dire advertisements saying that we'd better up our life insurance levels. Or else.

The minute you have a baby, the whole world knows about it. And I'm not just talking about your friends and family. I'm talking about people who you've never met, never did business with, and never want to run into in a dark alley.

Somehow, *they* always know.

It's almost as if the minute a child is born, the stork patrol lookouts send word via little stork phones and via stork e-mail.

In a warehouse somewhere in Topeka, Kansas, promotional letters are hurriedly printed entitling the new parents to a "great offer" to buy a bible with the name of the new family member delicately written on the front with a genuine glitter gun in pink or blue glitter.

In San Jose, the baby bootie-bronzing place starts melting more bronze in anticipation.

The guys who make the infant formula in Detroit start rubbing their hands together. "Hey Jake," the formula king yells to the head formula chef after getting off the stork hotline, "get another few cases together and ship 'em out. Gotta get 'em hooked on this stuff now. Gotta get 'em now. They try our samples, and they're ours forever baaay-bee. Cha-ching."

Not too long after I had my twins, little, unsolicited "gifts" started arriving in the mail.

We got fliers for things I never knew existed. Who knew that you could get a poem using each letter in your child's name in a beautiful pine frame painted blue or pink (it's always blue or pink) for just $59.99? Or a set of toy blocks made of 14 carat gold, engraved with rattles and teddy bears for four installments of only $99.19, sure to become a family heirloom?

Of course, we got the typical coupons for baby food, diapers, diaper samples, wipes and pain medication (to be used in the event that your precious little bundle drops one of those hefty gold blocks on her tootsie). Each package of coupons congratulated me – and it was always me, not my husband – on the new addition to the family.

But along with the promises of getting a whole $1 discount if you bought 48 jars of organic blueberry-rice-free-range-chicken baby food, was the unspoken message that by choosing their products and showing brand loyalty, I would tell the world that I really cared about my baby. If I didn't buy the organic food, then I was being reckless and wanted to fill my baby with sugar, starch and (*cue the sinister music*), pesticides.

Then came the formula.

Cases of it.

Delivered by UPS.

They were left all around our house. On the porch. In between the screened door and the front door. One case sat at our front door step for two weeks before we even noticed it (we only use the side door). And we never requested anything from them.

The junk mail kept coming.

We got pleas from so-called medical groups for us to save the blood in the baby's umbilical cord and store it at their facility for a small yearly rental fee in case our child becomes gravely ill in the future. Perhaps it would've been a good idea, but that note came a little too late. The cord had already been cut, but maybe the hospital could rummage through the medical waste pile . . .

But it wasn't too late to save our baby's first nail clippings so they could be glued to a little frame. The Nails-to-Frame-Keepsakes Co. could preserve our cherished memories for years to come, and at a mere $15 for a do-it-yourself kit.

The most diabolical of all the offers were the insurance pitches. Bearing cherub-like baby faces on the glossy brochures, the companies warned that if we didn't stock up on our insurance, we'd leave our kids vulnerable and unprotected. They used more subtle language, but the message was clear: Buy more insurance or your kids will wind up like the orphans on the 1990s drama "Party of Five," having wild teenaged sex, getting pregnant, arrested, drunk, unshaven and perpetually unemployed. If we had the right insurance plan, even if both my husband and I died, our kids could have Mary Poppins follow them around and feed them organic grapes for the rest of their childhood.

Most of the junk that filled our mail box landed in our circular file, which is lined with one of the 4,000 trash bags we got for only $89.95 with the guarantee that nothing we put in there, not even dirty diapers, would stink up the house and disturb the new, sensitive nostrils of a newborn.

The case of air freshener is on back-order.

Diapering Barney

It was 3 a.m. I was barely conscious. I was tired and very cranky. (I'm perpetually cranky, but at this moment, I was exceedingly cranky.)

My breasts were sore and brimming with milk that my newborn, twin infants were getting ready to consume. The last thing I wanted to look at or think about was PBS's Barney character, with that sickly cheery purple dinosaur face of his. But there he was. That purple Q-tip.

In my face.

Staring at me.

From the front of a diaper I put on my infant as I changed her. "What the?" I huffily muttered to no one in particular.

Apparently, I hadn't been in tune with diaper fashions. I hadn't really given much thought to the different kinds of diapers out there. In the few weeks that I'd been a parent, I'd just bought the cheapest ones without realizing what was pictured on the front. Now I was suddenly thrust onto the front lines of diaper chic.

But, for the life of me, I couldn't remember purposefully picking Barney diapers off the shelf and putting them in my cart.

During my next visit to the grocery store, I ventured down the baby/diaper aisle to see how I could've inadvertently purchased Barney diapers. As a brand, spankin' new parent, I was dumbfounded by the choices. It was much more than just a Huggies or Pampers world.

At first, I spent quite a while gauging the benefits of one brand over another, over certain models of diapers within a brand, over the "options" the diapers offered. "Options" is, I think the optimal word here, considering how much money the average parent spends on diapers per the lifetime of a child . . . an amount roughly equivalent to the price of a new automobile. The car analogy works rather well actually. Because, when it comes to diapers, you can buy the luxury model, the standard family car or the tin can econo-car.

Some top-of-the-line brands had quite a few perks: A built-in "special" layer of diaper rash prevention lotion along with softer material so as not to chafe sensitive bottoms, and a tiny audio sound system complete with computer chips that broadcast programming that teaches your baby how to speak Spanish, Italian and Cantonese. (One model in the top-of-the-line brand gave parents the option of playing Bach, Beethoven or NPR broadcasts instead of foreign language instruction.) The outside of these primo diapers was decorated with black and red pictures that scientific studies conducted by supposed professional experts say will mentally stimulate infants.

These top-of-the-line diapers cost $40 for a package of 12, but as the ads say, "They only have one infancy, so why be cheap?"

Those diapers were too pricey for me, so I moved on to the medium-priced diaper section, where the diapers there had computer chips that would only teach your kid how to speak Pig Latin and count to 10. They cost half as much as the luxury diapers, and, although they didn't broadcast NPR reports, they did have a black and white photo image of NPR newscaster Corey Flintoff from, "All Things Considered" on the front.

But I was still too chintzy to cough up that much for a glorified poop catcher, so I went to the cheap diaper section, offering models that only claim to keep a baby's bottom relatively dry, or at least keep any wayward excrement from sliding out of the leg holes. The one perk with this brand: Pictures of Barney on the outside. Ah-ha, so that's how I wound up with Barney. He was on one of the cheapest brands next to the store brand. I must've just seen the price tag, made sure the size was correct and threw several packages of them (I had newborn twins who went through 10+ of these things a day) into my shopping cart without thinking about the different models.

I didn't realize Barney was on them until 3 a.m., after being summoned by my daughter's cries that her diaper was soiled. I pulled one from the new package. There, under the glow of the nightlight, I saw him.

The irrational, angry woman trapped inside of me wanted, at that moment, to grab the phone and call the diaper company's 1-800 number to demand answers, like how these yo-yos could, in good conscience, mentally torment new parents by putting this creature on the diapers. I didn't want to think about Barney loving me or me loving Barney or Barney loving my daughter or anyone loving anybody. I just wanted to change my baby, nurse her and put her back in her crib, repeat the process with her brother, and then try to sleep for two hours before starting it all over again.

Was it too much to ask that I be able to tackle the aforementioned tasks in the middle of the night without being plagued by the likes of Barney?

But instead, I was haunted by this bloated purple face. I restlessly rolled around under the covers unable to sleep, trying to figure this out.

I love you. You love me. We're a hap-py fam-i-ly . . .

"Why would anybody put Barney on a diaper?" The question kept floating in my brain despite valiant efforts to block it out. "Why was his fat smile on diapers for newborns who can't speak, can't see more than a foot in front of them or recognize anything other than Mommy and Daddy?" My babies couldn't even hold their heads up, never mind look down at the front of the diapers to even see Barney, so what was the point?

Was this some kind of plot to brainwash my kids into becoming lifelong Barney fans? So, they could never use the bathroom without thinking of him?

Had I purchased the medium-priced diapers and had to look at Corey Flintoff, I can't say I'd be as upset. At 3 in the morning, his mug is forgettable. I could've easily gotten myself back to sleep. Then I'd only be humming the inoffensive NPR "All Things Considered" ditty instead of that whining Barney tune as I drifted off into what was now considered "dreamland" for new parents . . . maybe an hour or so of consecutive shut-eye.

Perhaps I should've turned the diaper inside out so my infants could show Barney what our family (or I) really thought of him. In reality, Barney himself would be, sadly, unaffected, as would his evil creators (unless of course I sent the results of my protest to them, but then I'd be jailed for making threats and my story would be reported on NPR by Corey Flintoff, characterized as a crazed, postpartum depressed mom who snapped at the sight of the loveable PBS dinosaur).

It would've made a mess, but I would've been able to sleep better, with a smile on my face.

Barney, reconsidered

Whenever I think of that saccharin purple blob with the incredibly grating voice, I literally cringe. But, as the years passed and my twins grew into toddlers, I had to put my intense loathing away in a lock-box.

I have long hated Barney. Y'all know who I'm talking about. That dinosaur. That one with hypnotic powers over kids. The one who's so patently absurd.

Who doesn't despise him, except for children and his creators who are laughing all the way to the bank?

Years ago, "Saturday Night Live" ran a parody of Barney featuring then-Phoenix Suns basketball star Charles Barkley playing a pick-up game with the pre-historic being. As Barney sang his anthem ("*I love you. You love me. . .*"), Barkley jammed over his head, ran into him and knocked him to the ground. It was funny in a sick way, funny, if you really didn't like Barney, which I didn't.

When I was pregnant with my twins Abbey and Jonah, my husband Scott and I vowed that our house would be a Barney-free zone, for Scott also found the monster repugnant. For the first two years of the kids' lives, we succeeded in keeping that vow (with the exception of Barney being featured on their diapers, but don't get me started on that).

We didn't allow Barney on TV. He didn't sing between our walls or appear in any form, including stuffed or portrayed on flat surfaces in the form of books or posters. Nothing, except for the poop catchers.

Then somehow it happened.

That insidious creature wormed himself into their lives. Maybe it was during that play date at a friend's house when she put on a Barney video and Abbey and Jonah stood, absolutely transfixed with the screen. Maybe it was at their play group when all the moms — as if they'd been sucked into a Stepford wives cult – would chant, "Clean up! Clean up! Everybody clean up!" when it was time to put the toys away. Everyone, it seemed, knew the song except for my kids and me, the Barney non-believers.

The final straw was when my neighbor — who'd been generous and fantastic about giving me her sons' outgrown clothes and toys — gave us a stack of videos, including some Barney ones. In a moment of weakness during a bout with the flu one afternoon, I popped a video into the VCR, not being able to stand hearing Elmo or "Blue's Clues" one more time.

And there was no turning back the Barney tide.

Not only were the kids enamored of him, but they actually learned some good things from the creature, like the dreaded "Clean Up" song, as well as stories about sharing and make-believe. The first time Abbey came over to me in her little squeaky voice and sang the "I Love You" song, giving me the requisite hug and kiss with innocent enthusiasm, I must admit, I melted. Not to be outdone, Jonah came over and gave me his rendition, complete with a hug and sloppy kiss.

I soon saw them imitating other things they'd seen on Barney, so I acquiesced and let them watch him on PBS. One afternoon, they lined up all their plastic kid chairs, put themselves and their stuffed animals in them and pretended to be on board a plane while singing a Barney song about airplanes.

Even I had to admit that as far as TV goes, this was a good thing. I liked the way they responded to the show. I liked the things they were doing and were suddenly interested in. Barney as a role model was turning out to be pretty positive. So, much to my chagrin, this former Barney hater began to warm (just a tad bit) to the pudgy plum mass, even if I simply couldn't stand to sit in the room when he was on.

The one thing I wouldn't succumb to: I won't sing that stupid "Clean Up" song.

Ever.

A woman's got to have some pride.

Princess no more: No sympathy the second time around

The first time around, I was a princess.

Untouchable.

The It Girl.

Friends and family made food for me, opened doors and cleaned things of mine that needed to be cleaned. I didn't have to lift a finger.

When I was pregnant with my twins in 1998, everyone from my husband to my family treated me like a helplessly fragile egg.

However, by the time I was pregnant for a second time (with one baby) in 2001, those days seemed like a hazy memory, a misty, surreal dream that must've really never happened except in scenes from sappy movies like "Father of the Bride: Part 2." And honey, I wasn't any stinkin' princess any more. Handmaiden would've be a better title, the omnipresent servant to my very impatient 2 year-old twins. Butt-of-the-joke would've also sufficed, as this last pregnancy became a source of great amusement to those whom I loved and cherished.

How was this pregnancy different from my first? Let me count the ways:

Omnipresent morning sickness: 'Twas, to my supposedly loving family, a laugh riot. Hey, let's shove a plate of liver and onions in her face and wildly guffaw while she gags. All things garlic make ya barf? Why don't I eat a clove and then breathe on you? Hardy-har!

Exhaustion: "Please, how can you be tired? What have you done all day? Watched another dozen Barney episodes and read a few nursery rhymes? Why in the world would you be exhausted?"

Started to look pregnant earlier than other women who haven't been all stretched out having TWINS: "Hey, you'd better call Goodyear because the blimp has some competition." What a crack-up. "Ya sure you're only carrying one? You're pretty big." Heartless bastards.

During my first pregnancy, when there were no kids at home

and no one making sacrificial offerings of diapers filled with steaming poop, I was pampered. I didn't know how good I had it. The second pregnancy — even though I was *only* carrying one baby – seemed much more difficult with no break from 24-hour parental duties and robbed of my husband's exclusive attention and doting.

Instead, I got a stand-up routine.

Truth be told, my husband Scott was a saint during the initial twin pregnancy. But with the second one? Ya know, when you mock a pregnant woman and write off her complaints as the crazed ravings of a hormonal psychotic person, you're just askin' for it.

When I was pregnant with Abbey and Jonah, every little thing that turned my stomach was quickly whisked away. Scott even stopped eating garlic, which he adores, because the garlic smell on him made me wanna hurl. I'd get home from working at a Boston newspaper, and he'd have a nice meal waiting for me. If he arrived home after me, he'd offer to make whatever I wanted and insist that I rest. I never had to slave away in front of a hot stove when I really felt like curling myself up into the shape of a "c" over the edge of the toilet.

During the second pregnancy?

Forgeddaboutit.

Just for the record, with Abbey and Jonah, I experienced frequent nausea but rarely actually followed through with launching substances into the porcelain receptacle. But during the second pregnancy, I was kneeling in front of the toilet with disturbing regularity. My hurling was so regular that Scott grew to find it amusing, but more on my darling spouse in a second.

I was so nauseated that I was unable to stand to be near almost all types of food. But being an at-home parent with toddlers, it was my job to make them three meals a day (accompanied by an untold number of snacks), limiting my vomiting to gaps between recipe steps. At night, I held off serving dinner for as long as possible, praying Scott would get home from work so I could barricade myself in the bedroom and burn rose scented candles after spraying orange room deodorizer everywhere.

One night at dinner, I was determined to sit at the table with everyone, a vain attempt to achieve some semblance of normalcy. Then I saw Abbey cramming chicken and rice into her mouth. It was all over. As I made a dash for the bathroom, I could hear Scott chuckling. When I came back ashen-faced, he said sarcastically, "Oh, so you've decided to join us?" he quipped. Then, looking at the kiddos and nodding affirmatively, he added, "Isn't that nice guys?"

Then there was my brother. On Christmas Day at my parents' house – where I ate virtually nothing and held my breath for nearly 48 hours for fear of being nauseated and blowing chunks all over the Christmas tree and my grandmothers – my brother thought it would be funny to thrust platters of appetizers in my face. "Hey Mere, want some shrimp? How 'bout some kielbasa? Chipped beef and onion spread?"

Five months into this second pregnancy, I frequently had the sensation that my heart was suddenly pounding really, really hard for no apparent reason. So I pulled out my handy dandy "What to Expect When You're Expecting" book and read that this symptom was typical for my stage of pregnancy. When I told Scott about it, his suggestion was to stop reading that book, insinuating that I was fabricating symptoms based on what I'd read, given that I was overly emotional and hormonal ya know. So this overly emotional, hormonal chick used everything in her power not to use that book to pummel him until he cried. Instead, the next time my heart started pounding, I grabbed his hand and pressed it to my neck so he could feel my pulse. "It's fast," he admitted (or maybe he lied to avoid a book pummeling).

The first time I was pregnant, had I expressed any teensy-weensy whimper, he would've come running with the first aid kit and the phone ready to dial 911. Not so with the last.

Perhaps there should be a special hot line for those women coping with second (or third, or fourth, etc.) pregnancies and our husbands and male relatives have lost all capacity for compassion. Either that, or they should be forced to wear a 30-pound fanny pack bound very tightly around their abdomens so that they can barely breathe, get lower back aches, suffer non-stop heartburn and feel fatigued by 4 p.m. On top of that, we'll make them run after kids in diapers all day, drink 15 glasses of water (as my ob/gyn has instructed me) and conduct mini-art classes with the tots, trying to comfortably bend over the burgeoning belly to wipe the finger-paint and Play Dough off the rug. Oh and try to potty-train them.

And when they complain, we can say, "It's all in your head."

To peek or not to peek?

When we told her, she cried.

For about 15 minutes.

The weepfest was followed by the most enthusiastic pouting I'd witnessed in my daughter Abbey's two years. It was followed by an uncharacteristically terse statement: "I'm sad Mommy and I'm going to go to sleep."

The cause of her despair? The ultrasound technician had just informed us that I was pregnant with a boy. My daughter Abbey — the female half of my boy-girl set of twins – was crushed. She'd concocted all sorts of fantasies in her head about having a baby sister. The harsh reality that she was going to be outnumbered by a duo of sweaty little boys settled into her little tiny brain like fog at dawn. But slowly, very slowly over the course of several weeks, she let go of the dream of a sister and began to relish in her role as the one and only daughter.

When I was pregnant with the twins, Scott and I expressly asked the doctors to shield us from gender info. (I wanted to know; he didn't. See explanation below.) But by the second pregnancy, we decided we needed to know the baby's gender because one of our kids was going to wind up bunking with a demanding poop and crying machine. We wanted to take our time, break the news to the aggrieved party gently, rearrange the room over a period of weeks and enthusiastically get the kid involved, you know, using all that parental illogic to con a child into thinking that he's really getting some cool bargain when he's really getting the shaft and has to share a room. It's like when we try to convince the kids that peas and broccoli are the most delicious things we've ever eaten, when we'd truly rather have some creamy mashed potatoes or maybe double-chocolate brownies.

And it's a good thing we asked the doctor to search for a little pee-pee on our unborn child. Had we allowed Abbey to continue to develop her fantasy of playing tea party and dolls with her sister, it's scary to think of how she would have reacted when informed that she was the proud big sister to a baby boy. I'd fear that in a moment when I was distracted, she'd try to dispose of him in hopes of getting a different version, something new and improved, which, would of course, come in the form of a female.

We didn't always think that learning the gender of a baby while it was still in utero was a good idea. Or at least Scott didn't. In fact I'm still not convinced that he thinks it was right that we found out for the second pregnancy. We had major battles when I was pregnant with Abbey and Jonah because I wanted to find out what their genders were while he, staunchly, did not. Given that these doctors all knew, I couldn't see why we shouldn't have known as well.

Yeah, I've heard all the arguments in favor of keeping it a surprise.

Please.

Surprises are highly overrated. After being in the pushing stage for three hours while vomiting during the birth of my twins, I didn't care about genders. I didn't care about who the children looked like, or how much hair was atop each baby's head. I just wanted to get Baby A out of there so I could deliver Baby B. In the hours immediately following the delivery, my main concern was about their health, not what was between their legs. After you've been in labor for 12 hours, big surprises aren't your top priority.

When I pressed to learn the gender of the twin babies, I wasn't harboring any deep seated desire to paint a nursery pink or blue, or to go out and buy exclusively blue or pink clothes. I wanted to know what the babies' genders were so we could make decisions about how to arrange the rooms and how many names to pick out. For example, just selecting two girls' names — complete with middle names with familial ties — was less daunting than selecting four names, two girls' and two boys' names.

But Scott adamantly did not want to know. "You can find out," he said after one of our prolonged discussions. "Just don't tell me." Well that's the same as telling me that I couldn't find out because there was no way that I could've found out and *not* told anyone. I couldn't keep news like that to myself. And throw on top of that the fact that I'm an atrocious liar, I would've blown it anyway.

I can just imagine myself in the midst of our name discussions and letting Scott get away with horrific name suggestions because I'd know we'd never use them. Take the Otis example. Scott was stuck on the name Otis for a while, despite the fact that I said I wasn't going to give my kid a dog's name. Although Otis Redding's "Sittin' on the Dock of the Bay" is one of my favorite tunes, I couldn't imagine naming my son Otis. If I suddenly acquiesced ("Sure, if we have two boys, the second one can be Otis.") Scott would've been very suspicious and probably figured out that we weren't having two boys.

He seemed to buy into the whole surprise argument, wanting the thrill of the "surprise" at the birth. Yeah, that's because it wasn't him pushing watermelons up his nostrils and bleeding all over the place. Yippee, big surprise, now please pass me the Percocet while you stitch me up.

So we didn't find out. (Damn it.)

With the last pregnancy, my lobbying effort – including the argument that letting the kids know if they were having a brother or sister ahead of time was a good idea – paid off, with one caveat. For a few weeks, Scott insanely insisted that we had to come up with both a boy's *and* a girl's name before the ultrasound, at 20 weeks.

"I don't want to put all this pressure on picking just one name," he said. (And I thought *I* was slightly addled by this pregnancy and the mélange of hormones coursing through my veins.)

"But you're putting more pressure on us by insisting that we pick *two* names instead of just one, and in much less time," I complained. It made no sense.

Needless to say, we didn't come up with two names by the time ultrasound day arrived. We did settle on a girl's name though. If the baby had been a girl, her name would've been Zoë Maria. And, what do ya know, we found out we were havin' a boy for whom we hadn't agreed on a name.

I asked the doctor to double-check to be absolutely sure it was a boy. She said, with utter certainty, that she could tell that the baby was male. Imagine my horror at spending months trying to prepare my son Jonah for a roommate only to have to renege and bring home a girl.

You've all heard about prospective parents who rush out and buy gallons of Martha Stewart "dove's belly pink" paint after being told they were having a girl, stocking up on scratchy frilly wear, doilies and dollies, only to find out that their son's pee-pee was playing a game of peek-a-boo with the ultrasound doc.

Before our son Casey was born, I had my fingers crossed, hoping that, come the delivery time, we wouldn't be treated to our own little version of "The Crying Game."

Great expectations

I got the relaxation tapes: The sounds of the sea.

I got one of those wooden, happy-faced massage thingies for my husband to press into my back during contractions. I had Jolly Rancher hard candies, CDs, the still photo camera *and* the video camera.

I had a birthing plan.

I vowed that my second childbearing experience was not going to be like my first. During the 12-hour labor with my twins, I didn't have a birthing plan to follow. The babies surprised everyone arriving 5 1/2 weeks early, weighing under 5 pounds each. As a result, there was a veritable throng of people filling my labor room. Each kid got a personal neonatologist and nurses, not to mention all the med   students eager to witness the birth of twins.

I didn't have a hospital bag prepared. I didn't have all the crazy stuff the pregnancy books say you should have for the labor, like a picture to focus on during pushing.

But the second time around, things would be different, I said. (Ha!)

By the time I reached the 30-week mark in my last pregnancy, I already had my hospital bag ready to go. As time wore on – my son arrived 11 weeks later – I kept finding more things to pack, things I didn't really need for the actual labor, like a baby book, my older kids' drawings, a journal in which to record my post-labor thoughts. I finally had to replace the small nylon bag I was initially planning on bringing with a much larger steamer trunk to accommodate my burgeoning collection of stuff I was accumulating. The longer the pregnancy dragged on, the more items that wound up inside.

"I want a quiet birth," I told my doctor. "Just you and a nurse, and the anesthesiologist when it's time for the epidural."

I planned for everything, except my real labor. The harsh reality is that with childbirth, as with child rearing, nothing *ever* goes as planned. I don't know anyone who has had a labor that went according to her original birthing plan.

Regardless of warnings from birthing plan naysayers, I crafted one anyway, dreaming of a fuzzy, five-hankie delivery like you see in primetime dramas. Instead, I wound up with a scene akin to bad TV sitcoms.

I started having some pretty nasty contractions five days past my due date. Let me tell you, they *hurt*, just ask my husband who fearfully cowed each time I let out a long moan resembling that of a sick moose.

When the contractions were about seven minutes apart, we headed to the hospital. By the time we got there, however, the contractions became sporadic. I was only two centimeters dilated. The doctor on duty (not my regular ob/gyn) told me I was in false labor (false labor my fanny) and essentially said I shouldn't return to the hospital until the contractions were consistently five minutes apart. Despite my claims that the contractions were intense, the contraction monitoring machine wasn't picking them up. I got the feeling that this doctor thought I was a whiny ninny.

Three hours later, the contractions were back in earnest. Lucky for me, my sister-in-law and her husband had stayed overnight at our house and took our nearly 3-year-old twins to the zoo the next day.

Curled up in a ball on my bedroom floor, I groaned and clutched the rough carpet fibers. I felt like I was being pummeled internally with a medieval, iron mace. A few hours later, the contractions were five minutes apart. Within 10 minutes, I was ready to push, and I was still at home.

Alone in the bathroom.

Scott stood frozen in place as I wailed, "Got . . . to . . . PUSH!"

"No, don't push. Don't push!" he shouted, quickly degenerating into cartoonish, panicked behavior. "I'll get the car. Don't push."

"I have to!" I howled as I disregarded his admonition and bore down anyway. His eyes bulged out like a blowfish.

"Nine-one-one. Call 911!" I blurted.

"No, I can get there faster," said my delusional husband, who literally had to drag me to the car because I could no longer walk.

In hindsight, Scott admits that he was not in complete control of his mental faculties at that moment. He actually thought that we could make it through a 30-minute car ride to the hospital in Boston in which I'd been planning to deliver. I couldn't believe my eyes when I saw him driving toward the highway. Had we attempted going to Boston instead of to the local suburban hospital closer to our house, we would've wound up on the evening news, likely as a cautionary tale.

While writhing on the car floor, I screamed for him to instead go to the nearest hospital some 10-15 minutes away. What was he thinking?

Scott even called my mother from his cell phone while driving 90 mph to tell her where we were going. The minute she answered the phone, I let out a gargantuan, "Oww!" and the phone signal began fading. All she heard was, "Different . . . hospital . . . in labor . . . Oww!"

I honestly don't know how Scott stayed on the road with me tearing at his arm as I screeched in pain.

Then the baby started coming out.

"No he's not," Scott said, shaking his head in denial and pushing the gas pedal harder. He pulled up to the ER entrance and dashed inside. "My wife's having a baby," he hollered to the woman at the desk.

She gently shook her head at him like he was another one of those overreacting new daddy types. "Okay sir, well you . . ."

"No!" he cut her off. "NOW. In the parking lot."

In less than a minute, I was pulled from the car, undressed from the waist down, put onto a gurney and wheeled into the ER. And indeed, I was right. The baby's head and the intact amniotic sac were protruding from my body.

After terrorizing the people in the ER waiting room with my animalistic wails, my son Casey was born less than 10 minutes later weighing in at a horrifying 8 1/2 pounds. I gave birth in the ER with only a thin curtain separating me from the rest of the viewing public, with a stampede of medical personnel buzzing around me. I suppose it was better than having the baby in the parking lot.

So much for the epidural. So much for the Dave Matthews CDs, the Jolly Rancher candy and the quiet birth. And we didn't even get to use the massage happy-faced massager. I endured hard labor on my bedroom floor on a carpet amid Cheerio tidbits and bagel shards my toddlers accidentally dropped that morning while stepping around me.

Just a few words of advice: The next time you hear the stork's wings furiously flapping outside your door in the form of any type of contraction, you grab that stork by the feathers, look him straight in the eye and say: "This ain't false labor, bub. I'm gonna get my epidural AND use my wooden massage thingie. I made a birthing plan dammit."

Mothers' Day for those who need it

Okay, so there you are on a bright Sunday morning in May.
That Sunday morning.

You've been up all night – the baby's teething and therefore not sleeping – and you look like you've just emerged from the dregs of hell. You've spent the week rushing around the mall and in an untold number of shopping hubs – unhappy kids in tow — trying to find the perfect cards and exquisite Mother's Day gifts for your mother, grandmothers and even your husband's mother. (God, ya can't forget her, then the dregs of hell would seem like a nice place to be.)

Not only that, but you've been on the horn with both families (yours and your husband's) for weeks trying to diplomatically negotiate plans for how you will all spend this bright Sunday in May. You've been trying to be accommodating, to make sure that Mother's Day goes smoothly for everyone. Except for you.

What do you, the mom of young kids, really want for Mother's Day? How about a chance to sleep as late as possible and then quietly read a novel in a spot of sunshine?

Not a chance.

It's Mother's Day, a day that is supposedly about honoring women for all they've done for their offspring. Unfortunately, when you get right down to it, what Mother's Day is really about is YOUR mother and mother-in-law, *not* you, the one who has the bags under her eyes as deep as the Red Sea and hardened teething cookie bits lodged in the fibers of the right arm of your favorite black, zip-up sweater.

I can't tell you how many mothers with wee ones with whom I've spoken who've have come to dread Mother's Day. They feel this onerous burden to make sure that their moms, grandmoms and moms-in-law are all taken care of — all at the same time, mind you, so no one feels slighted (oh the horrors of celebrating the actual day with *one* side of the family and not the other) — so that they're all treated royally, or maybe even taken out to brunch at some fancy place with cloth napkins.

Of course, it's these at cloth napkin brunches that the aforementioned young bundles of joy inevitably transform into an experience akin to ramming thin juice box straws under your nails. The kids — who'd much rather be eating PB&J in the sandbox (and you'd secretly like to join them) — pull down the blindingly white tablecloths, wing actual silver spoons at unwitting patrons nearby, get ketchup on the table and shriek for paper place mats and a fresh packet of crayons. The restaurant doesn't even have a kid's menu. "Why can't we eat at Old McDonald's?" they ask. ("Good question," you say to yourself.)

Or, worse yet, the newer moms, fearing a loathsome restaurant experience, have somehow been foolish enough to suggest that they host a Mother's Day event in their own homes. They wind up cooking and cleaning for everyone while their sweet little kumquats run about their humble abode wrecking everything in the joint.

And where are the dads? Well, they do their part. Kind of.

Many of them guide their kids in making sweet cards for Mommy, smeared with glitter glue and overflowing with innocent, bountiful love. Perhaps these big-hearted dads get some flowers and a nice card, or maybe a gift certificate for a massage or facial. The cards and gifts are placed on a tray (that used to be used for romantic breakfasts in bed in what seems like another lifetime) carried by the kids and presented to Mommy along with some toast and OJ and, if you're lucky, maybe an omelet and a still-hot cup of coffee.

After a few niceties and deliciously sloppy kiddo kisses, it's time for the mad dash to scrub the children clean and iron their clothes for the *real* Mother's Day, the celebration of the veteran moms (planned by their daughters or daughters-in-laws) who've already mastered the hard stuff and get to entertain themselves watching you try to keep your toddler from knocking over the tall vase of roses in that fancy, cloth-napkined restaurant. For them, it's quite amusing.

That's what gets me about Mother's Day. These veteran moms, they've already done their time. They've already wiped the bum-bums, kissed the boo-boos, served as Cub Scout den mothers, given the gray-hair inducing driving lessons and wept as their children walked down wedding aisles (while simultaneously emptying parental bank accounts with pricey wedding receptions). They no longer have bags under their eyes. They get to sleep all night long.

All. The. Way. Through.

Their bare feet don't accidentally come crunching down on Matchbox cars menacingly lying in the shadows in the middle of the living room. Their kitchen tables aren't perpetually sticky. Their couch cushions are always in place. And they can now have an entire conversation without ever having to stop to say, "Please, I'll get your snack in a minute . . . Just pull your brother's face out of the cat food. Oh, and grab that cup of juice from the edge of the table before you sp . . . ill . . . it. *Never mind.*"

The moms with the little ones are the ones who crave the day off. It's only now that these women have become mothers themselves that they understand what their own mothers and their mothers before them went through. In fact, they're in awe of what these women have accomplished, that they actually made it out of early motherhood with their limbs and mental faculties in tact. (Well, mostly in tact.) And these people didn't even have microwave ovens, sippy cups or disposable diapers. How did they possibly manage?

They now get that that motherhood is hard, oftentimes thankless, and is a vocation that needs to be honored. On this, everyone agrees. But it's these new moms who seriously need the holiday break. (Maybe the grandmoms will take the kids on Mother's Day? To relive the glory days of maternal madness?)

Ask a mom with little kids what she really wants for Mother's Day and here's what she's likely to tell you: A big hug and kiss from her kids, homemade cards and time for herself. If she could ditch the brunch and fancy duds, she'd take a nap and maybe have a rich chocolate bar. A whole one. All by herself. And she wouldn't have clean up after anyone for the whole day.

Sleeping thru the night? Yeah right!

(Written when I was deep in the throes of sleep deprivation in 2002. And you can tell.)

I need sleep.

Badly.

And my toddler won't let me have any.

Go ahead, ask me if I've tried the 100 billion "sure-fire" kid sleep remedies like: The Ferber method, letting him cry it out, a "no cry" sleeping technique, curbing excessive daytime naps, reading before bedtime, feeding him before bedtime, not feeding him before bedtime, letting him sleep in my bed, moving to Nome, Alaska until the kid is 12, etc., etc.

None of this has worked.

As my brain continues to operate on auto-pilot from over a year's worth of sleep deprivation, I've decided that if I hear one more person tell me not only what I should be doing, but how I've failed as a parent while *they've* succeeded in getting their baby to sleep, I'm going to dump my steaming mug of coffee – the only thing that's enabled me to continue to speak with any degree of clarity – over the offender's head.

Consider this your one and only warning.

When you tell people that you have a child who won't sleep through the night despite trying every method known to parentkind short of anesthetizing the tot or creating a soundproof home, everyone else thinks he or she is a veritable expert.

I'm not talkin' about the people who *upon request*, repeat, *upon request* offer suggestions. I'm talkin' about those folks who openly "tsk" when they hear that you haven't been able to get your kid to sleep through the night yet. These are the ones who started asking you, when your baby was a mere week old, whether she was sleeping well. By the time your baby is four months old, if his head doesn't hit the crib mattress and remain there for a solid eight to nine hours, you start getting the laundry list of questions:

Do you use pacifiers? If so, put a dozen in the crib so baby can easily find one in the dark and can soothe himself back to sleep.

Do you have a nightlight? If you don't, put one up. If you do, maybe it's bothering the kid.

Do you have a nighttime ritual, something soothing like reading the same book, singing the same lullaby? If you don't, start one. If you do, stop.

Is there too much noise at night? Too many odors that upset the baby? Too much stimulation?

Is the baby hungry? Wet? Gassy? Teething? Sick? Hot? Cold?

Is she sleeping too much during the day so that she's not tired at night?

And when these self-appointed sleep gurus get no satisfaction from grilling you like a smoked sausage, they then trot out an ungodly long list of recommendations.

If the torrent of recommendations isn't enough to bring you, the overwrought, sleep deprived shell of a human being to your knees, you can take a gander at a popular book by an English nanny who says she likes to "whisper" to babies, in which she purports to have all the answers as to how to get your kid to sleep soundly. The bottom line: If your kid's not sleeping, it's all your fault, you sap.

My son Casey still doesn't sleep through the night and he's 1. Around his first birthday, for no apparent reason, he miraculously slept all night long for four nights that week. My husband Scott and I donned his leftover birthday party hats and ran naked down our street with joy. I think Scott actually wept (so did my neighbors when they saw the spectacle outside their window).

After a week of bliss, our luck shifted dramatically. Casey suddenly began waking up again each every night in hysterics. Why? I haven't the foggiest idea.

My older kids didn't have this problem. They were sleeping through the night at roughly 6 months old. Sure, there were nocturnal interruptions when they experienced teething pain or were sick, but, all in all, they were pretty easy on us, sleep-wise that is.

Then there's Casey, who has turned me into a murky-headed

lunatic.

And there's no end in sight. Sure, he's not getting up as frequently as he used to any more, like 10 times, but he's still denying Scott and I a solid night's sleep.

Going without regular sleep for over a year has really taken its toll on what little remains of my mental faculties. I've forgotten people's birthdays. I've sent my older kids to preschool and forgotten to brush their hair. At times, I've been utterly embarrassed by my inability to carry on cogent conversations.

Scott and I have had major feuds over how to handle this (the problem kid, not my conversations). When Casey was about six months old and still nursing, Scott thought that I should stop breastfeeding the baby when he woke up at 2 or 3 a.m. I disagreed, saying that I'd rather get up to nurse him for 20 minutes instead of listen to him scream from the pit of his stomach, disrupting everyone's slumber and sending waves of tension through my muscle fibers with every holler for a solid hour. Since feeding him in the middle of the night wasn't working, I relented to Scott and withheld the breastmilk at night.

For four long months, we let Casey cry at night instead of breastfeeding him. Scott spent many of those nights sitting on the child's bedroom floor next to the crib, trying to calm him.

The kid got lungs.

Casey would scream to exhaustion. He'd shriek for upwards of 90 minutes without let up, fall asleep for a while, only to awaken a little while later and start yelling all over again.

I would lie in bed in the next room stewing. I couldn't go into his room because if I did, Casey would go nutty knowing that I could nurse him but wouldn't.

It was an abysmal failure.

After months of this psychological torment, I could not tolerate it any longer. I resumed middle-of-the-night feedings and we got a tad bit more sleep under slightly less stressful circumstances.

At his 12-month pediatrician's appointment, Casey's doctor recommended that we boost the fat content in his food, giving him as much food as he wanted, but nothing at night. We tried it. For that amazing week, it seemed to work. Even though I was still waking up at 3 a.m. out of habit, I was just starting to feel just a wee bit more alert. Then, as the week ended, Casey resumed waking up repeatedly throughout the night, screaming loud enough to peel the paint off the walls.

Several nights passed with Scott lying on the floor in Casey's room next to his crib trying to get the shrill cries to cease before we finally caved and put Casey in our bed, only to be roused throughout the early morning hours by feet kicking our faces or pudgy little fingers poking at our eyes.

We're still fielding questions about his non-sleeping habits, still on the receiving end of pitiful looks and uppity asides that, as parents, we obviously have no idea what we're doing.

Someday, I'll come up with some sassy comeback for these know-it-alls who get to snooze for a solid seven hours straight. In the meantime, I'll continue to buy 40-gallon bins of coffee and 300 cases of diet colas weekly, mainline the caffeine and try not to operate any heavy equipment.

Newborn brain

I locked my keys in the trunk.

I forgot my phone number.

I forgot that it was picture day at my twins' preschool, let them pick out their own clothes and then couldn't remember if I even combed their hair or wiped the grape jelly off their faces before dropping them off.

I accidentally put my minivan into the "reverse" gear instead of "drive" after picking up my order at a doughnut shop drive-thru window, terrorizing the driver behind me.

And it wasn't just me.

One of my friends, a mom of a baby and a toddler, absentmindedly left all the doors to her minivan open overnight — with the newly-purchased groceries still sitting inside – and drained the vehicle's battery. Not only was there some food loss, but she couldn't take her preschooler to class the next day because the van's battery was dead.

Why all this seemingly idiotic behavior? All because of that little phenomenon known as New Mommy and Daddy Brain.

Yes, I can hear all you non-believers out there, protesting that there's no such thing as a Mommy and Daddy Brain, and that to even suggest that a new parent's brain becomes hazy and foggy is somehow sexist, considering that most at-home parents are female.

Get over yourself.

Whenever you combine severe sleep deprivation with a baby's incessant need to eat every four hours, marathon crying, 400 tons of poop and spit-up covered laundry and all host of assorted other responsibilities, you have the formula for transforming one's brain into a porous, sieve-like item where only the most vital, short-term memories are retained, stuff like, "Oh yeah, I need to breathe. And eat. Breathe and eat."

While scientists scramble to figure out if there's a discernable physiological and chemical reason behind a new parent's tendency to forget things, there are others who try to deny that adding a baby to a home does not (albeit temporarily) turn an adult's brain into scrambled eggs. Groups who lobby on behalf of moms who work outside the home (while the others are working in the home for no pay . . . now there's a reason to go nuts, that no pay thing) like to say that there's no such thing as a Mommy or Daddy Brain, that the brain of a new parent works just the same as that of anyone else.

Hogwash.

Obviously, the people who protest the very concept of New Mommy and Daddy Brain have never actually had to care for and live with a newborn, or with a baby AND a toddler (try twin toddlers!) in the house. New parents are lucky if they can walk around with their pants zipped up and sleep crusts removed from their eyes, never mind remember the inane, endless to do lists of life.

When you have a baby in the house, your brain needs the Heimlich Maneuver.

Daily.

Your world is reduced to bleary moments at 2 a.m. in front of the tube watching "M.A.S.H." re-runs while trying to get the baby to sleep. (You figure, Alan Alda puts you to sleep, why not the baby?) It's forgetting what day it is and when your project deadlines are. It's putting yellow post-it notes all over the house to remind you that today is trash day, otherwise, trash day becomes a victim of Mommy and Daddy Brain and the heap of garbage (and stinky diapers) pile up, like the list of things you forgot to do.

One caveat on this Mommy and Daddy Brain theory of mine: Daddies get as murky headed when they're deprived of sleep and find their home life plunged into a whirling cycle of near chaos as their female counterparts. But it's been my experience that it's the mommies — regardless of their employment status — who wind up dealing with the bulk of the added responsibilities a baby brings, like pediatric appointments, laundering and feeding, especially if the food is emanating from mommy's body where whatever energy said mommy may have remaining is literally sucked out of her body. If that's not the case in your house daddies, you have my humble apologies.

If you step back and look at a typical day in the life of a parent of a baby, the list of things that must be done include one, stupor-inducing must-do item another. Let's just start mid-day, say, after lunchtime:

Throw clothes into the washing machine, or else no one in the house will have anything but stiff, smelly duds to wear.

Pay the credit card bill (and remember to not only put a stamp on the envelope, but put it in the mailbox near the doctor's office) or else you'll wreck your credit and won't be able to buy any more diapers, never mind send the little crazy people to preschool.

Feed the baby (breast or bottle).

Change the baby's clothes and diaper, as well as your own (clothes, not diaper) after the baby spit up on both of you.

Search for your car keys for 10 minutes in a panic. (Find them in, of all places, your coat pocket.)

Get baby into car seat and put into the minivan. Put hat on head and big coat over self to cover up the fact that you don't look your couture best today.

Go to closest CVS to buy diapers and baby wipes, or you're little love bug will be naked and diaperless, forcing you to mop up the floor after pee and poop explosions later.

Bring the baby to her doctor's appointment.

Get home, feed the baby again, liquids AND solids.

Put baby food covered bib in sink, throw dirty spoons and bowls in sink. Toss empty (you hope) baby food jars into the recycling bin.

Call pediatrician because you forgot to ask her some questions during your visit, and you've suddenly noticed a weird rash developing on the baby's wrist.

Move the laundry from the washer to the dryer and discover that all the items are pink because — considering you're going on maybe three consecutive hours of sleep — you missed the red butterfly pair of socks tucked inside a towel in the white load.

Avoid a phone call – you can see who it is on Caller ID – and change the baby's diaper instead.

Grab mail from the mailbox and curse because you realize you never did get that credit card payment into the mailbox near the pediatrician's office because you can still see the envelope sitting on the dashboard of your minivan.

Pick up the older kids from preschool and take them to an hour of soccer.

After soccer, race back home and try to delicately take the baby out of the car seat and transfer the child to his crib without waking her up. Older children are threatened with vocal cord severing should they wake up the baby.

Fold what you realize are multiple loads of now-pink laundry. (Damned red socks!)

Remember that you need to buy purple pipe cleaners for a craft project for preschool class that's due in two days. Decide to put it off another day, knowing you'll likely forget all about it.

Feed the now crying baby who'd prefer to assault you with his little fists (notice that he needs nail cutting when he slices the side of your breast with his little razor-nails and you bleed slightly) while the older kids whine that they're starving and need food now before they perish.

While giving the kids bowls of dry Cheerios to tide them over while you make dinner, you finally produce a semi-balanced, hot, homemade meal. And no one eats it.

Fill and start the dishwasher for the second time of the day. Pray that the unrinsed dishes will be free from the hardened food particles when the cycle is done.

Bathe the baby and the other skanky-smelling kids and shoe-horn them into pink pajamas because they're resisting, claiming they're not tired and would prefer to run about the house naked. Naked and screaming. And, oops, peeing on the living room rug.

Shove the folded clothes — that are now in a rumpled pile courtesy of your older kids — into a corner in the living room and pretend they are invisible. You don't have the hour you need to put them all away on their tiny little hangers and to wedge into their drawers.

Don your referee's jersey and whistle to officiate between your warring kids over which six bedtime stories you'll read.

Sing lullabies and tuck children in. Go to the living room armed with cleaners and paper towels and clean up the pee mistake.

Scrape the dried food off the floor, use a blow torch to clean the kitchen table. Decide to leave the pots in the sink.

Collapse onto the living room couch for a mindless few minutes of TV before the baby wakes up for the first of three times that night, wanting to eat and needing a diaper change.

Clean up the poop the baby has made in your bed – you were feeding her in bed — and wipe the spit-up from your sleeping spouse's ear.

At sunrise, repeat.

Yeah, and you try to remember exactly where you parked the car, that you're sister-in-law's birthday is in two days and that you're out of stamps.

The maternity ward meets the Vegas strip

Leopard print maternity thongs.

They're on sale, right now, alongside maternity strapless mini-dresses, maternity bikinis and virtually sheer lingerie cut to "flatter" a burgeoning pregnant midriff.

What's next, Victoria's Secret models with perfectly tight buns – sans varicose veins, cellulite or stretch marks of course — modeling the new maternity "Angels" lingerie line?

Okay, so I was among those who bitterly complained when I first went shopping for maternity clothes in 1998 and found my options limited to attire that was boxy and shapeless (think refrigerator cartons in a modest floral print and faux pearl buttons). I quickly grew tired of the iron-clad, industrial strength, hospital floor white maternity/nursing bras that sounded as solid as jail cell doors when being fastened shut with their 14 enclosures.

But in between the moments of puking, endless peeing, lower pelvic pressure and leaky breasts, I must admit, there were moments in my pregnancies and postpartum when I actually wanted to feel sexy and desirable. Fourteen-hook bras and T-shirts screaming "Womb with a View" just weren't cutting it.

During my second pregnancy in 2001, I was happily surprised to discover that maternity fashion had done a 180-degree turn. There was a veritable cornucopia of clothing from which to choose, much of it cognizant of the fact that pregnant women want to look and feel good, not industrial-strength, oversized, walking mushrooms in shades of salmon or taupe. Many of the duds were fashion conscious, snug-fitting and sometimes (*gasp*) sexy.

Even the nursing shirts for those postpartum days reflected this new trend. As someone who breastfed, the idea that I could purchase a shirt with some shape to it, that made me feel like something other than an unfashionable, large-shirted mammary machine was refreshing. As soon as I found out about the new lines of sexy nursing wear, I quickly got online and ordered a leopard print nursing bra and a tight, bright teal, V-necked nursing shirt (that didn't look like a nursing shirt) from a web site declaring moms "hot."

However while browsing these maternity sites, I spotted the leopard print maternity thong.

And I cringed.

This was a step too far. Who in their right mind would perpetrate *this* brainstorm on the pregnant public? Had these designers ever been pregnant? Hadn't they ever heard of the fact that many women experience a rather unpleasant side effect of pregnancy called hemorrhoids? Hemorrhoids trump visible panty lines any day in my book.

Now that I've stopped wearing nursing clothes and am not in the market for any maternity wear, I feel lucky. What I had initially welcomed as a liberating change in maternity fashion has now mutated into sex fetish nightmare.

Have you checked out the maternity and nursing wear recently? It goes well beyond the inanity of a leopard print maternity thong:

Try strapless maternity mini-dresses in "chocolate" that make pregnant women look like overstuffed, overcooked grilled sausages.

Or how about a baby doll nightie with matching bikini underpants where the clothing maker vows, "Wearing this will be sure to add a couple of logs to the fire." The sassy copy writer added for good measure, "Be naughty in midnight black. You can't get any more pregnant."

Then there's maternity yoga wear. Yes, I can think of nothing more I'd like to do than to try to stretch and twist a pregnant, bloated body into the Lotus position while wearing the sporty, belly exposing attire.

And we can't forget the low-rise maternity jeans coupled with a belly shirt. Gotta love the belly shirt to expose the burgeoning belly to the viewing public, with the low-rise jeans serving as a display shelf. (Did I mention this is being marketed as maternity wear?)

Then, my personal favorite, aside from the illustrious thong: The maternity bikini. Pregnant women unite. Go to the nation's beaches and show off your glowing bellies!

Don't get me wrong, I was proud of my pregnant belly during

both of my pregnancies. My husband took photos of me when I was in full mommy-to-be bloom. But who needs the pressure of also having to squeeze into a bikini without the benefit of 24-hour, real time air brushers following you around to cover up all your pregnancy flaws?

When I was pregnant with twins and needed the help of at least one strong adult to scale the dunes of a Cape Cod beach on my vacation, I came face to face with a young pregnant girl in an emerald green bikini. Her body was flawless. Her skin was perfectly tanned, lacking any visible pregnancy-related blemishes. Her bellybutton, which hadn't popped out as mine sadly had, was pierced.

As I grumbled and grimaced my way up the hill for the umpteenth time to the Sani-Can to relieve myself because my in utero daughter was crushing my bladder, I never felt so much like that clichéd beached whale. I had stretch marks from hell, bright red streaks from my belly button on down that one of my friends referred to affectionately as "war paint." Seeing that taut pregnant, bikinied being looking so sexy was maddening.

During my last pregnancy, not only did my twin-induced stretch marks return with a vengeance, but I developed new ones. I had so much pelvic and back pressure that I needed to wear a four-inch-wide, hospital floor white, Velcro belly/back support belt under my clothes. Imagine if I'd tried to wear a leopard print maternity thong, low-rise maternity jeans and a tight, V-necked belly shirt that would expose the edges of my Velcro belly belt? Oooh la la.

My husband calls me a raving hypocrite. He can't understand how I can be so thrilled that there are sophisticated, sexy maternity clothes on the market, while at the same time I'm ranting about the utter insanity of maternity bikinis and strapless sausage-like dresses.

What he doesn't get is that it's one thing for a pregnant woman to want to look good and feel sexy in her curvy, life-affirming shape. It's an entirely different matter to have young pregnant (or pretend pregnant) models with perfect bodies promoting sexy clothes that many of us wouldn't wear even if we *weren't* pregnant, putting pressure on actual pregnant women to look sexy while they're standing in line at the drug store to buy Preparation H for those damned hemorrhoids.

When you've been reduced to wearing a belly belt, the last thing you want to think about is leopard print butt floss.

Mum's the word

My bulging belly and I innocently made it up to the grocery store deli counter. I was verbally accosted before I could even place my order for a pound of peppercorn turkey breast. Thinly sliced if you please.

"So, ya gonna have an epidural or not?" the deli clerk inquired, giving my pregnant belly an up and down gaze. (Made me feel like I was in an entirely different kind of meat market.)

"Don't!" shouted the other female deli clerk from behind the counter. "Go natural. It's better."

"No, no, no," the first woman said, shaking her head in vehement disagreement. (She still hadn't taken my number ticket, even though I was the only one in line.) "Get the drugs."

Then they looked at me, their pregnant pause lingering in the air amid the aroma of tangy pepperoni and creamy feta cheese.
I just wanted my damned turkey.

"None of your stinkin' business!" I longed to shout.

After months of being public property, particularly after people found out that I was carrying twins, I was sick of everyone – friends, family, strangers at deli counters – doling out unsolicited advice and asking me intrusive, personal questions.

"I'll see what happens," I replied to the two deli ladies, praying the inquisition would end so I could go back to my apartment and put my aching feet up as I dined on a turkey sandwich and the barbecue potato chips I craved.

From breastfeeding to binkies, from sleeping habits to the pros and cons of making your own baby food, I absolutely despised being force-fed advice on how to rear my three kids. Not that I corner the market on parenting knowledge. I regularly solicit the advice of seasoned parents and parental peers about all kinds of things. I research issues, like how to deal with a kid who has night terrors. I read books, articles and web sites looking for advice on parenting, like on how to prepare kids for the death of a family pet.

One evening, when I became wretchedly frustrated with my

children's refusal to pick up their toys, I called my mom for advice. When I didn't know what to do when my twin 18-month-olds started leaping out of their cribs and landing on their heads, I asked every mother I could find (particularly moms of twins) what they would do. When my kids started biting one another, I went to my wealth of experienced family members, friends and the Internet looking for suggestions.

But when people just waltz up to me, instruct me on how to do things, or, worse yet, grab something (or someone!) out of my hands and started to say, "Oh, no, no, no, you've got to do [fill in the blank] this way," I go ballistic inside . . . sometimes on the outside too.

Now, after acquiring years of parenting experience, I find myself on the other side of the equation, absolutely brimming with parenting anecdotes and little tips I've acquired. I find that I love to talk about my pregnancies and births, about those insane, early days of sleep deprivation, which in the case of my youngest, lasted nearly three years.

And I don't have any place to go with that info.

As friends and younger family members start having kids, I actually find myself having to staple my own lips together and keep quiet. Sometimes, biting that lip is painfully difficult.

I struggle with the desire to have my own experiences and mistakes be a benefit to someone. I mean, come on, if I had to practically give birth to my youngest in an ER parking lot as his head and amniotic sac emerged from the birth canal, I want to be able to share the story and the lesson (don't let them send you home from the hospital if you KNOW you are having solid contractions and it's not your first pregnancy).

It took forever for me to learn to shove my baby's face into my breast if he or she bit me while breastfeeding (the shoving would cause them to open their mouths in order to breathe and then they'd associate the discomfort with biting, a lactation expert advised me). And after nursing the twins for a solid year and my youngest for 14 months, I wanted to share my nugget of info with someone.

But unless I'm asked, I have to keep my babbling tips to myself.

The torrent of stories and advice has to stay behind the flood gates until the new or expectant mom gently taps on that door.

When my sister-in-law Ellen was pregnant with her first child, I was so excited for her. I packed up baby stuff, parenting books, my maternity clothes, and handed them over. I told her which books and articles I liked the best, which nursing pillows I found most helpful. About 15 minutes into my breathless monologue, I realized that I hadn't actually been asked a question. Poor Ellen, hormones surging, her svelte body being transformed by the daughter inside, had merely said she'd be glad to take whatever I had to give her.

Embarrassed, I shut up.

When my brother and his wife had their first child, my nephew Gabe, the compulsion to launch into anecdotes about my three kids' infancies was extraordinarily strong. When I heard Gabe scream all night long one evening during a family vacation at Cape Cod, I wanted to go to their room and offer (*horrors!*) unsolicited advice, or, at the very least, to commiserate, to share my days of leaden eyelids with them because they now understood our common experience.

But no. I clamped my hand over my mouth and stayed in my own room.

And I won't be pestering pregnant women at grocery store deli counters with graphic stories, lecturing my sisters-in-law or hounding sleep deprived parents about what kind of techniques they've tried.

Mum's the word.

Mommy bodies

The big surprise of the 2005 Academy Awards ceremony (other than the fact that some poor saps had to accept their statuettes in remote, undisclosed locations in the Kodak Theater in Hollywood) was that Julia Roberts, mom of then three-month-old twins, appeared as an award presenter in a sleek, black Dolce & Gabbana gown that showed off her newly acquired curves.

Celebrity watchers who critique fashion choices on catty cable and morning news chatfests were agog over the Oscar winner's figure, how quickly she'd dropped her twins' pregnancy weight and how lovely her new mommy bosoms looked. The fashionistas likewise cooed when they saw fellow Oscar winner, Gwyneth Paltrow, another new mom who looked willowy in her pale pink gown that flattered her new mommylicious chest as she took to the red carpet.

When celebrities have babies, the public voraciously follows their post-baby body developments, or so say the TV ratings and glossy magazine circulation numbers. "When's she gonna lose that baby weight?" the celebrity reporters ponder out loud. If the weight doesn't come off "quickly enough" (whatever that means), there's a collective clucking of the tongues and a sudden use of somber tones often reserved for discussing the dead or gravely ill. And when some celeb moms burst upon the scene just a few months or weeks postpartum looking like elastic, spring-back-to-shape Barbie dolls (a la Roberts), fashion conscious observers avidly applaud.

Too many people look upon these celebrity mothers as role models who embody the message that being a new mom doesn't mean going to seed, that you can still be sexy (which is good and achievable for we mere mortal moms), *and* walk around in various, flesh and belly-exposing states of undress (which is, for most of we mere mortal moms, distinctly unachievable). If you work hard you can look like us, the images coo seductively. You can look like the celebs if you're dedicated, if your only job was not to care for kids and juggle work but to work out all day, if you live in Hollywood and are married to a plastic surgeon.

I have nothing against new moms, particularly celebrity mothers, who look and feel fabulous. I think it's great that they're psyched about "bouncing back" (I hate that term) from pregnancies and breastfeeding. What I do take exception to, however, is the illusion that most or all mommy bodies can just "snap" into their previous, post-pregnancy forms with nary a blemish, stretch mark, nor loose skin that doesn't respond to exercise. That looking like these hard Hollywood mommy bodies, slipping into a bikini postpartum is somehow just a matter of willpower.

The June 2003 provocative photo spread in *W Magazine* of "Sex and the City" star Sarah Jessica Parker, just 6 months after giving birth to her son, is case in point. The then 38-year-old actress did attempt to play down the return of her fab figure after giving birth with this observation: "I can afford a yoga teacher to come to my house. I can afford child care so I can work out for an hour and a half. . . I understand that as a culture, we cling to this idea that celebrities look exciting, but not only is the standard too high for most normal women, it's too high even for us."

Nice sentiments, but they were drowned out by the black and white photographs, one in particular showing the actress in a saturated state (literally, with droplets of water beaded up on her skin) in a bikini top and bottom, with the bikini bottom resting precariously low on her beautiful hips. Another image showed the actress in a tight white shirt and sweater hiked up to her belly button line while she wore a revealingly teeny bikini bottom. Flawless skin and body. No stretch marks or loose skin anywhere.

Great for her, but not for real world mommies like me who — while we might feel fine about the way we look in clothes — bear irreversible scars of pregnancy and birth on our bodies when we're naked. There's no way we could ever pull off a photo shoot like that Parker's. Despite what she said, her pictures provocatively screamed out loud with the false promise that you too could resemble her even after having a baby and breastfeeding. That anyone could.

But the reality is that no amount of sit-ups or yoga sessions will purge my belly of the loose skin from my twins' pregnancy. It's there for the rest of my life. Want a visual? Think of bread dough that's all soft and wrinkly. Now sew that dough to my abdomen.

No amount of exercise is going to move my poor breasts, savaged by a lifetime total of 26 months of breastfeeding (12 months for my twins, 14 months for the subsequent single baby), back to the same zip code from whence they came.

No amount of cream — even if purchased in 10 gallon drums — is going to erase the dozens of stretch marks that line my abdomen from the belly button down to my hips, as well as dot my upper thighs and breasts. While my stomach is kind of "flattish" when I am standing, you can still see the stretch marks, which remind me on a daily basis, of the grooves on a sandy beach left behind when the tide has gone out.

Permanently.

Of course no one who sees me fully clothed can really tell that I have all this loose skin on my belly or stretch marks marring my torso. The loose skin folds quite nicely into my pants, and I select clothing that covers the damaged parts. And although I've been able to get away with wearing a two-pieced bathing suit since having my children, the bathing suit had a *very* strong top that is so clever that it lifts AND covers certain areas, while the sassy skirt-styled bottom covers me from the belly button down. (Though I'm always paranoid about a stretch mark or two unmasking itself from the beneath the waistband.)

So when I hear celeb moms saying that they understand that they have certain lifestyle perks that enable them to look the way they do, their magnanimously humble words are nullified by images of explicitly exposed postpartum bodies, giving the visual suggestion that if only you other mommies would work out and stop eating, you too could look as sexy without your clothes on as they do.

The reality for many moms is this: You can still wear a lovely dress, but you just need to tuck and lift your boobs with sturdy packing tape and hold the loose skin down with aluminum siding pinned around your waist. However many moms plagued by stretch marks, myself included, can't walk around in anything exposing the lower belly. That includes low riding jeans, which I can only wear if I have a longer top on that covers the offending middle region.

If there's one celebrity mom who gets my vote for the most honest hottie, it's Patricia Heaton of "Everybody Loves Raymond." In late 2002, she wrote in her memoirs that in order to be a successful Hollywood actress – this coming from a woman who's had four babies and four C-sections — to be able to fit into gowns for the red carpet, she went under the knife to get a tummy tuck, breast reduction and breast lift. (She likened her postpartum tummy to "a big old wrinkly suede bag," in her autobiography.)

"It's really not fair — the image we present to the world — because it is so, uh, well, contrived," Heaton told *People* of other celebrity moms in a 2002 interview. "Women shouldn't look at people they see on TV and compare themselves to those women because you aren't really seeing those women the way they really are."

But then there's that little cliché that haunts many mommies when we're alone in the bathroom, gazing at what our pregnancies have done to our bodies: "A picture is worth a thousand words." It's hard to shake those Sarah Jessica images from my head when I'm seeing my the-tide-is-out-and-is-never-coming-back body in the mirror.

Maybe the best gift celeb moms can give to the rest of us mortal moms is a bit less of their naked unblemished torsos and a bit more of the truth, and maybe some really strong undergarments.

Growing Pains

Uh-oh

"Uh-oh."

In the sweet, squeaky voice of a toddler, this can be a precious little phrase. The first few times it's uttered.

My husband Scott and I were extremely shortsighted when we taught our twin toddlers, Abbey and Jonah, to say, "Uh-oh," like the Teletubbies. Every time something accidentally fell down, we'd overexaggeratedly say in sing-songy voices, "Uh-oh" and retrieve the wayward object.

In hindsight, a very bad move.

When Abbey finally used it on her own, and in the proper context, we swooned with delight. What a prodigy. I grabbed the telephone and tried to coax her into repeating it for Grandma, which, of course, she wouldn't, but I professed that it was an absolutely precious phrase to hear emerging from her darling, pudgy toddler mouth.

Little did we realize we'd created a soft-voiced little monster.

By the time we got to, "Uh-oh: Day Four," I was ready to play in traffic while blindfolded. Abbey had begun invoking, "Uh-oh" incessantly. It was no longer a quip made when something innocently fell down or was inadvertently knocked over. It had undergone a sinister metamorphosis into a shrill warning signal that Abbey was about to intentionally throw or destroy something. A pre-emptive, "Uh-oh." The meaning had changed from, "Whoops, sorry I spilled ketchup in your purse Mama," to, "Heads up!" just before ketchup was purposefully hurled at my chin.

Be careful of what you teach your children.

I had similar bad luck with the art of using a zipper. (Insert your own dirty joke here.) Toddler Abbey figured out how to use zippers by playing with one of those cloth activity books for babies, the type with buckles, Velcro, shoelaces and other hands-on items to teach wee ones how to use manipulatives. Just like mastering, "Uh-oh," after Abbey learned how to work the zipper in the book, it didn't take her long to apply that skill to evil enterprises, like unzipping her pajamas so she could strip herself every morning. I was never so proud of her as I was that fateful morning when I discovered that not only had she unzipped and undressed, but she'd relieved herself all over her sheets.

That same cloth activity book was also instrumental in teaching Jonah about shoelaces. He learned how to not only unlace his own shoes, but how to remove the laces from his shoes and subsequently wrap them around unsuspecting dolls' necks. Lucky for his sister that the laces weren't long enough to make it around her own neck, though he made a valiant effort to try to accomplish that feat.

The more I thought about it, the more I realized that we teach our kids all sorts of things that, in the future, we'll really wish we hadn't because the misapplication of all these skills will wind up tormenting us. (Think: Teaching the kids to make phone calls. Or drive a car. Makes you wanna shudder doesn't it?)

Even in the early months of our children's lives, Scott and I encouraged the babies to reach developmental milestones. Once those milestones were achieved and the kids eventually utilized their new skills for unsavory, unanticipated ends, we looked at each other and said, "Hey, why don't we pretend that you never learned how to turn a door knob okay? Now get your feet out of the toilet and go play in your room."

I never really understood why my friend Kerry – who has a daughter nine months older than my twins – warned me not to aggressively encourage Abbey and Jonah to start crawling, and later to start walking. I thought she was nuts.

Until now.

At first, Scott and I were proud when they became expert crawlers. But a few days after Jonah and Abbey learned how to crawl very quietly and nimbly, we realized that nothing would be safe in our home until the offspring move into their own apartments.

We made a terrible mistake when we introduced our toddlers to something we called, "Naked piggies." At night when it was time to get the kids into their pajamas, we'd make a game out of taking off their socks and ask, "Who wants naked piggies?" They'd scamper over to us, eager to be the first one to wiggle his or her bare toes in the air as we pulled their socks off with great fanfare. The unveiling was followed by a recitation of "This Little Piggy" for each foot.

This inspired a desire to have naked feet 24/7. Abbey began pulling off her shoes and socks several times a day and discarding the socks in random locations (though never together). She'd approach me, stick a bare foot in my general direction and wait with giddy anticipation for me to commence with, "This Little Piggy." Afterward, she'd go and wrestle Jonah's shoes and socks off his feet, put his shoes on her feet and start the process all over again. (It was easier to get his shoes off once he started removing the shoelaces.) At the library, she wanted naked piggies. At play groups, she wanted naked piggies. At the playground, she wanted naked piggies.

When Scott started pulling off his shoes and socks and saying, "Naked piggies," I decided it was time to place a strict moratorium on the unsolicited baring of naked feet.

Uh-oh indeed.

The boy next door

He was only four.

I'd informed Scott of this little morsel of intelligence on numerous occasions. But the fact that he was 4 years old didn't stop my husband from squirming.

Ben, the boy next door, was 4 years old. And he developed a crush on our 2-year-old daughter Abbey. Whenever he'd come into our yard to play, a giant smile would creep across his face so all you'd see were his little white baby teeth. He always greeted her first — before saying a word (if anything) to her twin brother Jonah — and would throw an exuberant hug around her slender shoulders. Ben's affection for Abbey even extended to his prized baby doll collection, where he named the biggest doll after her.

The sentiments were mutual. Abbey would inquire about Ben constantly, pointing to his house asking, "Where's Ben?" Never mind that Ben also had a 6-year-old brother named Alex who would also come over to play. Abbey only wanted to play with Ben. One afternoon, when she was in our front breezeway, she spied Ben in his yard. "Bennnn!!" she screamed while pounding on the window as though she hadn't seen him in years. (It reminded me of Dustin Hoffman yelling, "Elaine!" in "The Graduate.") Ben immediately scampered over and they went off to share the two-seated swing in our back yard together.

A few months later, Ben picked out a baby doll to give to Abbey for her second birthday. She promptly christened the doll "Baby Ben." "Baby Ben" became one of two dolls that *had* to be in Abbey's bed when she went to sleep.

All of this made Scott nervous. Again I'd say to him, "He's only four." But to my spouse, Ben represented all the boys who will come to our house in future years in menacing cars with reclining seats and take his precious little baby girl off into the night. Ben represented all the males who may break her heart, make her cry and, most ominously, make her heart race. Scott wanted no part of this. "After all," he'd counter, "*she's* only two."

Not to be outdone by his sister's love struck behavior, Jonah began obsessing over a pretty blonde woman (yes, woman) who, unfortunately for him, had just recently gotten married. And was about 25 years his senior. He first spied her across the dance floor at my sister-in-law's wedding. He raised his pudgy little hand, pointed his index finger at her and, in a hushed voice asked, "Who's dat?" When she learned of the little tot's affections, Lynne (a name we heard repeatedly in our house for the following six months) obligingly danced with him. Videotape of the moment shows Jonah (in the grips of his apple juice sugar high) gazing at her while she rhythmically swings his arms to the strains of Simon & Garfunkel's "Cecilia."

Jonah's crush on Lynne became epic.

In the months immediately after the wedding encounter, whenever Jonah would happen to glance at my wedding photos on a shelf, he'd get that giddy, goofy look on his face and ask, "Where's Lynne?" When I'd mention my sister-in-law Ellen (at whose wedding this whole thing began), Jonah would question me on Lynne's whereabouts, like I'd locked her away somewhere in a nefarious plot to keep them apart. He frequently asked to view the wedding video, the footage of The Dance. I was also occasionally asked to sing songs and insert Lynne's name into various stanzas. If I didn't, the little besotted one would repeat her name like a Buddhist chanting mantra until I acquiesced.

Now if Jonah were, say, 16 or 17 years old, believe me, I would've been worried and put a GPS tracker on him while he was sleeping. But at 2 years old, the little crush was kind of cute, even if it did seem a little stalkerish.

My mother, however, was the one ringing the alarm bells about this case of puppy love. "It's not normal for a 2-year-old, who isn't even potty-trained yet, to be like, 'Oh Lynne! Oh Lynne!'" she lamented on the phone one night. Every time I'd tell her that Jonah made another unsolicited Lynne request, she'd become very agitated, like it was her own little boy pining to leave the nest.

Honestly, it wasn't as if Abbey and Jonah were on the verge of hitting the road to Las Vegas for a quickie in an Elvis chapel with the objects of their affection. First of all, Ben was only four (I think we've covered that). He was a long way away from getting his driver's license. Second, he had a 5 p.m. curfew and wore Buzz Lightyear slippers outside in 95-degree heat. Third, he carried dolls. I thought Abbey's chastity was safe.

As for Jonah, well I hated doing it, but I had to keep informing the boy that Lynne was happily married. (That and the small fact that she was in her mid-20s and he was *two*.) The fact that Lynne really was with someone else hit Jonah squarely in the face when we were perusing some wedding photos many months later. He spotted an image of Lynne her kissing her new husband. "That's . . . that's Lynne . . . Kissing!" he yelled, with the most crushingly contorted look on his tiny face while he pressed his greasy finger hard on the image of her face. "Lynne kissing!"

My father joked that we should've taken a photo of Lynne and blown it up poster sized and put it up in his room. I thought, "Well, no freakin' way."

While Jonah may have been concocting ways to bust up Lynne's marriage – perhaps by going outside her bedroom window (a la John Cusack in "Say Anything") and singing his melodious rendition of the ABCs, counting to 20 or singing, "Row, Row, Row Your Boat" while wearing his Blue's Clues slippers – I honestly didn't think he had a realistic shot.

Prison break

It's not that I viewed baby cribs as a form of incarceration. Not really. (Well kind of, but incarceration is such a nasty word.) Let's just say that I saw them as convenient keep-your-kids-safe tools that prevented young, clueless cherubs from darting around their homes like wild monkeys hopped up on caffeine and sugar who were liable to accidentally hurt themselves, one another, or innocent inanimate objects like my fine china or my cherished television set.

Cribs, I believed, were perfectly safe places in which to place my toddler twins, up until the moment when the 18-month-olds started hurling themselves over the side railings and landing squarely on their noggins.

It was my nightmare scenario. I'd grown to cherish my twin toddlers' naptime as my opportunity to take care of adult affairs. (Not the kind of "affairs" you're thinking, unfortunately.) I'm talking about the chance to do some writing, reading, paying bills in some semblance of peace (meaning no shrieking) while it was still light out and I wasn't thoroughly exhausted yet. I didn't have to worry about key paperwork being pawed at by sticky angelic toddler fingers or covered with bodily secretions. When the kiddos were in their cribs, they were out of trouble, safe, and were getting some much needed shut eye. They weren't going anywhere. And they weren't fighting, as they were in separate cribs in separate rooms. Everyone was happy.

The beginning of the end of peace in my household came one summer afternoon when I thought things were going swimmingly. I was in my office when I heard a horrific slam in Jonah room. By the time I reacted and then raced up the stairs to his room, I found him playing quietly with some toys on the floor. (I had left him in his crib just minutes beforehand.) The only thing that indicated there was a problem, other than the fact that Jonah was no longer in his crib, was the bright red round splotch on his forehead. "Oh my God!" I screamed, fearing that he was just in some sort of daze and had sustained lasting brain damage. I ran my fingers over the red area.

No bump. He seemed fine, but I was totally shaken up.

Is he really okay? How did he get out here? Was this a fluke?

So what did I do? I put him back in the crib, prayed it was an aberration and returned to my office.

Minutes later, the prisoner escaped again, making another loud wallop sound on the floor. When I got to his room, Jonah was sitting in the same spot on the floor, silently playing with toys again. There was a second red splotch on another location on his forehead.

Being a complete and utter moron in need of an intravenous common sense infusion and perhaps a few smacks on the head myself, I put him back into the crib for a third time. It doesn't take a genius to figure out what happened next. But at least this time, I stuck around to spy on him to see how Houdini got out. Through a convoluted series of gymnastic maneuvers I didn't think were possible for someone as small and uncoordinated as this guy, Jonah managed to pull his body onto the crib rail with his arms while pushing off the mattress with his feet, teetered lengthwise on the edge of the rail, and then nonchalantly let his body fall toward the floor headfirst. (You would've thought that two face-plants in a row would've dissuaded him from going headfirst, but then again, I'm the brain surgeon who put him back in his crib three times in a row thinking we might somehow get a different outcome.)

I really wasn't ready for him to start sleeping in big boy bed yet. I can't tell you how much I wanted to wait until he was 10 years old before making that transition. I'd read an article quoting purported child experts saying that kids can't contain their impulses to run around the room and are apt to get themselves into dangerous situations until they're at least 3. And here was my bruised son at 1 1/2 playing circus performer with no net. Not good.

I suppose I could've gone out and bought one of those tent-like contraptions I'd seen in a baby product catalog that covers the top of the crib with mesh so Jonah couldn't get out. Then he would've been in his crib longer and stayed put. But I couldn't shake the feeling that I'd truly be caging him like the aforementioned wild monkey. I feared not being able to get to him fast enough in an emergency if the zipper got stuck. Yadda. Yadda. Yadda.

Sadly, my husband Scott and I agreed that emancipating him from his crib confinement was the best, safest option. We dragged a futon mattress I had in college into Jonah's room and put it on the ground next to his crib, just to test out if he really wanted to give up crib sleeping. Unfortunately, Jonah absolutely loved it. Talk about free for all. This kid was a little wind-up toy. Tell him it was naptime and you could watch him go like the Road Runner, running in circles and laughing. It was Jonah, unhinged and uncensored. Free.

We soon realized the necessity of installing a door knob cover on the inside of his bedroom door because not only was he spending naptime ransacking his room instead of sleeping, he figured out how to get out of his room and do God knows what in the rest of the house. Unsupervised. At 18 months old. (Play with the stove? Go through the trash? Drown in the toilet?) It was very unnerving to find him standing silently beside my bed clutching his beloved blue blanket one morning, staring at me until I woke up. I had no idea how long he'd been there. I bought the doorknob cover that day.

About a month later, Jonah's sister Abbey commenced her high diving act. The difference with this girl was that she bruised so easily that it only took a few leaps over the crib rail and onto her head before she looked like Rocky Balboa when he lost to Mr. T. I tried to brace myself to be on the receiving end of some strange looks from the neighbors when they caught a gander of her bruised forehead.

What was once my mid-day respite when the children napped suddenly became a non-stop safety patrol. I was a cop walking a beat, only with no lock-up to use to threaten the perps. Every thud or bang sent me flying into their rooms, trying to suppress screams when I saw things like this: Abbey broke through the child latches on her dresser, pulled her dresser drawers out, spread the drawer contents around the room and triumphantly scaled her dresser like Sir Edmund Hillary when he climbed Mt. Everest. Or the time Jonah turned his bookshelf over to use it as a diving board to leap onto the floor. (Yes, the floor.)

I had to buy Abbey her very own doorknob cover for the inside of her bedroom door when she started sneaking out of her room and into Jonah's room. (She was 18 months old people! Her ingenuity frightened me to no end.) I wouldn't realize anything was awry – she was smart enough to shut both doors behind her when she exited and entered the rooms – until I'd hear unabashed laughter and muffled voices and find the two giggling together. Sure, this was cute, at first, until they started destroying stuff, like Abbey's day bed (her crib was the kind that transformed into a day bed).

Most parents with kids Abbey and Jonah's age were still enjoying blissful naptimes while their kids were behind crib bars. A mom I knew with a child who was almost 3 still had her in a crib. But those days, were now gone. I was desperately envious.

It wasn't that I harbored fantasies of being my kids' jailer, but it was a lot easier to get things done when I didn't have to worry about them taking the furniture apart or staging prison breaks.

The girlie-girl

We were walking through a local furniture store when suddenly, she bolted away from us. My 2-year-old daughter dashed toward a children's furniture display. Strange "oohing" and "aahing" sounds emanated from somewhere deep within her.

When we found her, Abbey was sitting at a white, kid-sized table decorated with little pink ballerina slippers. "Ohh, I looove it!" she cooed as she literally wrapped her arms around the table in an embrace typically reserved for her dolls or close relatives. "It's my faaavorite. I want to take it home."

This was followed by similarly earnest declarations of love for the princess styled, pink lace canopy bed that stood beside the table. "I want this. I love this," she oozed. We had to tear her away from the display's pink luster as she cried and expressed her undying devotion to the color pink.

I didn't understand where this was coming from or who this stereotypical girlie girl was. Was this really *my* daughter? Abbey was becoming obsessed with the color pink and all things girl. The toddler had only recently started being forceful about her fashion sense and began shunning anything blue unless some portion of the fabric included a shade of pink, some lace or a ruffle to it.

She demanded to wear "a pretty dress" every day, whether we were headed for a birthday party, the sandbox or a walk in the woods. If I put out a pair of non-pink pants or shorts to get dressed for the day, and I'd have to gird myself for literal battle, to prepare to physically put those clothes back on her body multiple times that day because she'd strip herself of any offensive duds as soon as she was out of eye shot.

Abbey grew to adore her assortment of dolls and hardly gave her twin brother's Matchbox cars a passing glance, unless she was bored and wanted to torment him, in which case, she'd steal the entire line of cars and run away. Most of the time, she'd ignore the two tons of kid's sporting equipment that we had, despite my husband Scott and my attempts to stimulate an interest in sports by placing a toddler basketball hoop in her bedroom. No go. After a few tepid heaves of the ball toward the hoop, she'd skip off to play with her tea set.

For the record, I'm not a girlie girl. Yeah, I wear make-up, dresses, form fitting attire and heels when I'm so inclined. I look typically feminine, but when I'm spending the day at home with the kiddos, you're more likely to find me in a pair of jeans or shorts, T-shirt and a baseball cap than anything resembling a June Cleaver get-up. As a child, I had dolls (my favorites were the Donny and Marie figures), but, at a young age I also became obsessed with the Red Sox — in particular, their right fielder, Dwight Evans — and loved wearing my Red Sox jacket.

In fact, none of the adult females who Abbey routinely encountered in the first two years of her life were overtly girlish. Her grandmothers would wear pants on most occasions. Her aunts played women's basketball. One of them also played on a women's hockey team, in addition to participation in a softball league and part-time work as a ski instructor.

When the twins were born, Scott and I promised one another that we wouldn't stick them into gender ghettos by making Abbey wear only pink, frilly (re: scratchy) duds and play only with girl toys, or by making Jonah wear only blue, tough boy clothes and play with monster Tonka trucks. Their toys were gender neutral. Of the clothes we purchased for them, most, though not all of them were unisex (it made laundry so much easier). Their rooms were decorated in a gender-neutral fashion as well. His had a Winnie the Pooh theme. Hers had a celestial theme. Even the TV programs we let them watch when they were very young didn't promote gender stereotyped roles or sexist behavior.

We were very, very careful, and, upon reflection, more than a bit naïve.

Her second birthday, however, was when things hit the fan and we lost control. (We lost control a lot earlier than that but didn't really realize it at the time.) Abbey received three baby dolls as gifts from people who thought we were being too rigid with our informal doll ban. She was smitten. And seemingly overnight, she blossomed into a picture perfect girlie girl, exuding an inner sparkle.

Not only did her tastes sink completely into the depths of hellish pink, but her attitude did as well. She even started to occasionally alter her voice from its normally sing-songy happy tone into a kind of saccharin flirty pitch, complete with – I kid you not – eyelash fluttering.

Begrudgingly, I realized that I was going to have to steel myself for that inevitable trip that I knew I was going to have to take sooner rather than later to that creepy pink part of the toy store that has always made me shudder when I passed it. You all know the one: The Barbie aisle. But, despite my feelings toward stereotypical girlishness, I decided that I'd accept whoever my daughter would become, whether that be a baseball glove toting tomboy, or a femme fatale.

"Barbie," I said, "ready or not, here I come."

Baby no more

The first time around, I was militant. I had to be. I had twins. I was outnumbered and out-hollered at every turn. Scott and I devised a game plan of how we were going to muddle through the twins' first year of life and still maintain a modest modicum of sanity.

By the time Jonah and Abbey turned 1, we had them weaned and drinking store-bought milk from cups. Their binkies were gone. They were on quasi-regular nap schedules. They were in their own rooms.

Three years later, our littlest one arrived.

Our last one.

Our baby.

And we were militant no more. We had been defeated by the rambunctiousness and resourcefulness of parenthood. Our game plan of how things were "supposed to be" was in shambles.

Once Casey was born, he became the beneficiary of parents who were mellowed by three years of failed attempts to try to out-plot and out-strategize his older siblings. Our delusion that we could keep a handle on our household of three little people with rules and overarching guidelines was demolished. Our single goal was stripped down to the bone: We just wanted to get through the kids' early years with everyone in the family happy and, for the most part, in tact.

But as we struggled with the realities of being outnumbered by our kids, time did a funny thing. It sped up. And, without our really noticing, our baby was a year old.

Unlike Abbey and Jonah's infancy — where their needs were the absolute center of my world and every moment focused on them — Casey's babyhood passed like a 30-second TV ad for an overpriced sports car: Lots of loud noises, smelly exhaust, blinding lights and a quick fade-out.

I wasn't ready for my baby not to be a baby anymore.

As Casey neared mobility, I realized that I didn't want to rush the process. I didn't want to cajole him into crawling or walking. I wanted him to achieve his developmental milestones in slow motion, but everything in our house was hurtling forward at light speed. I wanted to enjoy every facet of my last baby's infancy just a little longer.

Though my oldest two were only in preschool, they'd transformed into individuals before my eyes with breathtaking alacrity. When I watched videos of them when they were wee ones wriggling beneath the baby gym, it seemed like a lifetime ago.

When you see pictures of yourself holding your firstborn(s), you look so innocent. You may be smiling in those photos, but behind that smile, you now realize that you had no idea of how your life was going to change. By the time that wrinkly little lump of love hit preschool, your pre-kid self seemed as foreign and outdated as your sophomore prom duds and the sitcoms you loved to watch at age 13.

By the time your last and littlest is cooing in your arms, you've (hopefully) acquired some wisdom, some experience. You know that not only do you want to cling to every little milestone, but to take the time to reflect on how the child is changing and growing. You forget about being militant or structured or about parenting guidelines. You now know that childhood, and particularly infancy, is but a sweet, fleeting moment to be savored, not rushed.

But trying to find the time for reflection oftentimes seems like an utterly ridiculous luxury, particularly when you have more than one small child. In a house buzzing with activities – dance class, preschool, play groups, emptying the odorific Diaper Genie and keeping the crawling baby from playing the toilet – it was a relief when they were all in bed and I could sit quietly for five consecutive minutes.

When all three kids were awake, I was in a constant state of torn loyalties. I wanted to make sure the older kids were playing with toys or doing activities that mentally stimulated them and physically challenged them so they'd flop on their beds at night from sheer exhaustion and give me minimal difficulty. At the same time, I'd see Casey chasing after his older siblings and worry that I wasn't doing enough age-appropriate activities for him, like pointing out colors and shapes. I spent an inordinate amount of time with Abbey and Jonah when they were babies reading to them, sounding out words, explaining what an octagon is and showing them pictures of bunnies and cows.

With Casey, I felt as though he was getting a raw deal. His nap schedule was disrupted so I could drive the older ones to school or to library story times. His age-appropriate toys were either confiscated by his brother and sister, or pushed aside by him in favor of cooler looking big kid toys. And then I had to worry about keeping any potential toys that were choking hazards away from Casey – who the kids nicknamed "The Menace" – so he wouldn't eat them.

Given that our lives circa 2002 were dominated by seamless waves of haphazard motion and sound, I didn't notice that my baby had hurried himself through his infancy until it was too late. When he reached the end of his first year, I was grossly unprepared for the fact that my little baby was now a toddler. I felt like I'd somehow missed his babyhood while I was tackling a mountain of laundry, driving Jonah and Abbey to activities and retrieving fistfuls of dry cat food from the recesses of Casey's mouth.

So, on his first birthday, I decided to make a concerted effort to slow things down, to leave the dirty dishes in the sink and the laundry in the dryer. I made time to take Casey's hand and point out the world to him. I'd take his hand and have him touch crunchy fall leaves, the moist blades of grass, the cool water in the puddles on the sidewalk. And he was thrilled by the simple. By life. I tried to remember to cherish that snapshot in time while he walked beside me, clutching my fingers and we shared the same breath of fresh air. Together.

Candy Land ain't so sweet

We bought into the whole ad campaign.

Hook.

Line.

And yes, let's finish the cliché: Sinker too.

We thought we'd have oodles of fun with our preschoolers, open their minds, spawn a few wholesome, family chuckles. We'd have so much darned fun, just like in those Milton Bradley TV commercials.

One weekend night, Scott and I pulled out one of the classic board games touted as part of a collection of children's "first board games." We thought we were joining the legions of families sitting in kitchen chairs — made comfortably sticky by half-chewed raisins, dried strawberry yogurt and unloved mystery food rotting in the wooden grooves — and sharing some character building moments playing Candy Land, a game of which I possess some fine childhood memories.

However, some 10 minutes into it, our then 4-year-old daughter Abbey realized she wasn't going to be the first to be welcomed with open arms by the generously girthsome if not jolly-right plump King Kandy at the famed Candy Land castle waiting at the end of the multi-colored lane. But what upset her more than potentially losing to her parents? Losing to her twin brother Jonah who was well on his way to bustin' down that castle door.

That's when her fury was gloriously unleashed. Everyone ducked to avoid the hailstorm, everyone except toddler Casey, who used the opportunity to scan the table for small things to stuff into his mouth including one of the colored plastic gingerbread playing pieces. The yellow one, I think.

Playing this game just wasn't as much fun as I thought it was going to be. Yes, I expected there would be disappointment when one of the kids inevitably eeked out ahead of the other. I knew that it would be a major bummer if one kid was on the cusp of passing through the Molasses Swamp — just six colored squares away from King Kandy – and wound up being sent all the way back to spend some quality time with the mischievous Mr. Mint, who spends his time vandalizing the Peppermint Forest like he was in a teenaged game of mailbox baseball (look at the game board and you'll see him wildly knocking down peppermint trees).

But the theatrics.

Though there weren't any table-clearing antics in the first years of board game playing – but believe me, if our early forays were any indication, board clearing is iron-clad guaranteed in my family's future – there were tears. Little lithe bodies flopped off their perches on the aforementioned sticky chairs and landed on the floor where they involuntarily curled up in the fetal position.

Screams were emitted. ("But I wanted the Queen Frostine card! Wahhhh!")

There was shoving. ("I want the red piece. NO! It's mine. I like red better," shouted in concert with a symphony of primitive grunting, accompanied by a dull-sounding thud of flesh hitting wood.)

Protests have been lodged. ("No fair, that's supposed to be my card. I get the card with two red squares! Red's my favorite. Tell him to give it to me! NOW!")

Lord Licorice and his ominous, dark castle had been cursed multiple times when the card bearing his likeness was drawn, sending some small person's playing piece back several spaces, precariously close to that delinquent minty guy. ("I'm not going there! I HATE Lord Licorice.")

My memories of childhood board games are highlighted by a fair share of tussles and playing card avarice, but the true struggles didn't truly emerge until my brother Sean and I were at least in the tail end of grade school. Real physical fights (or psychological ones) didn't commence until then because I'm four years older than my brother and, for a precious, sparse number of years, he did whatever I told him to do. If I told him that the gray squirrel inhabiting the Peanut Brittle House had become rabid, ate Gramma Nut, looted her wooden shack, and ordered that Sean go back 30 spaces, skip two turns and swear off peanut butter, he would've been sad, but he would've done it. And then I would win. (No wonder I have fond memories of playing board games when I was a young kid, that, and the fact that my parents would always let me win.)

I have hazy memories of the time when the fun filled games that always went my way gradually morphed into a horns-locked, blood curdling competition, probably at about the same time my brother started thinking for himself and rebuffing my dictatorial commands. Then he had the temerity to start winning games. And the ginger-bread men playing pieces started to fly.

During sessions of contortionists' favorite past time, Twister, it wouldn't take long for the games to turn into wrestling matches, with the person in the most advantageous position "accidentally" bumping the other, sending the unfortunate and losing sibling to the ground with a heart pleasing bang.

Any game involving play money spawned two sets of suspicious eagle eyes, always on alert for pilfering and unsavory, monetary tactics, with hair-trigger accusation activators. One member of a set of dice would accidentally nick the corner of the playing board and there'd be a 10-minute debate over whether the roll was legit.

It's not that we fought every minute, we just fought at some point during virtually every game. This has continued to current day, though Sean and I don't resort to shoving in order to win. Sarcasm and psychological torture have supplanted the physical aspect of competition.

At least once a year, Sean or I can be counted on to break out Trivial Pursuit or Scrabble at a family gathering and play until some-one falls asleep or is forced to wear the shape of an "L" on his or her forehead (L for "loser" of course). One summer, we had to invest in an official Scrabble dictionary because there was controversy about whether Sean, who was in law school at the time, was fabricating so-called legal terms that no one knew, suspiciously converting three-letter words into 564 point scores. (Yes Sean, you fabricated. This jig is up.) The following year, upon finally beating him, I post-ed the score tally on the fridge during a family vacation with great fanfare, took a picture of it and later placed it prominently in a family scrapbook.

Not that I'm a sore winner or anything.

And I can't figure out why my kids are already battling over who got the card with two red squares. Maybe, in fact, I was the one who was bitten by the ferocious, rabid Candy Land squirrel and neglected to get my rabies shots thus rendering me unable to play any board games without feeling as though I must win or I will combust.

Hopefully my kids' game playing won't be as competitive as it has been for my brother and me. Unfortunately, an absence of hot, competitive juices is about as likely to as Princess Lolly orchestrating a palace coup, dethroning the portly King Kandy and renaming the entire place Fantasy Land.

Timeout travails

Let me be plain about this: Timeouts don't seem to work. You know, "timeouts," the modern, gussied up form of the old parental standby, "Go stand in the corner," when a young child is behaving badly.

These are not to be confused with timeouts in sporting events, like basketball games when a team is getting crushed and needs a break. Actually, it is kind of like that, only that the kid involved likely sees the timeout as minutes spent in the penalty box like in hockey when you're sent there for behaving badly and not to get a chance to take a breather, while you, the parent, frankly, would prefer to slip out into the concession area and grab a cold one.

In the last half of the 1990s (which coincided with my first foray into parenthood), timeouts were advocated by pediatric experts as a good way for a parent and a young tot to take an escalating situation and diffuse it by removing the child from that situation which has spawned the fracas and afford the kid and the parent a chance to take a few deep breaths and "reflect" on the problem.

That's the theory anyway.

But from my experience with my three kids, I don't think they really work, particularly with toddlers and preschoolers who are completely and utterly irrational. Maybe it's a flawed technique. Maybe it's my kids. Maybe it's me. Or maybe it's the fact that 2-year-olds aren't supposed to respond to the logical consequences of their actions. Maybe it's all just poppycock.

When my daughter was 4, she struggled with containing her anger. Sadly, she inherited her mother's hair-trigger hot temper, coupled with the hearty helping of stubbornness. No amount of time spent "reflecting" in a timeout where she was standing next to a wall alone when she was a toddler or preschooler seemed to stop her from repeatedly doing things that: a) She'd been sternly told not to do a billion times, b) Would hurt her, c) Would hurt one of her brothers, or d) Destroy large (re: expensive) items in the house, like doors, furniture and major appliances.

It was almost as if she planned out her maneuvers in advance. "I'm going to torment Mommy until her eyes bug out and she's sobbing in the corner like a baby," I envisioned her thinking as she awakened each morning, looking deceptively like an angel with little, dark ringlets framing her pudgy face.

I knew it was going to be a banner day for so-called "positive discipline" advocacy when it began with Abbey openly doing negative things to get my attention. The child-rearing books said parents should ignore this behavior because giving her attention reinforced her negative efforts. But I found it exceedingly difficult to ignore her efforts when they involved things like smashing a plastic chair over her twin brother Jonah's head, framing her toddler brother for a variety of infractions (like ripping up books and then shoving the remnants in front of a quizzical looking Casey,) or pulling apart various pieces of furniture. It's not that she was a rotten or ill-mannered kid. She was, a spirited little lass, shall we say.

My unsuccessful struggles in trying to make the timeout technique effective with my older two kids, made me fear that I'd turn into one of those pleading parents who speak so gratingly and ineffectively in public places like grocery stores: "Paul, now remember what Mommy said. Please put that down now . . . Paul, Paul . . . Please put that down now . . . Hon-eeeey, please listen. . . Okay Paul, now if you put that down, I'll get you an ice cream . . . Okay, okay honey, I'll just buy it . . . Yes, yes sweetie, and the blue one too. Okay, okay."

I wanted to have a spine. (Last time I checked, it was still there, if not being used to its full capacity.) I didn't want to let my kids transform me into a walking, overcooked noodle who capitulated to them because I couldn't take one more moment of whining or screaming, or because I didn't want to play a supporting role in another daily installment of "Let's Have a Public Temper Tantrum." I also didn't want to become a screaming shrew who had nothing to say that didn't register below the shriek level.

Desperate, I attended parenting workshops in my early parenting years to find out what I was doing wrong. The experts then informed me, after I'd been using timeouts for four years, that a backlash against timeouts in the child development field had occurred. Experts now believed that they *shouldn't* be used as a disciplinary technique any more. One parenting instructor told a group of worried parents that instead of resorting to timeouts, we should remove our children from negative situations and "distract" them, all the while, cooing peaceful, soothing utterances to calm them. Threats, such as withholding TV or treats, we were told, were considered off-limit techniques.

I shook my head, trying to understand what this "expert" was telling me: I shouldn't send my toddler or preschoolers to their rooms or take away any privileges in order to discipline them. I wasn't supposed to yell or reprimand. Instead, I was supposed to bring the child who was likely kicking and screaming at me and just bloodied her sibling, into another room, maintain my cool and stroke her head calmly, while my other kid is bleeding onto the new slipcover and my youngest is making little, swirly smears in the blood drops?

I had three kids under the age of 5 at the time I was seeking out this advice. Did I happen to mention that? How was that technique supposed to work here on the planet Earth? Not only did I not have the time to take the "negatively behaving child" and accompany her to another room while giving her a veritable Swedish massage to put her in a Zen-like state, I didn't have the energy to do so every day, multiple times a day and not wind up speaking in tongues by 7 p.m. If I had to respond with TV Land faux happiness and phony calm to every infraction 24/7, I know that I would self-combust from the pressure. (Think of the mess that would make.)

And wouldn't all this special individual attention only serve to encourage negative behavior, if the child knows that I'd drop everything, leave the other two siblings' sides, and bring the ill behaving youth into another room to calm him or her?

In the abstract, of course it would be nice to sit down with each child when he or she is acting out, but in reality, that just wasn't going to happen. I operated in the real world, not in a sociological experimental lab with controlled conditions. And nannies.

So what realistic, applicable techniques were left in my parental tool box to use to teach my young offspring that hurtful or disrespectful behavior wasn't acceptable? The only tools I had were the now questionably effective timeouts and threats of the withdrawal of treats or privileges, things that parental experts now claim are old fashioned, but that parents had used for generations.

Perhaps, I should've just sought out Mary Poppins, or someone from "Nanny 911" to my house to turn my kids into the angels they resemble when they're asleep, because of course the accented nanny would know what to do in a positive, always smiling and educational manner.

Or, I could've just used Plan B: Realized that this is what being a parent is all about and give myself a timeout.

Twinkle toes

To say that my sparkly, pink-clothed daughter was tailor made for ballet classes was, my friends, a dramatic understatement.

To say that I was ready to be labeled a "dance parent," was, frankly, a laughable assumption.

To say that I was prepared for the transformation Abbey (and my wallet) would undertake during her time as a dance student, an equally laughable assumption.

When I signed Abbey up for a six-week ballet try-out at a local dance company when she was only but 3 years old, I didn't possess unrealistic expectations that she'd suddenly transform into Giselle and acquire grace beyond her years. I thought the teachers might instill in her some poise, all the poise that could reasonably be mustered by a preschooler. And while she wasn't exactly the portrait of smooth, gentle motion – she more resembled a well-coiled spring, think Tigger of the 100 Acre fame – she certainly had no problems adapting to the notion of dancing divadom.

In short order, she transformed from a toddler with an affinity for the backpack-toting girl explorer Dora and the cheeky, red-headed French girl Madeline, to one suddenly obsessed with Angelina ballerina, flowy clothes and dancing shoes.

I knew I was in trouble when, after our six-week trial ballet classes ended and I signed her up for a full year of instruction (making me an official dance parent), she suddenly cared about the type of leotard she wore. Initially, the plain pink leotard with the long sleeves and plain skirt I'd purchased for my little girl was a big hit. But as soon as Abbey realized that there were other types of leotards – sleeveless ones, ones with sparkly hearts (sparkly is big in the world of young dancers), ones with airy skirts — I was informed in short order of my grievous fashion error after she saw what the other girls in her class were wearing.

Once her ruffled feathers were settled regarding her mother's obviously passé sense of dancing duds (or maybe she was just distracted by seeing her reflection in the mirrored dance room),

Abbey was introduced to a new concept that would keep her, and her mother, in its grip for much of the year: The dance recital.

Deluded soul that I was, I thought that having a kid in dance class was about a cute leotard, dancing to a little of Tchaikovsky's "Nutcracker Suite" and a cute routine comprised of little girls nervously shifting their feet around.

Not even close.

About half-way through the dance year (which coincided with the school year), I was presented with an order form for a stage ensemble for my little tot to don when her graceful piggies set foot on the stage at her very first recital. Ah, the visions of spotlights and rosy cheeks, with Abbey waving to Mommy. The heart just melts.

Until I caught a gander of the costume's price tag.

To steal a line from a fellow novice, dance mom: This was the most expensive dress-up costume I'd ever purchased. It was lovely, I must admit, a lavender, velour number with spaghetti straps adorned with deep violet, blue and green silk flowers and matching chiffon strips flowing down the back. This was topped with a sparkly belted chiffon skirt and a set of lavender butterfly wings.

But when the costumes were delivered, every item for her pre-school class was two sizes too big. I had two choices: Pay for alterations or do them myself. (I wound up doing my own crude sewing job and, let's just say that it's a good thing that Abbey was up onstage, far, far away from the scrutinizing eyes of competent sewers.)

Then I got the 8-page recital handout, plus many more supplemental handouts. I started to get nervous. There were several deadlines, order forms, all kinds of schedules and people with whom to coordinate. Maybe I wasn't cut out to be a dance parent. My kid was only 3 years old for cryin' out loud.

As the recital grew closer, I suddenly realized that not only did I have to pay $10 per ticket for everyone to attend the recital (a common practice at dance schools throughout the civilized world apparently), but I had to order tickets quickly for fear of losing out on my family's allotment. That would make me the talk of the recital, the idiot parent with no tickets.

Delving deeper into my dance parent handouts, I learned that not only did I have to buy tickets to her premiere, but most parents get their kids a truckload of fragrant blossoms to rest in their dancers' delicate arms. I didn't know you were supposed to get a preschooler flowers. Had I not made sure that she had some precious petals (from grandma and grandpa) to hold as she emerged from her performance, I would've surely been viewed as a veritable scrooge.

On top of the costume, tickets and flowers, there was also the make-up question. I struggled over whether to let my preschooler wear make-up to the recital like everyone told me she should. Wouldn't it send her the wrong, beauty pageantish message? Would she think that she'd suddenly been given the okay to wear lipstick, eye shadow, mascara and blush when she wasn't on stage? (Luckily, she didn't notice the glitter other mommies smeared on their daughters' cheeks and shoulders before stepping on stage. Had she seen it in the dressing room, I would've been strong-armed into transforming her into a walking disco ball.)

So, as the apex of Abbey's first year of dance classes neared, on what did I, the newbie dance parent, cave? **Yes to:** A sparkly leotard, personally altered costume, flowers (my mom bought her pink roses), seven tickets, make-up, the "official" recital video and onstage recital photos at $45 for a 4 X 6 (no, just kidding, they were only $35 each, plus $20 shipping). **No to:** Sparkly make-up and an official studio portrait done off-site so Abbey could vamp for the camera.

On the big day, as I plopped my cynical self into my seat to watch my daughter on stage for approximately four minutes, I was surprisingly moved. As she twirled, waved to the audience, scratched her elbows in a brief moment of confusion and then remembered to point her toes and plie, I found myself wiping the tears from my face.

There she was.

Even though I didn't have any glittering make-up on my own face, I was temporarily blinded by the star in my eyes.

Safe at first

It's a swing.

And a miss.

Swing.

And a miss.

Swing.

And . . . ooh, almost . . . nope, it was a foul tip. Damn.

Twenty swings later . . . after his coach had thrown out his elbow, after his mother's head had sprouted exactly 22 new gray hairs, the boy finally coaxed the bat and the ball to connect. The ball dribbled earnestly down the first base line, still desperately clinging to fair territory. The boy successfully made it to the safety of the soft, squishy base.

Safe at first.

Finally.

A typical inning of beginner baseball or T-ball can last an awfully long, gut wrenching time, particularly for parents, with their nails dug into the palms of their hands or their fingers tightly crossed. Parents can do nothing but watch their progeny stand nakedly alone, unprotected next to home plate until he or she finally hits the ball.

Even though my son Jonah was simply taking a class to teach him the basics of baseball – where the rug rats stood at home plate until they actually hit the pitched ball — it felt like so much more.

My oldest son had been taking baseball for about nine months at an indoor sports facility. For months, he proudly took to the Astro-turfed field, trusty Red Sox jersey and baseball hat in place, clutching an impossibly small leather glove with his name proudly scrawled on the side in permanent black marker.

Each time he would leave me and his two siblings behind at the bleachers and excitedly take to the field, I found myself unexpectedly experiencing a vicarious sense of déjà vu.

Jonah – who had not yet been the last batter in a game when there were two outs and the potentially tying run was on base – hadn't yet experienced that pang of disappointment, that awful knowledge that one's own performance (or lack thereof) could be a game ender. He hadn't felt the sweat-inducing peer pressure to perform, and the perilous probability of mocking and scorn, particularly in the form of other parents' grumbling, if one's athletic play was sub-par. He'd never had the added strain of knowing that Mom and Dad were watching, making him deathly afraid of making a mistake that would embarrass his parents or guarantee another lesson at home on how to keep his "eye on the ball."

He was a total innocent.

It was me who was the wreck, worrying about his future anxieties, worrying about heartache that hadn't even occurred yet.

Yes, I knew it was only a teaching league. I knew that the kids were just getting schooled in the sport. It wasn't about competition. It was about cultivating a love for America's favorite past time.

It wasn't as though I was acting like the troubling sports dad-in-waiting who brought his kindergarten-aged son to class and shouted at him to focus on the plays or run down ground balls. His son, who didn't always pay attention, was like most of the little kids on the field. At any given moment, a number of the would-be players could be seen staring at their shoelaces, sitting on the ground, doing cartwheels or tumbling tricks along the baselines. If these kids were playing ball outside, I'm certain some would be doing random gardening chores, like pulling out dandelions or stomping on ant hills.

So the fact that most of the kids with whom Jonah was playing weren't natural baseball superstars, the fact that it took many of them 17 pitches before they could hit the ball should have been a comfort to me.

It should have been.

Then, upon the recommendation of the ever-patient coach, I moved Jonah from the 4-5 year-old class to the 5-7 year-old class. He went from a group where he was about average sized, to one where he was the smallest kid.

When he stepped to the plate in his new class, I would hold my breath. I found myself wanting to turn away because I was helpless up there in the stands. I couldn't wiggle my nose a la Samantha in

"Bewitched" and magically send the ball directly at the meat of Jonah's bat. I couldn't verbally pummel the menacingly bigger kids playing infield who rolled their eyes or openly griped about the length of time it took for Jonah to hit the ball.

I remained riveted in place on the aluminum bleachers, wanting so much for him to do well, for him to be pleased with himself, for him not to feel the pressure that I felt when I was watching him because I didn't want him to be disappointed in himself. He was learning and he was doing great. But standing there, solo at home plate, pride has a way of taking a hit with every pitch that whizzes by.

Intellectually, I could tell myself that the early tribulations one experiences while learning a new skill are character building. If everything just came easily to Jonah, then he really wouldn't learn the value of hard work, I rationally reasoned every week as we entered the sports center that smelled of a combination of ammonia-heavy store brand cleanser, sweat and adolescent sneakers.

With practice, I was sure my 5-year-old would come to understand the intricate dance, the precise timing between a pitched ball and a swatted bat. And even though he was not going to be a sports superstar, I hoped that his life in the world of extra-curricular sports would be filled with pleasure, devoid of the pressure and disappointment that too many parents like me pass down to our own kids. Jonah was bound to have moments of great accomplishment that would reside side-by-side with disappointment — the B side of Queen's "We Are the Champions" – in his heart.

As a mere bystander a couple hundred feet away from him, I wished I could wrap invisible arms around my little boy and let him know that no matter what happened when he was standing at home plate, he'd always be the champion of my heart.

Tooth dismay

Damned tooth.

Damned, crooked, hanging-by-a-thread tooth.

For a white pearl of enamel not even a quarter as wide as the nail on my pinky finger, that damned tooth consumed well over an hour's worth of my life, time I'll never see again.

Its last moments weren't pretty. Let's just say that there was blood, screaming and the swatting away of flailing hands that wound up with said tooth getting propelled into the air, onto the living room rug to finally come to a rest under a chair.

And now, after struggle, pain and the inevitable creation of a few more frustration wrinkles in my forehead, a very cranky Tooth Fairy has to cough up a dollar for this gem.

Okay, so here's the back story:

My 5-year-old daughter Abbey had already lost her first tooth a month before this incident. Two of her bottom teeth – the ones in the middle — were being edged out of position by her grown-up teeth and had been "wiggly" for some time.

And seeing as though she is the first of our three children to have any loose teeth, this was a matter of great import in our household. To her twin brother Jonah, none of whose teeth had moved nary a millimeter, as well as to her 2-year-old brother Casey, being in possession of a wiggly tooth was akin to having a learner's permit to drive. You were almost there, almost to that big moment.

There was much fanciful talk of the Tooth Fairy.

"Maybe the Tooth Fairy will bring me a whole box of new Barbies," Abbey said, clapping her hands together, before she lost her first tooth.

"Maybe I'll get more Legos or baseball stuff," Jonah mused.

I quickly had to put the kibosh on their entirely misguided notions. "The Tooth Fairy isn't Santa Claus. This isn't Christmas."

I tried to tamp down any talk of crates full of buxom, rubbery babes with pointy shoes and images of a truckload of primary colored building blocks being left in a tidy bow next to my children's beds.

"Maybe you'll get a quarter, or a dollar," I added, not sure of the current rate of Tooth Fairy reimbursement, as it had been quite some time since she'd visited my boudoir.

Then, quite unexpectedly on a Saturday morning, Abbey's first tooth was violently jettisoned from its delicate little socket when the little lass used her bottom teeth to pry two Legos apart. And she didn't even cry.

My husband, however, did. Well, not cried, but openly blanched when Abbey came to him with a big, bloody smile, proudly bearing in the palm of her left hand her first baby tooth. But Scott missed the smile, and the tooth, and saw only the blood.

"Oh my God!" he shouted, instinctively covering his own mouth as he started to panic.

Upon seeing Scott's reaction, Abbey started to cry. "Oh, Abbey," said the mommy who's much better at dealing with bloody situations than her spouse, "you lost a tooth! That's so exciting! Let's go get a wash cloth!"

Scott and I both talked up the imminent arrival of the Tooth Fairy that night. So did Grandma, Grandpa, Auntie Lisa, Uncle Sean and everyone else Abbey spoke with on the phone throughout the day as she shared her jubilant news.

This had two adverse reactions:

It sent Jonah into a fit of jealousy. "That's not fair!" he yelled, eyes brimming with tears. When he was reminded that not only did this mean that he had more teeth than Abbey, but that, once all her teeth were gone and the Tooth Fairy had come and gone, he would still be getting visits from the mystical lady, his tears magically stopped.

After hearing all about the Tooth Fairy from every adult she knew, Abbey soon grew leery of some strange woman-beast entering her room under cover of darkness and feeling around her pillow while the girl was asleep. After an hour of pretending to sleep, Abbey emerged from her room and said she was scared. We decided to place the special tooth-shaped pillow designated for this very occasion, with her first lost tooth inside, on the kitchen table instead.

So, having lost one tooth already, I thought losing all the rest of this losing teeth business would be a piece of cake for her, particularly because the first incident was so abrupt and bloody.

But the second tooth was overly loose for a painfully long period of time. For weeks, it gradually shifted position until it was virtually resting in a horizontal position in her mouth.

Then I made matters worse after I told her she should make sure to pay attention to what she was eating in case her tooth fell out in her food. "I could swallow my tooth?" she asked in horror.

Dumb mother.

No amount of explaining could assuage her that she wouldn't get sick from accidentally swallowing or eating her tooth.

"Well what would happen if you ate your tooth? How would it come out?" Jonah demanded, taking copious notes.

"You'd poop it out."

All together now kids: "Ewww!" (And I wondered why she chewed out of the side of her mouth for an extraordinarily long time?)

Finally, the looseness was getting to her. The tooth was barely hanging on. And she wanted me to help her to get it out. Or so she thought.

An hour later, after I had her bite down on two M&M cookies, a baby carrot stick, a cheese flavored rice cake and an ice cream sandwich (I wanted something to cool her overheated gums), she then projectile vomited.

No, just kidding. What she did was far worse. She begged me to take the tooth out myself, and then, when I'd get near her to maybe wiggle it around with my index finger, she'd start flailing, sobbing and kicking, or else she'd quickly turn her head away so I'd mistakenly scratch her face.

I repeatedly told her, "You don't have to take the tooth out. You can just wait for it to fall out on its own. It's up to you."

Her puffy red eyes focused on me. "What would you do Mommy?" Now this was a first. She'd never before actually solicited my advice on anything of significance.

"I'd take it out because it would probably bug me, but the choice is up to you."

It took another 10 minutes: Two seconds of allowing Mommy to touch the tooth, followed by 30 seconds of crying, two minutes of discussion and many more minutes of coaxing and calming. In the end, I had her lay down on the floor so I could put a wet paper towel on either side of the tooth when the ridiculous thing finally broke loose from the gum.

When the Tooth Fairy finally came that night, I breathed a sigh of relief. This dental drama was solved, at least temporarily. No other kids' teeth were loose or on the verge of naturally falling out any time soon. As long as we keep those Legos away from their mouths, the blood, gore and weird Tooth Fairy lady would be kept at bay.

"What does she do with all those teeth?" Abbey asked.

"I have no earthly idea Abbey. Now floss."

Whaddup Tooth Fairy?

Dear Tooth Fairy,

At first, I thought that you forgetting to visit our house when my daughter Abbey lost her tooth was simply an aberration, a random mistake. I thought you must've just had a bad night on the evening you forgot to come to our home, must've had a lot on your mind or perhaps you'd been besieged by the nasty stomach flu that's going around.

I was prepared to give you a pass. Then I found out that you've been missing other people's homes too, forgetting to pick up teeth all over the country.

So I have this one simple question: Whaddup?

It was hard to explain to my daughter Abbey why the Tooth Fairy forgot about her one spring evening. My little girl came bustin' into my bedroom in the 5 o'clock hour with tears running down her freckled face. After checking the little white, felt tooth container cleverly sewn (not by me) into the shape of a tooth that we leave on the kitchen counter (she loathes the concept of a strange lady sneaking around her room in the dark) and found her baby tooth still inside, she was crestfallen.

I quickly told Abbey that the Tooth Fairy must've been confused. You see, Abbey lost her tooth (I "helped," more on that later) just after dinner one night. Instead of putting the tooth in the special tooth container to be picked up that night like we usually do, Abbey really wanted to bring it to school to show her friends. So I placed the tiny tooth into a clear plastic baggie and told her that if she didn't return it home, the Tooth Fairy wouldn't come. She dutifully followed my instructions and brought the tooth back home the next afternoon and promptly deposited it inside the tooth container.

I told Abbey that by taking the tooth to school rather than putting it in the felt container the same night it fell out, she must've messed with the Tooth Fairy's mind. Even though the excuse sounded reasonable to the lass, Abbey continued to prattle on about the Tooth Fairy's slackery. So I told Abbey that I would go public about the Tooth Fairy's blunder. I promised to blog about it on my mommy blog, to tell the world about the error the magical tooth collector made in failing to pick up her tooth. And then, much to my surprise (as I thought this of sort of bungle only happened in my vastly flawed home), stories started to come in from all over about the Tooth Fairy's sudden forgetfulness. Her lack of a consistent work ethic, apparently, has become epic.

"The Tooth Fairy had to leave my niece an apology note saying she'd gotten caught in a blizzard in another part of the world and hadn't made it back to the United States in time to stop by the house the previous night," a woman named Jody wrote in to my parenting blog.

When fellow mom blogger Melissa Summers wrote about Abbey's saga, she lambasted the Tooth Fairy for "seriously falling down on the job." Writing on the Blogging Baby web site, Summers added that in her own Michigan home on the very same week, the Tooth Fairy had forgotten to leave money for Summers' daughter, and that this mistake had happened on another occasion as well. "I just don't think her heart is in it," Summers wrote.

These admissions prompted more parents to offer up their tales of Tooth Fairy absentmindedness:

"Hey, she missed our house a week or so ago too!" a California mom named Cee, wrote to Blogging Baby. "She did come the next night and leave a nice note and twice the going rate around our house."

(I didn't show Abbey Cee's comments for fear my grade schooler would be jealous that she only got the same rate – a dollar – for the tardy pick-up. I had yet to tell her about the gaping disparity in a different part of our neighborhood where I'd heard that the Tooth Fairy leaves, hold onto your hankies, a whopping $5 per tooth. There's something seriously wrong with that. How could the Tooth Fairy discriminate so blatantly?)

The Tooth Fairy even rooked at least one kid up in Canada, a mom named Kim reported to Blogging Baby, but that mother was willing to cut the Winged One some slack. "The Tooth Fairy is just one tiny little lady and she can only get to so many houses in one night," Kim wrote. "She often runs out of time before she gets all the way up here to Canada, as well. But she always makes it the next night, coincidentally."

No offense to Kim or any of the other Tooth Fairy advocates, but I'm sick of the excuse making. I'm tired of this Tooth Fairy getting the kids all excited, convincing them to save their bloody little baby teeth and put them under their pillows so that she'll visit the house that night, collect the tooth and leave some cash. And then she forgets all about it.

Losing a tooth, at least as far as my daughter is concerned, is a multi-day, full blown family melodrama. It usually involves a week or more of Abbey refusing to eat, or at least refusing to eat on the side of the mouth containing the loose tooth. She then insists on dining on only soft food. She whines. She moans about how much it *huurrrtts*, as you peer into her mouth and notice that the tooth is lying on her gum at a near 90-degree angle.

I usually offer to "take care of it" for her (I'm the Tony Soprano of loose teeth). And she almost always takes me up on my offer. Then she pulls back, covers her mouth and screams, "No!" Then, a minute later, a reversal, "Yes, yes! Okay, okay . . . Wait! No!!" Then she cries. While she's crying, I usually wind up putting pressure on the skin outside her mouth. The tooth comes out. And then she's thrilled. It's so predictable.

After all of this — the moaning, screaming, blood and the joyous release of the irritating little pearly white shard – we wait for the $1 payoff the next morning. For the Tooth Fairy to just forget about her part of the deal is inexcusable.

Maybe she's got too many commitments. Maybe she's stretched too thin. Maybe she needs to figure out how to focus, and not on silly things, like sleeping, eating working, caring for her three kids and watching the TV show "24." (I've read that she has three kids and obsesses over "24." I've got inside sources.) Maybe she needs some help, like a nanny, or someone to clean her house.

Sounds like the Tooth Fairy's desperate cry for help. Or for two pallets full of Starbucks whole bean coffee, and a quiet hour to read the newspapers in the morning.

I'm just sayin'.

Fashion weak

Time flashback to the year 2003: A precocious 4-year-old girl with her curly hair cut demurely in a bob, hitched up her omnipresent pink cotton shirt in order to expose her bellybutton. The preschooler then grabbed her size 4T flared jeans at the hips and inched them down her pelvic bone a bit to reveal more of her petite little belly.

"What are you doing?" I sternly inquired (trying not to utter the word "hell" in the middle of the question as I was aghast watching my daughter adoringly admire her hip self, literally, in the mirror). "You don't go to school showing your bellybutton like that!"

Her bright hazel eyes turned steely. "I like it this way."

In a move that I hated when I was a child, I ignored her self-expression-through-fashion and grabbed this product of my womb and yanked her shirt back down and her pants back up. "You don't dress like that. It's not right, especially for a preschool girl," I informed her.

She took a step away from me – which was prophetic more for the emotional rather than the physical distance suddenly between us – and replied, "I'll just do it again when I'm in school."

A year later, when she was 5, I was surprised to find her dancing in the family room to a Jennifer Lopez CD. It wasn't the dance music that caught me off guard (everyone in the house knew J.Lo.'s music by heart, though the youngins' had never seen her videos). It was her attire. If you'd suddenly burst into the room and saw the child, you would've thought that she somehow scammed a dusty old VHS copy of "Flashdance" and watched it, followed by 15 hours of MTV Hits while perusing a Victoria's Secret catalog.

She'd taken one of her preschooler undershirts, the one with the pink sparkly strip across the high neckline, and tightly secured it behind her back (exposing much of her midriff) with pink hair elastics while wearing a complementary pair of undies. Various other sparkly hair clips held up her ringlets.

This was not a home, mind you, where Mommy dressed in navel

exposing shirts or in flashy clothes. I didn't let my little Miss Abbey watch commercials or emulate those "Bratz" dolls who look like hookers ready for a booty call with their Botoxed pouty lips, big hair and ho clothing.

When material of a questionable sexual nature entered the house that I feared would unduly influence her, the material was trashed, or squired up into Mommy and Daddy's room. Things like my *Entertainment Weekly* subscription could be problematic with the magazine's ads, photo shoots and sometimes covers (like a cover featuring a near-nude nubile teen star sitting cross-legged with her private parts shielded by her limbs. That magazine cover, much to my husband's dismay, was immediately torn off the periodical and disposed of).

Occasionally, when I indulged myself in the fantasy that, on some days, I am somewhere on the edge of being kinda fashionable (I own too much L.L. Bean and Lands End cotton items to qualify as trendy), I've splurged on an issue of *In Style* Magazine. Inevitably, I'd have to rip out ads or just keep the magazine in my bedroom for fear that my daughter would gaze at the rail-thin, sexualized teen models standing in the middle of a city street wearing nothing but a gold necklace and a scarf and somehow think that this was normal.

In instances when my children saw some female in inappropriately, overly-sexy attire, I tried (in the best efforts of a former feminist that once tiptoed around the lines of militant) to teach them how to respond. See the cheerleaders at football games who look like they're ready to go swimming rather than cheering for their team in sub-zero weather that would freeze the spit off their pearly white teeth? "They should have more clothes on, huh? They look silly, don't they?" I'd say. (Full disclosure: I was once a high school cheerleader, but my midriff and rear end were always covered.)

Even when I read newspapers at the kitchen table each morning, I have to shield the underwear ads from the kids. I typically don't feel like having to teach lessons about how lingerie is not appropriate attire to wear in public while I trying to drink my first cup of coffee after being awoken at an ungodly hour by my 3-year-old whose first words to me on one particular morning were, "Stop breathing. Your breath smells bad."

If Abbey did get a glimpse of some slinky sisters in a newspaper or magazine ad and responded with an, "Oooh, look at the pretty ladies," my automatic reply was, "They are pretty, huh? But I think they forgot their clothes! That's nuts!"

In spite of my brainwashing attempts, I still found my daughter longingly looking at the teenagers at the local mall wearing low slung pants exposing parts of themselves that were better left covered in polite company (or perhaps spackled over so as to avoid inadvertently displaying unseemly crevices).

By the time Abbey turned 6, she and I all too often would engage in this twisted mother-daughter power dance over what she will wear to school. She thought I had no idea how to color coordinate separates, this kindergartener did. For the most part, I gave up trying to get her to wear anything that wasn't pink, purple or red, or any form of pants that isn't either: a) In any of the aforementioned colors b) Soft or c) Flared jeans.

But even when I worked within the aforementioned criteria, there was still routinely trouble:

Like when she insisted on wearing her pink, sparkly sandals to school for several days last fall during crisp New England weather. (After numerous shrieking arguments, I finally stooped to hiding the offending shoes.)

Like when she wanted to wear a thin, tank dress to gym class in January when there was two feet of snow on the ground and went crazy when I told her she couldn't.

Like when I presented her with a pair of pink jeans, pink shirt and oh-so-fashionable zip-up pink, sweater hoodie and she freaked because the pink jeans were "itchy" (although she'd worn them for previous months without complaint).

Did I mention that this kid was in *kindergarten*?

I thought I gave her plenty of latitude. In fact, I sometimes worried that she was the one who was running this asylum because her temper tantrums were exquisitely timed to coincide with the absolute moment when I had to get my brood out of the house in the morning. (She was not above agreeing to wear a mutually determined outfit and then appearing in different clothes when the school bus pulled up in front of the house.)

Was this premature teenaged rebellion? Was this going to be my lot in life for the next 12 years, arguing with my daughter over her clothing choices?

According to one national media outlet, she was less than two years away from that truly terrifying demographic group, the group known as "tweens," ages 8-12, the age when she'd be targeted with a bombardment of advertising and mature-before-their-time attire meant to drive a wedge between her parents and her, or at least between her parents and their money. Somehow I didn't foresee the advent of the "tween" years getting any better, at least fashion wise.

In response, I decided to pull my L.L. Bean turtleneck up high over my ears to provide at least some cushioning for when I continually banged my head against the wall.

Dirty lemonade

The senior department director zips through the electronic pile of resumes, as paper resumes are *sooo* 20th century here in the year 2020. One resume stands out. It's from some kid fresh out of college. He's got a stellar GPA, took interesting courses, and, get this: He's bilingual, is a Tae Kwon Do master, plays piano (loves jazz!), is on his college swim team (first place at the state competition!) and advanced to the Eagle Scout level. The director sends an Instant Message to my son Jonah suggesting an interview ASAP, and Jonah's new, fabulous career is all but assured, all thanks to some hyper, anal-retentive planning made by Mommy some 15 years earlier.

That's how I tried to rationalize this madness that I was trying my best to resist, this parental malady known as over-scheduling.

I'd read the warnings about over-programming kids, about signing them up for so many activities that they had no down time, no time to create their own back yard games, to fight with their siblings, to read comic books and to go on adventures in the woods which will inevitably yield some type of flesh wound or, at the very least, filthy clothes which sprinkle a variety of debris throughout the kitchen when the kids drag themselves in for dinner.

I wanted to offer my children the world but in offering them the world, I feared that I'd drain all the carefree joy out of being a kid with too many classes, courses and sessions. True kid-dom only actually lasts, what, 14 or 15 years, before the race to apply to colleges?

It's not that I didn't have extra curricular activities myself when I was a kid. At any given time during my childhood, I was a Brownie, a dancer taking jazz, a gymnast, a bad piano player (my Nana was the teacher), a center fielder on a lousy softball team and a singer in the church choir. My brother Sean played the trumpet, took karate, was a Cub Scout and played baseball, basketball and soccer. My parents, as a result, became coaches, den parents, Brownie leaders and volunteered for various things throughout the years.

But we didn't do all these activities simultaneously. Even when I was a Brownie, or was taking gymnastics once a week, Sean and I still had a ton of time to ourselves to mess around as we saw fit, to ride our bikes to the library downtown, to buy an ice cream at Friendly's, or to go to Duke's corner store where we would spend our allowance on 1-cent red Swedish fish and cheap balsam airplanes that broke within 10 minutes of use in the back yard.

Some of my best memories from my childhood involve not organized activities, but my own activities that I concocted with Sean, like transforming the living room into a "Star Wars" fortress, with darkened windows and Star Wars music booming in the background from our parents' giant record player as our Star Wars action figures lurked in "caves" made out of blankets and pillows.

Together, we sold dirty lemonade (mixed by hand, literally, when we claimed we couldn't locate a spoon) from our red, wooden wagon parked on the sidewalk in front of our house, for a paltry 10 cents a cup. (The E.coli was free.) Neighbors, kids and an occasional driver passing by (including the guy driving the ice cream truck) would cough up the change to do business with we pediatric, unlicensed lemonade purveyors.

My childhood wasn't programmed with a future college application in mind. It wasn't perfectly choreographed so that when I went after jobs with my college diploma in hand, that I'd naturally bubble up to the top of the heap because I had a set of skills that few others possessed. (Avoiding E. coli infestation, should I have put that on the old resume?)

So what was my problem once I became a parent? It was the fact that my desk soon became littered with applications for Tae Kwon Do, ballet school, spring soccer, T-ball, baseball, indoor baseball, swimming lessons, sports for preschoolers, drama club, piano lessons and Spanish classes for the very young. I felt overwhelmed by the abundance of possibilities, like I was holding my three children's future on these thin pieces of paper between my fingers, and that if I didn't act, other parents would and my kids would be at a disadvantage.

Take Spanish lessons. When I took Spanish in middle and high school, I came away with precious little real knowledge. After five years of Spanish, the only things I remember are the Spanish phrases for "shut up," "poor thing," and a colloquialism that roughly translates into something like, "Oh what the devil!" but that's only because my grandmother spoke Spanish and said these things in my presence. Research on children's foreign language education largely indicates that the best time for kids to pick up a new language is when they are young. If you wait until high school for foreign language instruction, like I did, it's harder to grasp the language.

So, as I looked at the application for Spanish classes for my young children, I couldn't help but think that I needed to sign them up immediately, so their learning would be easier and they'd develop a marketable skill that would help them out in the future.

Not that they had any burning desire to take such a class. Not that it would easily fit into an already full family schedule. ("Mustn't over-schedule," I had to keep repeating to myself. "Mustn't over-schedule.")

During my twins' kindergarten year, here's what I had on the family's plate: In the fall, Abbey signed up for a nine-month-long dance program and eight weeks of autumn soccer followed by eight weeks of spring soccer. Jonah signed up for the soccer in the fall as well, but with a gap in his schedule during the winter months, he took eight weeks of Tae Kwon Do and then T-ball in the spring.

I could rationalize all of these choices. Really, I could.

Abbey's dance class, for example, gave her physical poise, taught her discipline and hard work. She loved dancing, but, to be quite honest, sometimes shied away from formalized instruction that I thought, occasionally constrained her energy. Halfway through her kindergarten year of dance – which she'd been taking for 2.5 years at that point – Abbey informed us that she was interested in taking up gymnastics. Scott and I told her that after pouring cash into her dance program (and paying for her recital costume), she had to see the program through to completion, through the dance recital. We'd discuss other activities later.

Why did I sign her up for soccer, in addition to dance classes? I wanted her to participate in a team sport, in something that wasn't overtly girly, in an activity that gave her a sense of physical power as she clocked the soccer ball into the goal (plus she was good at it).

I could justify Jonah's activities as well as to why they're good for his development.

It was during this same time that my 3-year-old preschooler began hounding me for hockey lessons, which, thank God, he was too young for. When he finally reaches the appropriate age, we'll be looking at a price tag of, get this, thousands of dollars for the privilege of having him learn how to hit small objects with sticks while trying to remain upright on a slippery surface.

And we can't forget the non-sports-related activities that I knew would be good for them, things like piano lessons, Brownie and Cub Scout memberships. I knew that music education could help kids thrive in mathematics. Shouldn't I have been promoting piano lessons, especially to Abbey, who didn't appear to have the great interest in math? Shouldn't I have urged Jonah to join the Cub Scouts, to gently prod him into getting involved in more group activities to nudge him out of his shell?

Then I took a step back. ("Mustn't over-schedule. Mustn't over-schedule.") I surveyed the possibilities and tried to remind myself that limiting the insanity to one — okay, max two — activities per kid during any one season was in everyone's best interests.

They've only got one shot at this childhood thing and I thought it was a bit early for them to be held hostage by a Palm Pilot or their future college applications. Let them get dirty. Let them get into arguments. Let them play outside without adults hovering over them. Let them daydream. Let them be free. Their resumes can wait.

Going to the dark side

I resisted its siren song for years.

Buy me. You know you want to. I'll make your life easier . . .

"No way in hell!" I vowed.

But I am so very spacious, dearie, great for hauling around your kids' junk!

"I'm a grown woman who is not, I repeat, NOT going to be seen by the outside world as simply *another mommy,* a vanilla suburban parent, even when my kids *aren't* with me in a minivan. I'm still cool! Damn it."

But you can put all the kids inside me when it's raining, climb in, easily shut the sliding door and then buckle them, my dear without getting yourself wet . . .

"I won't melt."

Then reality hit in the form of my pregnancy with my third child and the task of trying to fit three car seats – two for my toddler twins and one for the baby – into our beloved, teal Honda Accord sedan became an onerous one. Once that pregnancy with my son Casey was deemed healthy and viable, my husband grabbed three car seats and went to multiple car lots trying to cram the car seats into the back row of various sedans. Any sedan would've worked, as long as the vehicle had air bags and a good safety/reliability rating.

No minivan.

No way.

We didn't listen when our friends extolled the virtues of minivans' spaciousness, their convenience. We were not going to go to the dark side. We weren't going to become one of those gas guzzling, minivan types of people who you could clearly identify, with pointed fingers and lips curled in derision, that they are *suburban parents.*

I, for one, didn't want to give up the illusion that, somewhere, deep inside, I was still a carefree woman who, when she wasn't tending to her small offspring, could blast loud music (*not* kids' fare) while inside a vehicle, put down the windows and not be pegged as a mommy (although a closer inspection of the car with its safety seats, random Cheerio distribution, extra diapers and plastic purple box of wipes knocking around on the floor would belie any such carefree status).

But the minute anyone plops one's fanny behind the steering wheel of a minivan — regardless of whether or not the kids are in tow – that person immediately transforms into *just a parent, just a mom*, not a woman with a whole set of her own interests outside of her beloved offspring. I didn't want to be a walking cliché (or maybe I was just in deep, deep denial).

When I learned of my pregnancy with my third child, I knew the days for my Accord were numbered. It got great gas mileage. It was reliable. It was easy to park. But fitting three car seats into the back: Wasn't gonna happen. And believe me, we tried. There was one sedan my husband found where, if we put one of the seats in a little crooked and I used my hip to push down on the arm of a car seat, the seats could fit . . . barely . . . if all the kids held their breath and everyone turned slightly to the right.

Now keep in mind how long kids are supposed to be in infant car seats, then regular car seats, then booster seats. The Center for Disease Control (CDC) web site says children who've "grown out" of safety seats should be at least 58 inches tall and weigh 80 pounds (that's roughly around age 8). "[C]hildren 10 years old and younger should be using a booster seat after they have outgrown the child safety seat," their web site reports.

It's not like the days when my friends and I would pile into the back of my dad's cap-covered red Ford pick-up truck or jockey for spots in the "way back" of a friend's station wagon. Nowadays, if your kid isn't buckled with sanctioned restraints, not only can you get ticketed, but you risk being socially scorned and possibly risk the child's death because those front-seat air bags can inflate with lethal force.

So with my belly growing exponentially, we stowed our vanity in the glove compartment of our Accord. In a serendipitous coincidence, an inattentive driver blew a stop sign and crashed into the passenger side of the Accord, rendering it totaled. (No one was hurt in the accident.) With the Accord transformed into an accordion, we put our quest for a new vehicle into high gear. And, as you may have guessed, became one of THEM. Those minivan people.

It's been several years since I got a giant minivan that was only slightly easier to park than an oil tanker truck.

I still hate the fact that it sucks down gas so greedily.

I hate that it's so hard to park. (See that minivan parked way in the back of the parking lot, away from the other cars? That's mine.)

However, there are many unexpected joys of going to the dark side:

I truly can shove all my kids inside during inclement weather, jump in, shut the door and then make sure everyone's buckled in safely. There was ample room to breastfeed my baby in private while his siblings played. Grandparents can pile in and accompany our family to restaurants or events. There's plenty of space for our possessions during family vacations or when we're spending the day doing a gazillion activities. And I love the fact that when I'm driving at night, I'm sitting higher up than I was in a typical sedan so truck headlights won't be aimed squarely at my eyes in the rear view mirror.

But I still hate that I've been stripped of the opportunity to look cool when driving solo in the van. That's one thing convenience can't erase. Despite my many years of resisting the siren call of the minivan, my husband and I were forced to answer it.

I knew you'd come . . . and, by the way, you left cool behind quite some time ago, dearie.

The flood

I couldn't find that ridiculous flier. The one that was accompanied by about 15 other compadres inside my kids' backpacks at the end of the twins' kindergarten and the youngest's first preschool year. The flier that contained the list of school supplies I was supposed to purchase over the summer for my children's new school year.

I didn't know where all those pieces of paper had gone. The ones about long past sign-up deadlines for summer camps. Notices from my kids' teachers about what their classes had done in school in that last week in June. Their report cards. I actually found the report cards, but as for the other papers, never found 'em.

I knew that crayons were on the supply list and seemed to recall that the list required particular brands or colors, and, what, pencils, maybe? Rulers? Glue sticks?

I was, to say the least, a tad disorganized when it comes to my kids' school papers. After my twins' first year of kindergarten, I realized I needed to spend the summer checking out filing systems in anticipation of The Flood from their first grade classes.

What is The Flood, you ask? It's a pulp-driven torrential downpour that I knew was headed in my direction, like a hurricane that weather forecasters can spot on the Doppler radar on TV days in advance, only I hadn't nailed plywood over the windows or stocked up on bottled water yet (or actually bought the filing system and binders) before the next school year began.

I knew that, in short order, my three children's backpacks (you gotta include the preschooler in the mix) would be stuffed on virtually a daily basis. With paper. Paper that I could never seem to get a handle on. Papers with deadlines that I always seemed to miss because I was consistently overwhelmed by the volume of stuff.

What kind of stuff?

Here's a sampling of the school-related material that came into my home when my littlest one started preschool and my twins started kindergarten (at least the twins shared a classroom so I got only one copy of some papers, when they switched to separate classrooms, the paperwork nearly doubled):

A thick booklet on the status of the public school system.

PTO sign-up sheets – separate ones for both preschool and kindergarten — for parents to volunteer to participate in classroom activities, chair art shows, organize spring events, plan a pumpkin decorating evening, as well as a puppet show, book fair, family dance, etc.

Bus route information.

Information on exactly when and where we could drop off/pick up our children at the various schools.

Announcements on soccer league signups.

Fund raiser announcements/requests for donations or goods.

Information on providing healthy snacks for my kindergarteners, as well as notices on which classrooms contained members with food allergies (my twins' classroom did, so I needed to keep that particular piece of paper to remember exactly what foods to avoid when it was my turn to provide classroom snacks).

School calendars.

A pamphlet on the kindergarten curriculum.

Solicitations for donations of food and household items for the local food pantry.

A parent handbook.

School Committee agendas.

A request that parents submit monthly letters, poems or collages about their child explaining how the student reflected the theme of the month, like respect, honesty, friendship, etc. (Being well-organized was not on the list.)

Lists of books being read in the classroom and songs being sung, along with lyrics.

Class portrait information.

Now, let me say this up front: I really appreciated knowing what was going on in my children's classrooms. For example, it was great to know what songs my preschooler was learning so we could sing them at home. It was also wonderful to know when my kindergarteners' class was going to focus on science or on phonics or math.

I likewise thought it a stroke of genius when this material was put together in one packet and came home only once a week. I could put the packet aside and read it in its entirety later and it wouldn't become a scattered mess. (However if there was dated material to which I needed to immediately attend, my system fell apart and I inevitably missed deadlines.) I also loved the fact that the quality of my children's education was enriched by so many wonderful activities.

But (and here's the not-so-nice part, well, it's more like a plaintive wail): I needed help. I was drowning in all this paper. In all these requests. For money. For time. For baked goods. For parents to do unexpected projects with the kids. For parents to provide stuff for math day. For parents to help celebrate the square root of pi.

It began to feel as though I was working in an office from hell, where you keep getting memo, after memo, after memo, followed up by e-mail, after e-mail. You get so much correspondence that nothing seems individually important. Everything gets lumped together. Put in a pile. Pushed aside.

I don't remember things being this way – let's all climb aboard the memory machine – when I was a child. Sure, my parents volunteered for things. Had parent-teacher conferences. Came to school to see my special projects. Signed permission slips. Bought things they didn't need to support the PTO. But, is it just me, or does it seem like there's an excess of events and requests nowadays?

In an attempt to not fall prey to the same disorganized mess, I tried to plan ahead. I purchased a 3-ring binder for each kid, bought a red wooden wall-mounted filing system in which to store those binders, as well as a separate binder labeled, "Miscellaneous, Kids." I volunteered to do a couple of school and soccer-related activities that fit into my schedule, hoping that I won't succumb to mommy guilt when I didn't volunteer for every other event that came down the pike.

Halfway through the school year, when my twins were in separate first grade classrooms and the youngest was in a new preschool, those binders were chock filled and had to have their contents rotated to a filing folder in a cabinet each month. The papers started piling up each week around the kitchen. Taunting me.

I took one look around and actually thought about buying an oxygen tank, goggles and flippers (or starting a bonfire), and reading up on that Noah guy.

Not your mother's summer reading list

There was a very tall pine tree to provide cover, along with a second cover, this one fashioned out of a paper grocery store bag.

And there was surveillance. Okay, maybe surveillance is too strong of a word. Let's just say that I was on the look out. Constantly. For my mother.

I couldn't let Mom see that I, a pre-teen girl, was reading Judy Blume's book Forever. My mother had heard about this book through the grapevine of parents and I knew I wasn't supposed to be reading it.

I'd already devoured Blume books, particularly the one that was considered "edgy," Are You There God? It's Me, Margaret. My friends and I had re-enacted what the 11-year-old protagonist, Margaret Simon, had done with her group of sixth grade friends: We'd gone out with our moms to buy "training bras" and had, in unison, done our, "We must, we must, we must increase our bust," exercises. And we had made a pact to tell one another when we finally got our periods. It was scandalous to us, reading about bras, periods and "sanitary napkins."

But if Are You There God was edgy, Forever was fatally, razor sharp. We'd heard that it was about a high school couple that had sex and actually named the boy's, you know . . . his . . . well, we girls couldn't even bring ourselves to say the words out loud. He named his (*leaning in closer so you can hear me whisper*) . . . private part . . . Ralph. That was as risqué as it got when it came to literature for young girls in the late-1970s.

One of the girls from my social studies class somehow got a copy of Forever. I can't remember if she's the one who put the paper bag cover over the front or if I did, but by the time her copy got to me, I made sure to hide the book inside my book bag until I was in my back yard, under that pine tree, facing away from my house.

Recently, I've been thinking a great deal about Judy Blume after seeing an increasing number of news articles lamenting how books for middle school and high school aged girls have become graphic and valueless. I read news stories about a book called, <u>The Rainbow Party</u>, by Paul Ruditis, about a high school sophomore girl who decides to hold an oral sex party where boys would get gratification from girls. (I read it. It was awful.) I read about an explosion in series of books that try to, as one book blurb said, imitate "Sex and the City," only for the young, where pre-pubescent and high school girls' love for extraordinarily high-priced couture is surpassed only by their love for being really, really cruel to one another.

Author Naomi Wolf took aim at the current popular fare peddled to young girls in a *New York Times Book Review* essay, saying that the problem with these new books "is a value system in which meanness rules, parents check out, conformity is everything and stressed-out adult values are presumed to be meaningful to teenagers."

These have got to be exaggerated assessments, I thought. As Generation X parents — the ones who grew up reading Blume books and watching, "The Love Boat" on TV — get older, we must just start thinking more like our parents: That the youth culture is devoid of values and is full 'o smut. But it couldn't really be *that* bad, right? I wanted to check it out for myself. Thus began my youth lit reading project.

First I started with the golden oldie, <u>Are You There God</u>, followed by <u>Forever</u>. It had been decades since I'd opened these books. The junior school girl in me remembered Margaret and her friends as being really cool. But when I re-read the book from my thirtysomething perspective, everything just seemed quaint, "old fashioned" is how one local bookstore employee described it. The book was so sweet that it made me feel as though I was raised in the Pleistocene era.

I ventured into <u>Forever,</u> a book aimed at an older audience though many junior high girls still read it. (The children's book department manager at a bookstore I visited said middle school aged girls usually read older fare because their reading skills quickly advance beyond younger reader material.) Aside from its rather shocking lead sentence — "Sybil Davidson has a genius I.Q. and has been laid by at least six different guys." — the book is a coming of age story about a girl losing her virginity, where the lead character is thoughtful, respectful and really thinks about what she's doing.

Flash forward from the 1970s to now.

My initial foray into contemporary youth lit was the first in the series of exceedingly popular books called The Clique, featuring seventh grade girls who attend an exclusive private school in New York and spend way too much time obsessing over how to spend their parents' money, whether to cancel their spa appointments for their bikini waxes, whether the new $800 halter top they bought matches their skin tone and how they can be the cruelest creatures on the face of the planet. Though the girls in the book – which Amazon.com listed as appropriate for ages 9-12 – don't have sex or drink, they are among the worst, most self-centered people I've ever had the distinct displeasure of reading about. The cruelest thing that girls did in the Are You There God book was when one of them lied about getting her period. In the The Clique book, the In-girls dumped food all over an Out-girl to humiliate her.

Feeling as though those The Clique girls would savage my thirtysomething behind for *my* lack of couture, I moved on to another trendy girls' series, Gossip Girl. Early on in the book there was a party scene at the mansion of yet another rich New York City family where the teenagers were liberally drinking scotch from crystal glasses (the parents allowed this "European" behavior, under the guise that early drinking would get the kids "used to" drinking). One of the lead characters – who maintains a web site where she traffics in fabricated rumors about her private school classmates under the moniker of "gossip girl" — purges an exquisite meal (again) that had been prepared by the servants. Her boyfriend, who's about ready to cheat on her with an old flame, fondly remembers when the whole group of friends got drunk in eighth grade. This was a place where the cool kids wore the super-short skirts and the girls ate lunches of lemon yogurt, tea with lemon and sugar, and a plate of lettuce, with a bit of bleu cheese dressing. On the side.

When I started worrying that I am truly disconnected from

today's young girls, that they are all too cool for me, I got to <u>ttyl.</u> (For the benefit of the grown-ups reading, "ttyl" translates into, "talk to you later.") The book is comprised of Instant Messages sent between three high school sophomores. Aside from the IMing, these girls were more my speed. They seemed like normal, high school girls, worried about their clothes, boys, what people thought of them, etc. They weren't mean. They weren't obsessed with out-of-reach couture or with mercilessly judging.

But they weren't like my old friend Margaret, the 11-year-old who had her mother bring her to the department store to buy her a "Gro-Bra."

Are you there Margaret? It's me, Meredith. I miss you and your innocence. I hope that my daughter Abbey finds girls like you when she's in middle school and not those nasty beings from the <u>The Clique</u> or the <u>Gossip Girls</u>. While you and I may be quaint and old fashioned, reading books outside under a pine tree, at least we didn't grow up too fast. The Gro-Bra fit us just right.

On the Home Front

Zone defense

If I was a good mother, I would never allow my young children to endanger themselves. Not even for one single moment. They would only breathe purified air, only drink beverages that had been certified to have been boiled, pasteurized, de-bugged and de-infected in every conceivable way, and only live in a world of soft corners and cushions.

If I was a really good mother, that is.

But I apparently wasn't a good enough mother to my infants or toddlers, otherwise, I wouldn't have left my twins alone in the living room when they were only 1 year old so I could use the bathroom. Granted, I usually took quick trips to the loo, but this particular one when the kids were 1 was not quite quick enough. You see when I came back into that very same living room after relieving myself, I found toddler Abbey standing atop a chair with no pants on, bouncing up and down while chewing on a heavy curtain cord and threatening to jump over an arm of the chair, smack dab onto the hard wood floor. Her brother Jonah was busy climbing atop his yellow plastic, kid-sized truck preparing to scale the tall bookcase on the other side of the room. At least he still had his pants on.

When you are a parent of small children in the new millennium, it's not enough to try to protect your kids by putting those plastic covers over all the electrical outlets. It's simply insufficient for you to relocate all the household cleaners and poisons from your lower cabinets and make sure all your prescription medications have childproof caps. If you go by today's parenting magazines and baby product catalogues, you have to not only transform your home into a fortress, but you can't leave your offspring alone in a room until they are 21. And even then it's still a crapshoot.

After the bathroom/semi-nude circus act debacle, I perused several parenting periodicals and web sites, ripping out and downloading several safety-oriented articles. I grabbed a big pile of them and, with a notebook in hand and the children at my side, I went on a safety check around the house looking for hazards.

They were everywhere.

I had my pen at the ready.

"What was I thinking in keeping plastic bags in the house?" I thought when I looked under the kitchen sink, behind the double-locked cabinet doors (locked with a white plastic gadget threaded through the handles outside the cabinet *and* locked with latches from the inside), and spotted the bags I'd collected from the local grocery store. The kids could've easily broken the locks I'd installed, grabbed the bags, stuck their heads inside and suffocated. Although I'd been told if I didn't save and recycle these bags I'd be contributing to landfills and poisoning the environment, it was either them or the kids.

I quickly wrote a note to myself: "Return plastic bags to store. Invest in re-usable cloth bags with happy-faced trees on them."

"And what about those living room windows? How could I have been so reckless?" I shouted to no one in particular as the kids looked on glumly. I hadn't placed safety bars across them. The kids could've climbed on the windowsills, pushed the screens out, fallen and broken their necks or limbs. Or both. Despite the fact that, at the time, we lived in a one-story, ranch-style home, you just couldn't be too careful, I thought. I dog-eared the page in the baby-proofing catalog for window safety kits and moved on.

Then there was the big fat television (one of my favorite inanimate things in the house) sitting on a television table that had wheels on the bottom (a vestige of Scott and my lower income days). A big safety no-no. What if my crumb-crunchers teamed up to pull it over on themselves? What if the TV landed on their little piggies and they wound up with 11 stitches in their insteps?

"No TV," I wrote. Sure, it might seem like a sacrifice, but hadn't I just read an ominous report from a group of pediatricians saying that television should be banned for kids under that age of 2 anyway? "No more Teletubbies guys," I had to tell the toddlers as they fervently clutched their Teletubbie dolls. "The TV is too dangerous."

And we could forget about the battles I'd had with my husband over the position of the toilet seat. We had two choices, according to the parenting magazines: Lock up that toilet in a closed position or remove it altogether. Toilets are big hazards, the safety experts warn. Kids can fall inside and drown.

I had a friend who had a child safety toilet lock that wrapped around the side of the toilet seat and lid, something I discovered at an inopportune moment during a visit to her house for a play date with my twins. Holding the urgent urge to pee with the every muscle left in my pelvic region after the twin pregnancy savaged that area, I ran down the hallway to summon her assistance while I silently cursed the many cups of coffee I'd just consumed. I realized afterwards, that my pain while holding in the urine waiting for my friend to show me how to unlock the toilet was a just punishment. How could I have dared to indulge in hot coffee when my very small children were so close by? I could've spilled the scalding java on them, scarring them for life.

I made another notation, "Get a lock or ditch the john." We did have some wooded areas in the back of our house . . .

Even in the kids' bedrooms, I found death-traps-in-waiting. In addition to their bureaus – which one of the catalogues suggested we bolt to the walls so they won't fall (or be shoved) over – there were the baby cribs themselves. I'd already made sure that the cribs met safety standards and kept soft, plush bedding away to avoid suffocation hazards. But then I examined the crib sheets and remembered an article I'd read about crib sheets that came untucked and fatally choked a child. I had to remember to buy sheets that had ample room in the corners and tucked more than two inches under the mattress to assure that they wouldn't slip off and get wrapped around the children.

Next notation: "New, extra long, deep pocketed safety crib sheets. No Teletubbie patterns. (See TV note above)."

In the laughably named master bedroom (like my husband and I were the masters of anything during that period), I found not only more un-wall-bolted bureaus, but also pieces of jewelry in containers on top of those dressers that could be potential choking hazards. I then shuddered when I looked at my bed and remembered how I'd brought the kids to sleep with my husband and I when they were babies so I could breastfeed them. Another scientific study had come out around this time period warning that parents could accidentally kill their babies by rolling over on top of them and suffocating them in bed. A government agency was admonishing parents — regardless of the positive message advocates of "family beds" promoted – to never let their babies to sleep in bed with them.

"Get rid of jewelry. No kids in bed," I scrawled in my notebook.

When my list was done, I pulled out the telephone book — keeping a close eye on my mischievous tots in the room — and looked up the number for the nearest pediatric body guard/child-proofing safety service. Once I had Commander Ed, the head pediatric body guard, on the phone, I requested that he dispatch a team to my home. ASAP. STAT.

After Ed and his crew arrived, I made them strip down and shower with anti-bacterial soap while I washed their clothing in a special detergent to ward off any toxic chemicals, offensive odors and potential biological warfare agents while simultaneously running a criminal background check on them as my children were safely strapped into their stroller alongside me. You never know.

Once the agents were deemed clean – physically and criminally — I assigned two agents per child and sketched out a zone defense for them to implement. By that time, all the childproofing mechanisms I had purchased arrived by super-fast, same day delivery services. I asked Ed and his team to install them, while I assumed one of the guard's positions in the zone child defense plan. Once the team completed their work, and all the offending items had been bolted, locked, cushioned or removed, Commander Ed took my spot in the zone defense.

Then, and only then, could I safely go into the bathroom to pee alone, with the door closed.

What a good mother I am.

Toy revenge

Her eyes dart back and forth. Her ears are perked. She's completely alert. She is *(*dramatic pause*)* on a mission.

With great precision, she picks up what appears to the uninitiated to be an endearing, cuddly, plush chocolate colored monkey. But inside there's something sinister. Spying the red tag dangling from its limp hand that says, "Push my belly," she does so, releasing the inner demons that plagued the poor creator of the toy, and with it, a hideously loud, awful screeching sound. Customers browsing in other aisles drop their purchases and grab their ears in horror, thinking that an air raid siren has been activated. Cell phones go haywire. Small children cry.

However the noise doesn't faze *her.* Not in the least. She smiles and tosses the monkey into her shopping cart. This is the moment for which she's been waiting almost 30 years.

It's revenge time.

Sure, there were other less offensive, noisy toys she could have chosen for her beloved grandchildren, like the soft yellow chick that chirped softly, evoking visions of a peaceful summer morning or the tan kitty with black spots that purred demurely. But those just wouldn't do. It had to be a teeth-grinding, bone chilling sound effects toy, something that would cause hearing aides to combust upon activation.

In addition to the monkey, two little lambs that sang, "Here Comes Peter Cottontail" in the most obnoxious tone an adult could imagine, were also placed in her cart. This shopping trip was complete.

But those three tokens of her love and devotion weren't the only loud, obnoxious toys my mother purchased for my twins during their first two years on earth. There was the animal "orchestra" which had a keyboard that made various, extremely high-pitched animal sounds. (The noises made by the bear sounded like the cry of someone getting stabbed or doing something obscene with an ostrich.) There was the noise-making, yellow and red plastic ride-on bus that forever chimed, "School time is fun time," in that oh-so-pleasant electronically generated voice. (Behind closed doors, Scott and I applauded when it ran out of batteries and we lied to the kids that there were no more batteries that fit that particular model.) Oh, and we could never forget about the duck pull-toy which chirped, "Quack" 15 times in a row to a horribly catchy tune that unsuspecting people discover they can't shake from their heads. Try engaging in adult conversation when all you hear running through your mind is a sing-songy, "Quack, quack, quack, quack, quack, quack, quack, quack, quack, quack, quack, quack, quack . . . (*wait for it, another moment*) quack, quack!"

If the toy made noise and it was in our house, it likely came from my parents, more specifically, my mother.

They (she) consider(ed) this payback. I have long considered this psychological torture. Several decades ago, I convinced my parents to buy me this now infamous toy metal gun that glowed red and made red sparks inside a plastic window whenever the trigger was pulled. It made a sound that I remember as resembling putting a soda can in a food processor. When I think of that toy gun, a smile still comes to my face. We'd been on a family vacation on Cape Cod when they acquiesced to my pleadings in the middle of a store in downtown Provincetown to purchase the coveted item. Even now, when we pass that same gift store in the seaside resort town, they remember the gun. That gun – which made what my mother called "the most horrendous racket in the world" – became their albatross. I played with it constantly. My mother became so tormented by the sparky gun that she finally "lost it" for me. As she put it, "It fell through the hole in the toy box."

As penance for that purchase that I badgered them into making when I was about 9 or 10 (remember, *they* are the ones who bought it, not me, they could've said, "No" and bought me a quiet toy), my kids, practically as they were emerging from the womb received boatloads, no, make that tidal waves of noisy, audio impairing toys. This was hardly my idea of fair play. While I clearly remembered my mother bestowing upon me "The Mother's Curse" when I was a curmudgeonly adolescent — the old "I-hope-you-have-a-kid-who's-just-like-you" whammy — this was a little much. My kids couldn't even ask for particular toys and they were getting them by the gross. By the time the twins reached 2 years old, we were nearing the point where we needed to add a sound-proofed wing to our house and outfit the kids with ear plugs before they could play with all these toys.

Maybe these purchases were simply part of a master plan to drive me insane. The U.S. military uses incessant, loud noise as a form of torture, of extracting information from would-be terrorists. Remember in the 1980s when General Manuel Noriega was holed up in his compound in Panama? The Americans surrounding his compound played earsplitting music 24 hours a day outside of the building trying to drive him out. I don't know about you, but 24 hours of their choice of songs – like Linda Ronstadt's "You're No Good" — would make me want to flee even the cushiest compound. If they'd had the monkey, the twin singing lambs and the animal orchestra all going at the same time at full blast, I'll be Noriega would've been out in an hour.

Don't play with your food

I remember the scene fondly: The giant fan standing in the corner of the kitchen on stale, hot summer days. Soggy, murky green canned peas sitting on my plate in a lukewarm heap. The mischievous twinkle in my brother's eyes. The barely stifled laughter as we chucked the peas into the fan, sending mushy shards back out all over the kitchen.

As I looked back from a parental perspective, the pea shard antics outright terrified me. Not only did my brother and I throw peas, but we threw a few other food items into that fan as well, though none had quite the same visual panache as the despised peas. Had our parents caught us in the act of playing with our dinner in such a manner, we would've been in major trouble. But nowadays, a kid mashing a fistful of food, say, between the pages of a book could argue that he was just doing what his toys told him to do.

Literally.

When my twins were toddlers, a bizarre genre of books and kids' products came onto the market, sending children a message that runs directly contrary to the stern dictate we heard growing up: Don't play with your food. My first exposure to this phenomenon occurred when a relative gave my then-1-year-old twins The Cheerios Play Book. Knowing that young kids and Cheerios are as natural a combination as baseball and Cracker Jack, this well-meaning, gift-giving person thought it would be cute to give my children a book bearing bright drawings and (*here comes the ominous part*) spots in which to place *actual* pieces of Cheerio cereal. The first time I let the kids put the cereal in the book, they just ate the Cheerios and ignored the book. The second time, they dumped the Cheerios out, ate them off the rug — the hideously peculiar odor of Cheerios clung to the carpet fibers — and flipped through the book after the food was gone. The next time, they mashed the cereal in the book and spread the remnants around the room while stomping on them.

Who in their right mind would encourage small children to put food into books rather than their mouths? And how stupid was I to be letting my kids – who already ate the *books* themselves, rendering the so-called sturdy board books into soggy, gnarled messes – do this?

In addition to the Cheerios book, there were other books aimed at toddlers that invited children to put Goldfish crackers, animal crackers, Sun-maid raisins, Reese's Pieces and M&M's in between the pages, albeit not all at the same time. Putting food in books was being *encouraged*. Was I the only one who thought this whole thing was simply wacky?

Not only did I find the food book thing odd, but I soon discovered plenty of other products that offered up entertaining ways for children to consume food. Kid's yogurt was being sold in squeezeable, soft tube-like containers. Macaroni and cheese was made in the shape of Nickelodeon's Rugrats or Blue's Clues characters. I read about odd candy ranging from plastic ears that one would lick to obtain the "ear wax" candy and "booger" candy, with the motto, "You think it's candy, but it's snot." There were even battery-operated lollypop holders that spun around so America's youth didn't have to burden themselves with the onerous task of actually moving the lollypops around themselves and having to do the horribly difficult task of licking the candy on their own steam.

True, there have always been some pretty weird children's food products out there. Fruit roll-ups for example, came out when I was a kid — a sticky, kind of bumpy, sickly sweet concoction rolled out flat on plastic (like peeling Naugahyde off a couch and eating it) that now strikes me as vile. The new version of these roll-ups that my kids have started eating has an odd component: The "tongue tattoo." This "tattoo" of a cartoon character is actually an ink image printed on the roll-up. To get the tattoo, the kids are supposed to press the image onto their tongues. (That can be quite a sight, I tell ya.) Then the image barely remains on the tongue for a nanosecond before it turns into liquid and dribbles onto the table.

Other odd foods populated my childhood, like electric green drinks with names like Ecto Cooler, a colored juice named after a plot line in the movie "Ghostbusters." And there have always been fake eyeball candies and cartoon character cereal. But kids my age were never under the impression that their breakfast cereal was a toy.

After surveying the array of play-food books out there, I decided to conduct a little experiment. I purchased the Goldfish, raisin, animal cracker and M&M books and put them alongside the Cheerio book. I bought the requisite food items. Then I let my toddler twins at them, overseeing each activity as they did exactly as the books instructed. The results:

Sticky.

Gooey.

Crummy.

Salty.

A parental nightmare.

The Goldfish book — used only a few times with the actual crackers — wound up covered with greasy stains. An abundance of bright, orange-yellow crumbs were scattered throughout its pages, lodged in the book's spine and all over the floor when my kiddos began fighting over who could hold the book and who got the most crackers.

The M&M book became a slimy mess. Ever seen two small kids hyped up on sugar as half-melted chocolate goop coats their hands (because as they'd chew, some bits of the warmed chocolate candy would fall out of their mouths)? Not pretty. I was lucky that I noticed Abbey trying to slide the contaminated volume into my purse or not only would I have never been able to open the pages again (as they would have been permanently fused by spit and semi-hardened chocolate), but a family of insects likely would have begun following me around and taken up residence in my bag.

After just a few forays into the food-as-a-toy world, I decided that I needed to stop the practice in its tracks. If I had continued letting my kids put their food into their books, who knows where it might have led. The last thing I wanted to spend my time on was rooting around the house in search of the smelly, moldy raisin book that somehow slid under the living room couch with several drool-slimed raisin "buttons" stuck to the picture of the gingerbread cookie boy. Of course then the Cheerio, Goldfish and animal cracker chunks that were already under there wouldn't have been so lonely.

Pocket full of rye

What normal person would talk to a child about grabbing a bunch of blackbirds and stuffing them into a pie and cooking them alive? Who would spin tales of ladybugs perishing in a fire? Kids dropping dead of the bubonic plague while dancing merrily in a circle?

Me and millions of other addled parents, that's who.

No, I'm not a sadist with a basement full of dead animals and a DVD library full of slasher movies. I just happen to be in possession of several books of nursery rhymes, the golden oldies recited throughout the generations, some of which just so happen to be twisted and sick. And of course, being the good parent that I am, I've shared these bizarre poems with my impressionable children.

The actual meaning of some of these rhymes didn't really hit me until one day, after reading "Sing a Song of Sixpence" aloud, I tried to see it from my kids' point of view:

Sing a song of sixpence, a pocket full of rye
Four and twenty blackbirds baked in a pie.
When the pie was opened, the birds began to sing.
Wasn't that a dainty dish to set before the king?

So let me get this straight: My kids were supposed to imagine a pie filled with live birds which start singing after the pie is cut open? That it's normal to serve pies stuffed with live animals which can double as dinnertime entertainment? (Why didn't I think of that? I could use this as motivation to get them to eat their dinner, telling them that if they don't eat the chicken on their plate, it will start singing to them.)

Then I started examining other poems I'd been reading aloud with a critical eye, like this one found in a Winnie the Pooh nursery rhymes anthology:

Ladybug, ladybug fly away home.
Your house is on fire.
Your children are gone, all except for one, her name is Nan.
She crept under a frying pan.

The moral here? Perhaps the parent ladybug shouldn't have left her tiny insect kids home alone (quick, someone call children's services. . . do they have those in the insect world?). And maybe Smokey the Bear needs to retool his fire safety directions to include telling kids NOT to hide under a frying pan in the event of an actual fire, despite what this rhyme says.

Then there's another one that my kids just adored:

Tom, Tom the piper's son, stole a pig and away he run.

The pig was eat and Tom was beat and Tom went howling down the street.

A poem that extolled the virtues of child abuse and the slaughtering of a stolen, chubby pink animal, how quaint. Maybe I could've instead switched to "Peter Pumpkin-Eater" who kept his wife hostage inside an oversized gourd, or "Three Blind Mice" where the farmer's wife chopped off the tails of disabled rodents after they irritated her. (Where's the animal rights crowd when you need them?)

My interest in what I was actually reading to my kids was piqued after my husband saw some documentary that mentioned "Ring Around the Rosy." It said the song was something kids sang about people who died of the bubonic plague, which gave its victims rose-like rashes around the neck, hence the ring part.

Maybe instead of reading these weird little rhymes, I should compose my own set of poems designed to scare the pants off the kids when they don't cooperate with me. There could be one about a Time-Out monster who takes little kids who don't listen to their parents to an evil place where they have to sit absolutely still for 24 days while dressed in their itchy dress-up clothes and offered only kale and prune juice to eat. Or I could pen one about a boy who didn't share his toys and was sent to a prison forever and had to watch other kids play.

Come to think of it, I could really milk this warped genre of nursery rhymes to my advantage, either that, or start reading them some of the less innocuous material, like a Stephen King novel.

A million pieces

I wasn't trying to be ungrateful.

Really.

It was just that there were all these pieces of things.

Everywhere.

They were hard and sharp and plastic and inevitably found their way into the tender arch of my foot in the middle of the night, or when I was carrying 15 loads of laundry up the stairs.

And if my kids got any more toys that came with a boatload of tiny pieces that never, ever, make it back to their rightful place once the box was opened, I threatened to stage a gigantic, environmentally toxic plastic bonfire at which I vowed I would stand back and laugh.

You know exactly what I'm talking about. Let's not pretend that you really ever got the toys that had tons of little pieces back into their rightful containers. Sure, maybe you'd keep all the pieces of the train set together for a week. Let's say a month (I'd roll my eyes as you profess this because I wouldn't believe you). But the minute your kid decided to take a Thomas the Tank Engine train to bed, or to see how the zoo car ran along the linoleum on the kitchen floor, all bets would be off.

Maybe you have spent an ordinate amount of time tracking down these tiny plastic grenades in waiting. But have you typically gotten *every* single one of them and put them back in their rightful containers, in their rightful places? Have all the Legos really gotten back into that sturdy plastic container from hence they came? How about the cars from that Little People toy garage? You mean to tell me that the cars have never double parked outside the Matchbox track, or made their way beneath couches and kitchen tables and in between bed sheets? If you have more than one kid and they're closer together in age, I for one, assert that accomplishing these tasks is impossible.

I defy any parent to tell me with a straight face that he or she has actually kept a handle on the insidious little things that come in all shapes and sizes:

Hard green Legos.

Edgy wooden puzzle pieces of barnyard animals.

A billion Matchbox cars that have the added bonus of having wheels (all the better to trip you with my dear).

Miniature metal forks accompanying a tea set where the teapot has an even smaller porcelain flowered top and is practically invisible when left on a floral carpet.

Slippery magnets in the shape of woodland creatures.

Dolls that have separate little socks, gloves, shoes and hats, some with Velcro that cling to rugs and furniture.

Plastic, sequined dress-up hats with feathers and embedded hair combs that feel especially nice impaling my right big toe.

Pink plastic rings, barrettes and toy jewelry.

Blocks of every description.

Play food, from plastic tacos and pizza, to egg rolls and bananas with narrow little black tips.

Action figures with little guns.

I tried to keep the hordes of tiny amusements under control.

I was a frequent shopper in the home organizing aisles of local mega-stores. I bought a ton of those clear, plastic bins. I bought stacked drawers. I got crates. Baskets. Buckets. I spent hours pouring over my kids' toys and figuring out the most logical place to put them. After thinking about where in the house each type of toy was most frequently used, I put them in a nice, neat fashion near where they could be enjoyed and then put back in place easily, without much effort.

Every few months or so, my husband would take the kids out of the house for a few hours while I organized the toys. Once I was done, I'd usually have this silly, inhuman *Better Homes and Garden* smile on my face, proud that I, to the outside world, seemed like I had it all together. My home looked like a Pottery Barn Kids catalog. Kind of. As long as you didn't look in the closets or under the carpets. And I dimmed the lights while you squinted.

All the wooden alphabet puzzles had 26 letters in place. The play food was organized into dairy, snack and entrée sections. The Matchboxes were lined up by make and model and no road rage was evident. The different train tracks were put into the correct bins along with the matching trains.

Then the kids came home.

Within an hour's time, I could see my hard work quickly slipping away.

My daughter would put a few Legos in her pink beaded purse and pretended that they were money.

My older son would stage a race between a Thomas the Train and a flaming red Matchbox Corvette in the hallway, a floor away from the neatly organized bins of trains and cars.

My toddler son would take each wooden puzzle and laugh uproariously as he overturned them one by one over his head while several pieces slid under furniture or were intentionally shoved between the metal heating vents in the floor.

When my twins were toddlers, it was slightly easier to keep the pieces of their toys under control. I used to spend a half-hour each night after they went to bed carefully putting each piece of toy back in its rightful place. But then again, they were just toddlers. They weren't going up and down flights of stairs. They weren't moving toys from room to room. They (and their toys) were easier to contain.

Then three things occurred: They mastered scaling the child safety gates, the volume of gifts containing small parts exponentially increased and then their younger brother arrived.

It was never the same. Aside from a few moments of maternal insanity when I thought I could truly organize my home like they recommend in all those magazines which feature matching, cloth-lined baskets and cooperative family members, my house was constantly populated by heaps of toys thrown in various containers. There was no logic to any of it.

Legos? Everywhere. Train tracks could be found in any room in the house. Play food could be discovered in the laundry basket, the cat's water bowl or in the back yard. One never knows what could turn up where.

I'll probably find all the pieces to all of the toys some time in the next decade or so. By then, the kids will be onto other items, like CDs, car keys, their own cell phones and my wallet. But in the meantime, I put this out to the world in the hopes that someone is listening: Please refrain from adding to the avalanche of toys with a million pieces. And no, I don't care if they're educational. (This means you, Grandma!)

Adventures on the potty seat

He preferred to do it while he was buck naked, with product catalogs featuring sporting goods at his fingertips. Occasionally, a crumpled-up, outdated magazine would suffice. And there was to be no singing. Na-da. Not one note or he would've been outta there.

She, on the other hand, preferred to belt out a tune or two while swinging her legs and grinning mischievously. Several rounds of "A Hunting We Will Go" (she heard it on a kids' tape) and "Row, Row, Row Your Boat" were among her favorites at the time. And even if she was sitting there trembling because she was cold — for she too preferred being au natural — she would push your hands away if you tried to drape a sweater over her shoulders. She knew that as long as she sat there, she wouldn't be made to do anything else, like take a nap, or have lunch, or get ready because we had an appointment. As long as she sat there, she reasoned, she was golden.

Why? Because our home had transformed into the Potty Zone: The irrational, ridiculous and utterly absurd world of tinkle, poo-poo, bribes and gobs of toilet paper that clog your plumbing.

The concept of trying to teach two toddlers how to pee and poop in a giant porcelain bowl, or in the little plastic replica on the floor, seemed patently bizarre to me when I first attempted this feat. How exactly was a parent supposed to teach a child to poop while perched on a potty seat? I never saw a definitive set of guidelines on this. Was I supposed to lean my own ample behind over a toilet, grimacing like I was passing a kidney stone the size of Alaska, and pretend I was pooping so the kids would understand what they were supposed to do? You certainly didn't let the child witness actual defecation, right? (For the record, I didn't.) How was I supposed to describe the feeling you get when you need to pee so I could explain it to a toddler so he or she would learn to recognize it, hold the urine inside, make a mad dash to the potty, disrobe and *then* let it go? A whole industry has been built around the fact that millions of adults can't even hold their own urine in their own bodies, so how was a 2-year-old supposed to do that?

Then there was the whole nudity issue. Was it a problem for my son Jonah to see me peeing on the potty, even though he wasn't really "seeing" anything? My husband Scott wouldn't teach our daughter Abbey how to pee by example, even if he sat down on the toilet seat so no offending body parts were visible. He has outright refused because he said it was wrong for him to ever be naked in front of her . . . yet, somehow, it was okay for me to pee in front of Jonah? (For years I had to use the toilet and take a shower with the bathroom door wide open so I could hear what the kids were doing so I was afforded exactly NO modesty.) When it comes to deliberating what degree of parental nudity was okay in front of one's offspring, the discussion gets – how shall I say this? — *sensitive.* If you ask other parents if they have ever urinated or defecated in front of their children while trying to teach them how to use the toilet, you're apt to seem like some kind of sociopath pervert-type and can likely expect children's services to come knocking on your door in a few hours asking if you've ever looked at porn on the Internet.

So when I had to teach the twins how to use the potty, I felt largely left to my own devices to figure out exactly how I, the mommy, was supposed to, among other things, teach my son how to pee standing up without a demonstration or manual assistance (talk about feeling creepy).

When I was in the throes of this potty-training madness, I secretly wished I could've just sent them to potty-training camp. It seemed like something rich families would do to get all the messiness and nudity ambiguities over with. (They'd save a bundle on carpet and furniture cleaning to boot.) A few days, and *boom,* they're out of diapers and I wouldn't have to worry about teaching them how to push waste out of their bodily orifices or worry that my son will have nasty flashbacks when he's 20 of his mommy peeing in the same room as him. (I can just hear the therapist now, "You mean she thought it was okay to sit on the toilet while you were in the bathroom? Didn't she know how psychologically damaging that image could be to a young boy?")

Scott and I embarked down the potty-training road with our

twins when they were 1 1/2 And when I say embarked, it was a very little embarkment, an embarkment with no plans. No rhyme. No reason. We just had a plastic potty seat sitting innocuously on the bathroom floor. If the kids wanted to sit on it — which was rare at first — it wouldn't be for very long. Eventually, we got Abbey to sit there, but Jonah would have nothing to do with the monstrous-looking thing with the wide mouth that looked like it would swallow him up butt-first and suck him into the evil Land of Poop.

We puzzled about how to do this potty-training thing for quite a while. Then, about three months into the official declaration that our home had become a Potty Zone, I witnessed a friend of mine bribing her 2 1/2 year-old daughter with stickers to get her to pee on the potty. "Bribing," I thought, "that's always a good way to go." So I bought a bunch of stickers and fashioned what I dubbed the "Potty Sheet" featuring my kids' beloved "Blue's Clues" characters. Whenever they peed (they weren't quite to the pooping in the potty seat), they could chose from a wide array of stickers and plaster one on their personal Potty Sheet. A couple months into the sticker-inducement phase, Abbey's sheet was covered with stickers. Jonah's was practically barren, except for a few pity stickers he was awarded after spending half-hour bouts on the potty where nothing in the form of pee or poop came out of him, though he and Mommy had enough time to select a new wardrobe from an old Land's End catalog.

By the time the twins were 2, they weren't yet potty-trained, as I so desperately wanted them to be. I calculated that, conservatively speaking, by the age of 2, they'd gone through well over 8,000 diapers. (Don't make me go over the math. It's too damned depressing. And no, I didn't calculate how much money this cost. It was a whole lot.) But the more I pushed, the more they resisted, so I decided to pull back.

But, according to a self-proclaimed Potty Guru, a mother who used to go to my kids' play group, I should have been very worried. I should have bought every book on toilet training, hired a team of consultants to tell me how to make the potty area more attractive, as well as have counselors do a mental and emotional assessment of the kids and me. This Guru, who had a penchant for spontaneously launching into unsolicited and unwanted parenting lectures, dogmatically told me that *every* child can be potty-trained at 18 months. "All you need is one day in the bathroom," she proclaimed. "That's all it takes." (Well, after one day in the bathroom with her, I can tell you I'd do anything she'd ask to get out of there.)

But Scott and I were determined not to rush things. The peeing and pooping in the potty, we reasoned, would come in its own sweet time. However if the kids weren't out of diapers by the time they were in elementary school, I vowed to send them to the Potty Guru for the weekend. She'd certainly know just what to do.

Adventures on the potty seat: Part II
(Written five years after Part I)

If there was a potty-training hell, I was smack dab, in the middle of it.

My patience was gone.

My sweet, Mommy's-so-understanding tone of voice, was kaput.

There would be no more bribes. No more stickers, incentive sheets, M&Ms or any form of molded plastic toy would be dangled in front of a certain someone if he pooped and peed in a porcelain receptacle on a regular basis.

My Diaper Genie was on its last legs – it was well over 6 years old – and I was teetering on the edge of sanity wearing 2-inch heels in an ice storm.My youngest son refused to be potty-trained.

Damn it.

He was 3 1/2 and showed no interest in moving his bowels or evacuating the contents of his bladder into a toilet. So (imagine an image of me on your TV screen, while waving a tattered, stained white dish towel) I gave up.

Between my twin 6-year-olds and He Who Would Not Use the Potty, I calculated (calculating gave my misery more validity) that I had spent over 42 months of my life trying to teach my children how to become official members of civilized society (i.e. — People who don't look you squarely in the eye while you're sitting at the kitchen table eating scrambled eggs and toast, grimace and then fill their pants with odorific material).

My daughter Abbey, after a little more than six months of effort, finally mastered potty-training by 2 1/2.

Her twin brother Jonah took much longer. He was a month shy of 3 years old when I was ready to break out the bubbly because he was on the verge of ditching the diapers. But the celebration came to a grinding halt when Jonah completely gave up on using the toilet and demanded the return of the very same diapers with the annoying purple dinosaur that was pictured on the front of his brand new baby brother Casey's diapers.

The process of potty-training my twins made me feel like a ludicrous performing circus monkey. I overenthusiastically talked in glowing terms about pee and poop in a way no self-respecting adult should have to do. With a sparkle in my voice I'd say, "Who wants to read the potty book and try to make pee?" I took the kids to the library and checked out cheery potty-training books and videos. I made sticker charts. Scott and I bought containers of M&Ms and doled the candies out as a reward after Jonah and Abbey used the toilet.

But the kids eventually rendered the incentive part of the potty venture useless when they started peeing about one one-thousandths of a milliliter of urine in order to qualify for a sticker, only to return to the toilet 10 minutes later to eek out a teensy bit more pee and get another reward. It was an endless loop of insanity.

I would announce to the entire household when I had to make poop and would make exaggerated faces to drive home the point that I was moving my bowels. We would all wave, "Bye-bye" to the waste as it descended into the Land of Poop. We sang songs while naked kids sat on the potty (their preferred method). We leafed through countless crumpled catalogs while we crammed ourselves into our tiny bathroom.

When I changed my last Jonah diaper, I felt tremendous relief.

Only one more kid to go.

But with Casey, I decided to take it slowly. I wasn't going to push. I was, as many of the so-called experts (I secretly loathe those people) urged, going to let him indicate to me that he was ready.

Not that I didn't offer to have him sit on his little plastic potty seat.

Not that I didn't read him selections from our potty book library while he was hanging out on the little plastic potty.

Not that we didn't pick out cool Spider Man underpants together.

Not that I didn't offer him an M&M every time he peed or pooped in the toilet.

"Mommy and Daddy won't push him," I kept repeating to

myself. With Jonah, I thought we pushed too hard and made the entire process longer than it needed to be, particularly after he lapsed all the way back to full diapers when his brother was born.

Thousands of diapers later, when Casey was 3 1/2 I felt like that manipulated circus monkey again, only this time, Casey was holding my leash. When the little man started preschool he wasn't potty-trained, but the school still took him (thank God!) as long as he wore Pull-Ups and I agreed to rush to school to change him in the event of a "Poop Alert." And, while he would pee at school (or least pretend to), when he got home, nothing, not a drop, when I was around. When Daddy was home, Casey would head to the toilet, lift up the seat and demand his father serve as his adoring audience. With me, he'd make stinky poop (akin to a smoke bomb being hurled into the house by excrement terrorists) and dart around the house vociferously denying that he was the source of the smell.

I was stymied.

Yes, there were plenty of know-it-all parents and "experts" who claimed that training could be done in a day if you just let your kid run around naked while he pees and poops on everything in sight. For days and weeks on end. In fact, the illustrious Dr. Phil aired a segment on his TV show at around the time of my Casey potty-training crisis where the august doctor set out to demonstrate how any kid could be trained in a day. Attention Dr. Phil: I would've gladly shelled out $1,000 if you had come to my house and trained Casey in 24 hours. With all due respect accorded to a friend of Oprah's, couldn't be done sir.

I tried the naked days without diapers. I tried putting him on the potty every 20-30 minutes for several consecutive days so I'd catch him when he needed to pee. I tried having his brother and sister role model positive toileting behavior. I pointed out the kids at school who were trained.

Failures. All.

Not that I was pushing . . .

When the little lad was 3 1/2, Casey and I were at an impasse and neither one of us blinked. So I just gave up. As long as the school would take him with his Pull-Ups, my wallet and I (those Pull-Ups cost big bucks) could outwait him, though we were both getting a little tired.

I did, however, hold the line on the Diaper Genie, that broken, sobbing Diaper Genie that was begging to be put out of its misery. I would not surrender on that point. I would go down with that Diaper Genie cause I wasn't buyin' another one, because if I did that, then I'd let the potty-training terrorists win.

Postscript: Casey was finally potty-trained through what I affectionately named "Potty-training Terrorist Camp:" Several days of hard ball in the summer before he turned 4. It was a hellish week. I'm surprised my neighbors didn't call the authorities as there was much loud squawking and foot stomping from the small person. But when it was over, there was never so much satisfaction as there was when Scott and I officially sent the Diaper Genie to Diaper Heaven.

Home sweet home

I knew my naïve ideas about housekeeping were long gone when I found a perfectly washed, intact pea in the clothes dryer.

Between the petrified chunks of oatmeal-coated carpet fibers and other pieces of food inadvertently left to harden in random spots around in the house, I learned when my twins were but mere toddlers that when you have little kids, the concept of "clean" is a largely unachievable mirage, regardless of what those insidiously seductive Pottery Barn Kids catalogs will tell you. (The kids in those catalogs aren't real anyway. They're just display models.)

Don't get me wrong. I've never been a Martha Stewart clone, though I wish I had her money, clothes, chef and staff to do my bidding (I could do without that pesky criminal record thing though). In our Pre-Kid days, Scott and I used to manage to keep our apartment, and later our house, relatively organized and clean. But once our twins, Abbey and Jonah, reached toddlerhood — never mind when their baby brother Casey was born a few years later — just trying to keep the house operational became a Herculean task.

This shift from a mostly neat abode to a slight step above chaos was hard on Scott. I felt badly for him, mostly because my cleaning style – if you could even call it a style – was the antithesis of his, particularly when our children were very young. The poor man suffered from the delusion that preschoolers could be clean if only someone took the time to "work with them," like I had nothing else to do with my day other than spending hours trying to teach a 2-year-old to pick up all the crumbs on the floor or to just teach the preschoolers not spill stuff. (I'm a grown adult, and I still haven't yet mastered that how not to spill stuff.)

It bothered Scott to see the floor beneath the kids' seats covered with a mishmash of crumbs, sauces and whatever else they attempted to eat at lunchtime or simply chucked to the floor in the response to an innocuous question. When he would see them munching on a snack in the living room — the inevitable aftermath scattered around the rug — he would quickly dart over to clean it up. Me? I would only literally run to clean something up immediately if the spilled or dropped item was foul or a liquid, like a poop explosion or projectile barf. If the kids got Goldfish cracker shards around the floor, sure, I would pick up the big pieces by hand and vacuum later (more like use the little hand vac) when the despoilers had gone to bed, otherwise I would've wound up spending my days doing nothing but changing diapers, making meals and cleaning. Maybe that worked in June Cleaver's world, but not in mine.

My laissez-faire attitude would've disturbed many people, as it did Scott when we had twin preschoolers and a toddler. (During that period of our lives, Scott once claimed – and I'd never let him forget it — that I would've been happy living in squalor.) To my uber-neat brother-in-law (who had no kids when mine were little), whose response to finding my 18-month-old's chocolate fingerprints on his foyer wall was to repaint it, my behavior was an example of unimaginable slackery.

I didn't understand how or why some parents would have the time to wash their kitchen floors even if no one was coming to visit. These were the people who vacuumed after every meal and snack, and consistently had all their laundry done, not to mention folded *and* put neatly away by size, color and clothing type. (I can't tell you how long my kids' clean clothes, to this day, sit in the laundry basket ... Who am I kidding? The clothes *start* in the basket and then slump over onto my bedroom rug until they cover an area about as big as our minivan and we walk around it for a week. The pile is sometimes so deep, my kids can leap from our bed into the heap and emerge unscathed.)

When people are slated to visit my house, it's a different story. We try to make all the toys and books look neatly organized. We dust and vacuum, clean the fridge and cram the baskets of clean clothes into the closet and threaten our guests not to open the door for fear for their personal safety. We chuck the mass of disorganized bills, magazines and other various paper pollution into my or Scott's office and quickly shut the door. Voila! We've created a Martha Stewart illusion, as long as you don't look under anything and you leave your white gloves at home.

But on a day-to-day basis, even though my kids are older now and supposedly have more control over their limbs and their hands, I truly do not have the time to do anything other than the mere basics of cleaning. When I do have a moment to myself after the kids are in bed, the dinner dishes are clean (or at least in the dishwasher) and most of the toys are put away, the last thing I want to think about is washing the floor, vacuuming, dusting or organizing the pantry. My moments of peace are too precious to me, now that I have so few of them, to spend them on house cleaning.

Instead, I opt for the "as clean as it absolutely needs to be" rule. We need clean clothes, towels and sheets. We need clean plates and eating surfaces. We certainly can't live with large chunks of food lying around, or anything that will eventually smell, grow exponentially or lure small animals into the house (neighbor children don't count). But the rest of the innocuous stuff can wait, at least until the kids are able to competently vacuum by themselves.

Whoever it was who said that cleanliness is next to godliness couldn't have been a rational parent of young children kids and most certainly never found a perfectly washed pea in the clothes dryer. I thought that pea was pretty godly.

Handmade Halloween? Hah!

Around the end of September, once school has commenced and the fall leaves have begun to transform into a tapestry of autumn brilliance, children's minds turn to thoughts of that sugar-ladened October holiday. (You know the one.) Not only do the little people start rubbing their hands together anticipating how much candy they'll rake in from the neighbors in the time honored, annual extortionist trip (otherwise known as Halloween) around the 'hood, they'll start clamoring for costumes.

They may not care what kind of candy they get in their hollowed out plastic pumpkins, as long as the candy is sweet – although there is an informal caste system when it comes to candy (Reese's Peanut Butter Cups, M&Ms, Kit Kats and anything chocolate *good*, anything with raisins or oatmeal *bad*) – but they do care about the costumes.

Here's where the juvenile trick clashes with the holiday treat.

Do you, the unassuming parent, buy a costume or do you make one? And if you deign to ditch your sewing kit and glue gun and replace it with a handy dandy credit card at the costume shop, do you go for the expensive costume or the "inexpensive" one, on sale now for a mere $30?

This is a tricky topic in Mommydom. Questions such as, "Don't you care enough about your child to hand-make an amazing costume?" dance relentlessly in your head. And while parents try to figure out what option they're going to take, they're greeted with an onslaught of goading articles and television segments purporting to show viewers and readers just how *very simple* it is to make a kid's costume, complete with darling photos of smiling children, children who you believe are secretly thinking, "Come on you idiot. Even the most moronic adult could make a costume like this one."

It's enough to make you want to commit hari-kari with a Twizzler.

Inevitably, confused parents are shown diagrams and photos of what seem like simple directions, told to buy a few items, cut a few things out with kitchen scissors, fire up the glue gun, and they're in business. Any parent can make a stellar, amazing costume, they lie. And of course, your children won't be able to express their gratitude enthusiastically enough once you present them with the finished products.

Yeah, and I'm the Easter Bunny.

Let's take something like a "simple" lion costume. Directions might go something like this: Buy brown pants and a matching brown turtle neck shirt, along with a similarly hued hooded sweatshirt, a black face paint crayon and some brown or tan felt. Cut the felt into strips. Roll the strips up and steam-iron them so they make ringlets. Sew or glue the ringlets to the hood. Once the child dons all the brown clothes, pulls the hood onto his head and the parent smears on the face paint (in the form of whiskers and a lion-like nose), you will have a darling little lion.

One of my loveable, very clever friends "Mandy" — who always make me absolutely verdant with jealousy with her creativity and natural artistic ease — actually created this very same costume for her toddler son once. She stayed up late on many an evening, cutting, steam-ironing and gluing, her heart filled with anticipation. But there was a hitch. Once her son put on the sweet ensemble, he refused to pull the hood onto his head. It was too heavy, too much glue, you see. So at his Halloween party, Mandy had to spend the whole time explaining to other mothers that her son was dressed as a lion, even if you couldn't tell with his weighty mane draped down his back.

After Mandy's experience, no matter how hard she tried and how genuine her desire to make her son happy, I determined that I would be hard pressed to ever contemplate making a Halloween costume, particularly considering how absolutely pathetic of a sewer/crafter I am. I was convinced that if I invested all the time (which would be double Mandy's because I have not a drop of clever costuming talent or patience circulating in my blood) it would turn out lousy and my kids would hate it anyway. Then I'd just be angry. But then there's that nagging voice in your head – that nasty Type-A mommy voice – which says that if you don't make your kids' costumes, you're a mommy failure and you really didn't try hard enough.

My mother proudly remembers how she labored over my costumes for days on end before Halloween each year. There are photographs of me in handmade costumes, dressed as a pumpkin, as Raggedy Ann, a die (as in dice) and a fluffy bunny (I refused to wear the hat with rabbit ears but did carry Mom's handmade carrot shaped candy bag which I later brought to bed, slept on and melted all the candy inside). And what did I, the ungrateful lout, complain about? That other kids had store-bought costumes of the characters du jour, the flimsy ones with the scratchy, too small plastic faces and pinhole eye openings.

Which brings me to the store bought costume dilemma.

If you decide to go the store bought costume route, should you buy the less expensive costume or the ornate one that sets you back the monetary equivalent of the price of 30 pounds of the GOOD chocolate bars (not including the subsequent dental and nutritionist appointments)?

Case in point: When my son Jonah turned 4, he was given a videotape of the movie "Toy Story" and became obsessed with Buzz Lightyear. Weeks after his birthday party, when we were in the party store (go figure) and the Halloween costumes were on display, he spied a Buzz costume. He HAD to have it. I hadn't even begun to think about Halloween yet, but figured I'd buy the costume to: a) Quiet him (because there was no way I'd be able to make a decent Buzz costume) and b) To cross "Halloween costume for Jonah" off my to-do list.

All was fine until he went to a Halloween party and saw a kid in a much more elaborate (i.e. – mucho expensive) Buzz costume. It had wings (Jonah's had none). It had boots (Jonah's didn't). It had contoured shoulder puffs (Jonah's, again, sadly, none). Jonah looked down at his thin, nylon, hooded costume and grimaced, "I want a costume like THAT!"

Where was that piece of Twizzler?

But even if parents attempt to supplant their guilt for not

making a costume with buying the expensive duds (that no one will really see under cover of late-autumn trick-or-treating darkness or beneath a jacket because it's too chilly) you can still be left out in the cold. One of my friend's children got a gift one year, a luxurious, authentic, Disney Captain Hook costume, with crushed velvet, heavy material, the works. Must've cost a small fortune. Only problem was, the kid was afraid of it. Wanted absolutely no part of it. It sat around, unloved and unworn while my friend tried to concoct excuses for the relative who bought the costume as to why she hadn't yet seen snapshots of the child wearing said ensemble.

The lesson here? No matter which way you go with your Halloween costume choices, your kid will likely spot a costume on some other juvenile and loudly lament. So before investing your heart, time and hard earned money into trying to conjure up the costume of your child's dreams, be sure to lower your expectations.

Why not just be preemptive? Treat yourself to your own Mommy or Daddy stash of Halloween chocolate weeks before the spooky holiday. And when your sugar high hits, you can flip through the pages of the parenting magazines purporting to tell you how to easily make a costume for your child. And guiltlessly chortle.

Holiday Hangover

I was certain that I'd be finding shards of shriveled up cranberry skin and popcorn kernels for months on end. Forever, actually. Tucked into every nook and cranny in my house. Until my husband Scott got our AARP applications automatically sent to us in the mail.

True, most people who decorate their homes with live Christmas trees typically find pine needles wedged under sofas sometimes into mid-summer. That's a normal occurrence in a normal household. That's in a house where people walked by the Christmas tree when it was in its full glory, stopped to admire the beautiful ornaments and perhaps accidentally knocked a stray needle or two to the floor. But in my house, after the Christmas when our twins were 2-year-old terrors, I found not only pine needles, but bits of cranberries and popcorn everywhere. That's what happens when one's Christmas tree is under constant and vicious assault from a pair of determined destroyers the moment it crossed the threshold.

Keep in mind, as the December holidays rolled around — long before we bought our Christmas tree that year — Scott and I thought we had planned our interfaith celebrations carefully so as not to overwhelm our toddlers our Christmas and Hanukkah traditions. We tried to keep everything low-key. We tried our best not to interrupt nap schedules and meal times or over-stimulate them with too much newness. We thought we had everything well under control.

But the best laid plans went drastically awry.

Let's start with the tree.

I'd heard from a couple of moms at Abbey and Jonah's play group about this great, classic New England Christmas tree farm not too far from our house. They lauded it as "the perfect place" to take little kids. You get a sleigh ride, cut your own tree down while tromping through a snow covered field. (Envisioning Currier and Ives yet?) With somewhat sketchy directions, we took off at 5 p.m. (I know, I know!), on a weeknight, in search of the tree farm. We got lost. After over an hour of calling attention to every home decorated with a high-wattage display like maniacal General Electric shareholders in an attempt to avert a twin meltdown, we finally found the tree farm which, as it turned out, was only 10 miles from our house.

And it was closed. (And it was now dark . . . one couldn't really go tromping through a tree farm in the dark, now could you?) After getting the kids all pumped up to get the damned tree, we went home empty-handed with two really cranky toddlers in tow. We had to get the tree on another evening, after going to two different places, with Abbey in tears after we left the second one sans a conifer. But our winter holiday extravaganza had only just begun.

Once we finally had the tree firmly planted in its drug store bought plastic container, we set the new, post-kid tannenbaum rules: We strictly limited tree decorations to non-breakable ornaments, relying heavily on white lights and homemade garlands of strung cranberries and popcorn (that Mommy and Daddy made when the kiddos were asleep). We soon discovered that we are woefully dim people. I don't even remember how many times we found the kids with their faces in the tree or standing on tables that they dragged next to the tree, heads plunged into a tangle of branches with their mouths twisted around the garlands. Half-chewed pieces of wet cranberries and popcorn that were spit out in gooey pink gobs became a common site throughout the house.

In response to the woodland animal impersonation my twins were practicing, I moved the garlands higher and deeper into the tree. It was no use. (Why I didn't just take the tree down, take off the garlands or just put a safety gate around it, I have no idea. Chalk it up to sappy holiday sentimentality. Or stupidity. Coupled with sleeplessness.) When the kids weren't leaving naked, noose-like threads where popcorn used to be, they were stripping the tree of all of its remaining soft ornaments and organizing them in clumps on one side of the tree like miniature armies ready to overthrow the tyrants who were trying to rob them of their popcorn and cranberry feast.

When they weren't trying to eat the Christmas tree, Abbey and Jonah were busily spending the holiday season gorging on chocolates from their daily Christmas advent calendar booty and the eight days of Hanukkah gelt (otherwise known as the little chocolate coins wrapped in gold foil) that I bought them. Yes, I bought them, the Advent calendar AND the gelt. Because I am a stupid person. At every meal throughout the month of December, they'd beg for Hanukkah and Christmas chocolates in lieu of whatever was being served. And they were relentless.

Speaking of not eating . . . during the actual holiday celebration dinners, the two toddler celebrants marked them by the ambitious consumption of crackers, grapes and apple juice. The kids ate virtually nothing else. No Christmas or Christmas Eve dinners. No Christmas breakfast. No Hanukkah food. No potato latkes. Nothin'. Nada. No matter what delectables family members placed in front of them, they wanted nothing to do with them. Chex Mix was much preferred, thank you very much.

So they're filled with cranberries, popcorn, chocolate and Chex Mix, they're not eating full meals, they're pumped up about this holiday business, so they thought it was a perfect time to give up their naps. Fun times.

Then, the over-tired, over-stimulated, over-chocolated toddlers decided they weren't going to be opening any gifts. I kid you not. When confronted by a mountain of presents from Santa, their parents, grandparents and relatives, they opted to instead open the first toy that wet their whistles and turn their backs on everything else. We begged them to open the much-agonized over Christmas and Hanukkah presents but to no avail. Scott and I got the pleasure of opening a wide array of gifts ranging from Billy the Big-Mouthed Bass (that singing plastic fish mounted on pressed wood) to an incessant Blue's Clues radio that we secretly hope would be accidentally dropped in the toilet. And we had to smile while opening the gifts. Each and every one of them. As we talked about how nice they were. And how fun they looked. Because the toddlers were elsewhere.

Add to that the non-stop questioning of exactly when, where and how Santa was going to visit and, "Is it time to light the Hanukkah candles yet?" and I was close to imposing a two-year hiatus between us and the next celebration of Christmas and

Hanukkah. If I had to sing or hear "Frosty the Snowman" and "Rudolph" one more time, I threatened to voluntarily exile myself into a long winter hibernation with express orders to wake me up when it was July.

Lessons from "A Christmas Story"

When Christmas time rolls around, ever feel like you need some refuge from the gauzy Yuletide perfection extolled virtually everywhere you look?

First, how about a little quiz?

Which description best describes you?

A) A person who has picturesque Christmas gatherings in a professionally decorated home, with imaginative gifts wrapped in handmade paper with crisp red satin bows (none of which resemble gnarled chew toys) sitting beneath a pristinely symmetrical tree as nary a cross word passes through the chap-free lips of your loved ones while a plump turkey sits on a Williams Sonoma seasonal platter and delicate, epicurean side dishes cook on a sparking stove.

Or,

B) A person who gets kind of tense around Christmas as high doses of pressure and a mountain of nearly insurmountable tasks menace you, to which your only response is a string of mad dashes through various stores, late night Christmas card writing sessions until you can't see straight and desperate pleading with the delivery guys to please, please, please send the item you ordered ASAP because one of your cherubs has just changed his must-have "big" gift from Santa . . . five days before Christmas. ("Santa will know because he's magic. He's got that crystal ball, right Mom?")

If you fall in category B, then, my friend, you're in fine company. And I have the answer to what ails your soul.

"A Christmas Story." The film is my favorite winter elixir. In case you have lived on Neptune for the past few decades and have never come across this holiday staple, you can probably catch it on cable TV during one of its innumerable showings. For the past few years, one network has aired it for 24 hours straight on Christmas, like a soothing salve to ease the insanity occurring that very day in millions of homes across America. People struggling with dinner and internalizing negative feedback on gifts can ignore their guests and laugh as the 9-year-old lead character Ralphie had simple dreams of getting a coveted BB gun from Santa and thwarting the neighborhood bully.

The 1983 movie is the antidote to the bombardment of saccharine, tear jerking Christmas images blanketing the media with the false promise that with the right gifts, gourmet dinner featuring pomegranate ginger cranberry sauce and free range turkey, argument-free holiday parties, starched snowflake napkins and matching homemade snowflake cookies in homemade bags with embossed gift tags for each guest, you and yours will be happy.

Where else other than on the fictional streets of an Indiana suburb circa the 1940s can you find the antithesis of holiday perfection featuring a kid who got his tongue frozen to a flag pole, oral discipline in the form of Lifebuoy soap, prolific artistes in the medium of profanity, a lamp in the shape of a sexy fishnet stockinged female leg that got "accidentally" broken by a wife who despised it, a scary Santa and a kid who ate his mashed potatoes at the dinner table like a pig?

At the heart of this classic movie lies one, consistent message: We American families are flawed, but pretty funny, particularly when you throw Christmas stress into the mix. We might not be the greatest cooks. We yell at our kids. We fight with our spouses. And, despite our best efforts, our well planned family celebrations can result in hilarious, epic disasters like the one that befell the Parkers in the film who, after their Christmas turkey was consumed by the neighbor's marauding hounds, dined on what they dubbed "Chinese turkey" that was decapitated on the table in front of them at The Chop Suey Palace.

This film offered a more realistic Christmas image with which many can relate. It was a warts-and-all picture imbued with love . . . and a few bleeped-out cuss words. When I think about some of my family's Christmases, most would not qualify for Hallmark card status, and, frankly, I wouldn't want them to.

Then we wouldn't have had the Christmas of the Sweet Potato. My then boyfriend (now husband) Scott was trapped in the TV room (only accessed through the kitchen) during his first Christmas with my family, when my parents became embroiled in a full-blown shouting match as they peeled a pot full of cooked sweet potatoes. Who was right and who was wrong is really irrelevant, but suffice is to say that the dispute was capped with my mother invoking what "A Christmas Story" dubbed "the queen mother of dirty words, the 'f' dash, dash, dash," followed by her hurling hunks of sweet potato toward the sink, missing my bespectacled father.

Scott began looking for a way out of the den (the window perhaps?) so my folks wouldn't know he'd heard the whole exchange. When the coast appeared clear, he tried to innocuously slip through the war zone, but was spotted by my father who became red-faced, realizing there had been an auditory witness to the lack of Christmas cheer.

Or perhaps it was the beef tenderloin incident that solidified for me the notion that I belonged in the "Christmas Story" fellowship where nothing goes quite right in December.

Several years ago, my parents splurged on two top-of-the-line beef tenderloins for the Yuletide feast. My dad had big plans for those tenderloins when he handed them to my brother Sean on Christmas Eve with instructions to put them in the extra fridge in the basement. Flash forward to late Christmas morning when my dad went to the basement to fetch the roasts and discovered that Sean had put them in the freezer.

Can you say beefsicles?

Scott, my brother, my mom, my toddler twins and I were sitting in the living room amidst the 4 tons of gifts the grandkids received when we heard my father bellow from the floor below: "Jeeeezus Chrrriist!!" followed by the sound of angry footfalls bounding up the stairs, reminiscent of the dad in "A Christmas Story" as he battled the persnickety furnace.

Feelin' that Christmas spirit yet?

I could recount a number of unChristmas-like tales from O'Brien family lore, from one holiday featuring the severely backed-up kitchen sink, another with an extinguished pilot light on the gas stove requiring the services of a repairman on the night before Thanksgiving, my father's first Christmas Eve at his future in-law's house where he ate so much of my Grammy's food (so as not to hurt her feelings) that he vomited profusely that night and missed Christmas dinner, to the countless times Scott and I have tried to take pictures of our "cheerily" dressed children in front of our festooned fireplace as our offspring weep and their noses run while we offer pained smiles to the camera.

You can take all the pressures to make the Christmas season flawless, to pick the most fabulous gifts, to have the best greeting cards and toss them into the refuse, where the pink bunny suit Ralphie got from a deranged aunt belonged. I'll take "A Christmas Story" Christmas, with fuse boxes that went out, crooked Christmas trees and ruined dinners punctuated by unexpected laughter over forced perfection any day.

The movie's DVD case says it all: "The funniest thing about Christmas . . . is spending it with your own family."

And that's where you'll usually find me on the 25th of December, with my family, laughing my fanny off, trying not to clog up the kitchen sink, tossing sweet potatoes at my husband or freezing any tenderloins.

Poison Control's got my number

So, how many times have you called your local version of Poison Control because your kid ate something she shouldn't have? Surely you know Poison Control, the telephone help line staffed by people who sit in little offices and hospitals all around the country fielding questions from hysterical parents in absolutely ludicrous situations they would've never in 10,000 years believed they'd be in when their children were nothing more than little tax deductions flailing around in their mommy's womb.

I've often wondered if those people, sitting there in those offices and hospitals ever keep scorecards or itemize the weirdest phone calls they've taken. I've secretly feared that the Poison Control folks mock parents who have sought their services, that they roll their eyes at one another and make hand motions indicating that the person on the other end of the line clearly has an intellectual deficit.

In fact, I'm one of those addled parents, one of the faceless thousands whose children have eaten things that would make the idiots on the reality shows — who VOLUNTARILY eat live slugs – squirm.

"Do they know who I am?" I always ask myself as I'm on hold on the telephone line awaiting their instant diagnosis. If I call too many times, do red "stupid parent" flags go up, prompting men in white coats to burst through my front door, handcuff me and take my kids away to Willy Wonka's factory, where everything is edible . . . just stay away from that chocolate drainage pipe that sucked that German kid away to an uncertain fate.

Unfortunately, I've called Poison Control a number of times, and I feel quite guilty about it. You see, I don't keep an unbroken, steady eye lock on all three of my children during every waking moment of every day. There are times, I'm ashamed to admit, when I want to and do, go to the bathroom, all by myself, shower even, without dragging my kids into the room with me. (I really don't need the questions that abound about "hairy places" and incisive inquiries such as, "Why do your boobies look like that?") There are times when they're playing in another room and I am not watching their every move, in fact, I may be doing something else that's domestically riveting, like washing the dishes or putting 25 loads of small people's clothes away.

This is why I must be on the stupid parent list somewhere in the bowels of my local Poison Control. I don't and can't keep an eye on each of my offspring all the time. But, there's actually a better explanation for my stupid parent status with the Poison Control folks. I can just blame my mother, or my brother, well, my whole family, really.

Between my father drinking contaminated farm water from a white bucket when he was a kid — which induced lovely, gut straining vomiting and diarrhea — and my brother Sean's legendary knack for ingesting chemicals unfit for human consumption, I suppose I was destined to be forced to post the Poison Control number in every room in my house.

Take Sean's sordid history. Time after time when he was a toddler, he would lie in wait for my mom to use the bathroom, answer the telephone or be otherwise distracted so he could sneak into the cabinets, peek under the kitchen sink or dash into the bathroom to snatch some illicit substance, smear it on his tongue or guzzle it down, all while emitting nary a sound. "He always used to have no reaction," my mother says. "I thought his taste buds were dead."

A sampling of his toddlerhood buffet:

Thick globules of the acidic smelling Head and Shoulders dandruff shampoo which he grabbed from the ledge of the white, tile bathtub.

White, liquid, roll-on shoe polish run over his tongue after he retrieved the bottle from a dented old wooden container of shoe repair supplies tucked way in the back of the kitchen coat closet behind the gargantuan bag of dog food.

Ammonia directly from the bottle after my mother – who had been washing the kitchen floor with a tasty combination of ammonia and water – dared to use the facilities. ("To this day, I can't smell ammonia without having a visceral reaction," Sean reports.)

Scented Ban roll-on, the only substance that elicited an "ack" from the precocious tot. ("My tongue smelled good though," he now says.)

It got to the point where the first thing my mother would do in the mornings was to make sure the Poison Control phone number was still emblazoned on Sean's forehead in thick, black permanent marker. (If you look really closely at his hairline, you can still, some 30 years later, make out some of the outline of the 1-800 number.)

While I only plagued my mother with only one incident of rogue chemical ingestion – I personally ate nearly a whole bottle of prescription, fluoridated vitamins, necessitating the issuances of the vomit-inducing ipecac coupled with orders for my parents to keep me up all night – I'm now being visited by the ghosts of my family's Poison Control past.

A generation later, I have become my mother (on the Poison Control front, as for everything else, don't get me started). I too have been tempted to start the day off with a fresh cup of coffee and the clean scent of permanent marker after writing the Poison Control number on my youngest child's forehead. At least two of my three kids have been, shall we say, orally fixated. Translation: They stuff anything and everything into their mouths, much like their Uncle Sean, who'd better pray that his sons don't follow in Daddy's footsteps.

My first foray into the legions of Poison Control fellows was when my twins were toddlers. Abbey, clearly under-fed, decided to satiate her appetite with Huggies, scented, aloe vera-covered baby wipes. Here was a kid who scoffed (and still scoffs) at perfectly good meals, turned her head away from any form of chicken that doesn't resemble a gnarled chicken nugget and nearly everything in the vegetable category. And she ate baby wipes. It boggled the mind.

And let me tell you, there's no more idiotic feeling you can have than when you dial that Poison Control number and utter the words, "Um, yeah, hi (*nervous, inappropriate chuckle*). My 18-month-old just ate baby wipes. . . No, I don't know how many. . . Well, I was in the bathroom . . . peeing." (Did I just hear laughter in the background?)

The feeling I had after reporting that my kid ate wipes was later trumped when I had to call and report that my youngest kid had fished a Lysol brand, orange-scented toilet bowl cleaner contraption – the kind that clips onto the side of the bowl and cleans with every flush – from our toilet and sucked the liquid cleaner out. I found my then 1-year-old son Casey in the bathroom (someone had left the bathroom door open and he took full advantage of the error), spotted the empty toilet bowl cleaner thingie lying on the rug, sniffed Casey's little mouth and detected the distinct odor of orange mixed with the pungent remnants of the strawberry yogurt that he'd eaten during breakfast.

Months earlier, when Casey was but a mere crawling baby with an affinity for crying, his older siblings thought that the perfect solution to his crying spells was, of course, to administer some liquid, infant Tylenol to him while Mommy was busy cleaning the dishes. I'd stupidly (Did I mention that I'm a stupid parent?) left the Tylenol bottle wedged between the infamous Huggies wipes box (Yes, the box was at the ready.) and the wall next to the changing table, which my then-3-year-old son Jonah had climbed. Upon discovering the Tylenol, the twin pediatric geniuses decided to take matters into their own hands.

There have been other instances, alternately horrifying and disgusting, where my offspring have eaten things that would make your blood curdle and your hands reach out for the Poison Control speed dial number. The tamest of the examples was the consumption of houseplant leaves (I wasn't sure if the plant was poisonous), followed by crunchy Cat Chow for older kitties (Casey was a big fan), various pieces of unknown items from the trash, beach and sand box sand, wood chips, books (literally *consuming* books), the occasional chomping on various toys like Legos and hardened cat vomit they found in the floor one morning.

I have admitted that I'm a dim-witted parent who, like my mother before me, cannot seem to stop my children from eating things that they shouldn't. So please, nice Poison Control people, don't laugh when I call with my next preposterous report that one of my kids has eaten my car keys. And please don't send the guys with the white coats here, unless they're going to be taking my kids to the set of a reality show centered on the consumption of horrific items. Then, maybe we could make some money. While I'm thinking of it, maybe you should give my brother a call too.

Homespun politics

The Jib Jab obsession served as my wake-up call, the moment when it finally dawned on me that perhaps my household was a bit...unusual.

During the summer of 2004, two enterprising animators created an online video parody of Woody Guthrie's "This Land is Your Land" song, lampooning the presidential candidates — Republican President George W. Bush and Democratic Senator John Kerry — with cartoon caricatures of both men singing the ditty in ridiculously exaggerated accents. Once the news media featured the Internet short on various shows, where Bush called Kerry "a liberal wiener" who has "more waffles than a house of pancakes" and Kerry called Bush "a right-wing nut job" for whom a brain "can come in quite handy," I decided to take a look.

With some judicious editing of a few unsavory parts (re: I either covered the computer screen with my hands or loudly hummed over certain lyrics) I let my then-6-year-old twins and 3-year-old watch it. Not only did the kids reenact the JibJab.com video more times than I could count (I officially began to hate "This Land is Your Land"), but the video prompted vigorous discussions about election issues over bowls of breakfast cereal.

Hardly atypical for our household.

It was my fault. All of this odd behavior. Considering that the kids couldn't even read at the time but could identify our state's governor, our U.S. senators, the president and vice president. I'm a politics junkie. Even though I've grown quite cynical about the political process since my years as a student of government and as a political reporter, I stubbornly and idiotically cling to a Jimmy Stewartesque, "Mr. Smith Goes to Washington" idealism about American politics; I love its promise, not always its messy practice.

And when I had kids, I vowed to explain to them the crucial importance of voting and how one should always be well informed on the issues. My twins' first exposure to politics was sitting through hours and hours of President Bill Clinton's impeachment hearings on C-SPAN. Of course the kids were just infants at the time, so hopefully they didn't retain any of testimony in the deep recesses of their brains, though Abbey still has an odd aversion to dresses in any shade of blue . . .

I bought a "School House Rock" CD and attempted to hook the wee ones on that "I'm Just a Bill" song ("I'm just a bill, yeah I'm only a bill and I'm sitting here on Capitol Hill"). I frequently show them newspaper photos, read them stories and play selected TV news footage about current events. Following the presidential primaries in early 2004, when former Vermont Governor Howard Dean torpedoed his Democratic presidential campaign with his primal, poll-busting scream after he lost to Kerry in the Iowa caucuses, one of my kids' favorite pastimes became impersonating Dean's maniacal shriek. And I know I'm probably the only nerd on the block whose children can complete this sentence: "If it's Sunday . . ." (Answer: "It's 'Meet the Press' with Tim Russert," my kids reply in unison, referring of course to NBC News' august political journalist.)

But the world of politics can be nasty.

During the 2002 governor's race in my home state, the patriotic melodies of "School House Rock," the all-American discussion about freedom and the colonial Revolution fell by the wayside to partisanship. Mommy and Daddy, who were rooting for opposing candidates, were asked by Abbey and Jonah which person would make for a better governor. Treading cautiously, we tried to delicately discuss our candidate preferences, trying not to taint the kids' points of view. But when we all watched the gubernatorial debates together, the matter became almost humorously polarizing, as we didn't hide our cringes or our (my) outbursts when we (I) talked back to the TV screen.

We told the kids that no matter who Mommy and Daddy supported, the children could support the candidates of their choosing (although I secretly wanted them to pick the candidate I supported, but resisted lobbying them). In the weeks before the gubernatorial election, Jonah, Abbey and I did a craft project: They made their own "voter registration forms" and picked party affiliations, as I attempted to neutrally explain for what issues and topics each political party stood. (We're pretty sure that Jonah picked the Green Party because he thought a party with a color was cool.) With a nod to Florida's hanging chads in 2000, the preschoolers and I made up paper ballots and the kids cast their votes for governor. Abbey chose the female candidate ("Because girls rock") and Jonah the male candidate ("Because boys rock").

Our gubernatorial election mania got a bit hairy when our family walked into the high school gym to vote. The two boys were with Daddy and our daughter was with me. Jonah and Abbey demanded to know where their homemade ballots were and, upon being told that only Mommy and Daddy were given authentic ballots, insisted that they get their own to fill out. Seeing as though we didn't want to go all WWF on the nice senior citizens manning the polls in order to acquire faux ballots for our preschoolers — never mind the fact that there was a nice police officer hanging around — we hushed the kids up with menacing parental glances, explaining the you-must-be-18-to-vote rule once we were outside.

The following morning, after I broke the news to Abbey that her candidate lost, she shed her first political tears. Jonah, who had not yet fine-tuned his gloat-o-meter, started chanting his candidate's name in staccato-like shouts, fists punching the air like exclamation points.

Two years later in 2004, we found ourselves smack dab in the middle of a close, contentious presidential campaign. And Mommy and Daddy were on opposite sides again. Not wanting to poison the rhetorical well or destroy our children's innocent, idealistic views of government, we tried to temper our viewpoints and tamp down our comments, at least at the dinner table. But the kids came down on gender lines again. Abbey supported Mommy's candidate. Jonah and Casey supported Daddy's guy.

So when the Jib Jab parody came along, it had the perfect mix of humor, politics and song. It blended all of the elements of our brand of homespun politics and brought the whole family together. Our three kiddos became obsessed with the parody. It was hard to explain to people at the park, mommies at play groups and the attendees at our Labor Day barbecue why exactly, our 6-year-olds and 3-year-old were clamoring to perform bits of political satire.

Still, there was something about our 3-year-old yelling, "I'm Howard Dean! I'm Howard Dean! Arrrgghhah!" and my kindergarten twins pretending to be Bush giving Kerry a shot of Botox in the cheek (it was in the parody) that was a bit odd.

Politics makes for strange kid-fellows, at least in my house.

New beginnings

It wasn't what I expected it would be. Moving to a new house. Moving into said house with three small children. In the dead of summer.

Who would've envisioned that our last, nostalgic night in our old house would feature the entire sweaty family sleeping on pillowless, frameless beds in 100 degree weather (98 percent humidity) on the floor, while giant dust bunnies and stray pieces of packing tape danced around our heads?

Who would've predicted that I could be found days later, in my empty old house, sobbing loudly as I washed the walls of the kids' bedrooms? Not I. This whole new beginning thing, the anxiety of this new shift in our lives, came as something of a surprise to me.

As Scott and I, veterans of many previous moves in our PKE (Pre-Kid Era), prepared to move a mere five minutes down the road to a new home – but in that five minutes we crossed the town AND county line – we were not delusional about what we could realistically accomplish. We knew we'd need to hire movers. On one too many occasions, we'd tapped the well of hearty friends and family members willing to lift, sweat and grunt while lugging our stuff on and off of rented moving trucks, all for some greasy pizza and cheap beer. We also knew that to get stuff done — pesky moving stuff, like packing, cleaning and painting (to cover up the colored chalk all over the walls courtesy of our charming children) — we'd need to distract the kids. Ninety-eight straight hours of the whiny, yellow spongy creature who lives in a pineapple under the sea on television, with wholesale club sized boxes of Goldfish crackers and a pallet of juice boxes just wasn't going to cut it. Thankfully, some friends kindly offered to host play dates to help me out. That worked. For a few afternoons. After that, they were stuck with Mama and 45 gallons of every variety of cleaning fluid known to mankind.

What I wasn't anticipating in all of this planning was that the level of stress from my kids, and consequently for me, would completely unhinge us all. When the kids learned that we were actually going to move – confirmation occurred less than a month before the closing date – uncertainty settled in, like the bad breath that inevitably follows the four helpings of garlic mashed potatoes you had for dinner. My twin kindergarteners, who had been looking forward to going to the same school building where they had preschool, with friends from their hometown, were thrown by the news that they'd be headed to a different town, with different kids and a different school building. My youngest son Casey, who had just turned 3, was so utterly confused, that he kept asking whether the vacation house we rented in Cape Cod earlier in the summer was our new home, one that came complete with Grandma and Grandpa Jack and going to the beach every day. During "moving week" the little people saw all their belongings packed up. They found themselves being dragged back and forth between the new house and the old house. Dinner came in Styrofoam. Drinks in juice boxes and bedtimes were all over the map. Things were just not right.

I'd seen "tips" for moving with kids, articles stating that moving is among the top five most stressful life experiences. The advice included having the kids pack some of their own things, allowing them to help set up their own rooms and involving them in the process. I did some of the suggested tips. Kind of. Actually, I made up my own. I bought those cheerful kids' books about moving and read them earnestly. We discussed how the children wanted to set up their rooms, colors and themes. We picked out some new bathmats, towels and accoutrements for what would be designated as the kids' bathroom (Mommy and Daddy were *finally* going to get their own bathroom). But as for packing with my 3-year-old "helping," I'd rather have carved my eyes out with a dull spoon. Neither of us have that much patience. My 6-year-olds would've inevitably gotten into a wrestling match over who got to put which toys in which box and, frankly, it would've made me crazy (okay, more crazy). I had enough on my plate without partaking of that little chestnut of "helpful" moving advice.

Between the few days we had to clean the new house before we moved our stuff in, through the last night in the old house, sleeping on those dusty bedroom floors (the movers had taken most of our stuff, including pillows, away in a truck overnight to some parking lot somewhere when they were supposed to move the furniture into the new house . . . it's a long story), it was pure chaos. During the insanity, I tried to appease my dictators. I set them up with the DVD player, bags of toys and coloring books in one section of the new house and left them to their own devices while I tried to clean the remainder of the abode as quickly as possible. Ever try to steam clean rugs while kids are chasing you through the house? Clean bathrooms when your 3-year-old thinks it's fun to surprise you by "cleaning" the walls with a toilet brush doused in bleach?

Once the movers finally delivered all our belongings to the new house (and didn't make off with the truck filled with our home contents as I feared) we tried to soothe the kids' fears by setting up their rooms first. I spent one of the first mornings unpacking their play room to increase their comfort level.

But it didn't really help.

My daughter uncharacteristically wept for the first few weeks of school, wrapping herself around my legs when it was time for her to get on the bus. (I had to literally place her on the inside of a bus seat, put her twin brother Jonah on the outside, and then jump out of the bus so she'd stay in her seat.) My 3-year-old started preschool and starred in repeated encore performances of "Let's Grab Onto Mommy and Sob Wildly." Why should his sister be the only one to provide theatrics?

Despite the fact that we moved to a house that would better suit our growing family's needs, the new beginning was rocky, and not just for the kids. One afternoon in the old house after we'd moved out, I was cleaning the walls in the bedroom that had originally been the twins' room and later the boys' room — the one with the Classic Pooh border, cream walls and slate blue rugs. There, at about thigh level, I spotted a perfect, dirty handprint on the wall. In movie montage-like fashion, images hurtled through my mind: Taking my babies over the threshold of this house for the first time, their first steps in the living room, giggling games of chase down the hallway (most of which ended with blood, bruises or bumps), almost giving birth to Casey in the tiny bathroom, celebrating their first birthdays in the decorated back yard with family, Abbey losing her first tooth.

And I lost it. How would we ever feel the same way about the new house? We'd never have so many "firsts" any place else.

After my weepfest, I actually toyed with the idea of having the whole family go into the family room of the new house, empty a box of Cheerios on the floor and have a family mash-a-thon to make the place feel more like ours. But after having lived in the house for a little over a month, I realized that we didn't need the crushed Cheerios. By then, we'd already had two incidents of writing on the walls (one in pencil, one in red pen) and had the downstairs toilet clogged twice with copious amounts of toilet paper from an enthusiastic bum wiper. I found a tortilla chip under the boys' dresser.

Felt just like home.

Of spilled milk and talking wallpaper

A parenting quiz in reverse order:

Answer:

1) Spilled milk that insinuates itself into every crevice of the kitchen table, streams over the edge where it lands with a faint splat on the floor (in between the wooden flooring slats, and all over the table and chair legs) and down the heating vent where it will smell to high heaven when the heat is turned on.

2) Pieces of penne – slathered in olive oil and Parmesan cheese – that somehow slime their way off of a young child's fork, slide off the table and land *plop* into the cat's water dish where, after the penne lands, a large splash of water is sent in all directions. (The ensuing juvenile "clean up" inevitably winds up with the soaking of the previously dry cat food sitting in an adjacent bowl, thus making the whole kitchen smell like the inside of a soggy Cat Chow bag.)

3) Toys that come smashing down to earth and break into a thousand jagged pieces that cannot ever be reconstructed with any semblance of order, despite the tidal wave of tears enveloping the play thing's tattered remains and the desperate pleadings, "But Daaa-deee, you're such a good fixer . . . We've got glue."

4) Trying to help, yet not really helping. In English: A kid tries to help a parent with some task, let's say, sanding something in the back yard, yet the overanxious child prematurely grabs the power sander, turns it on and not only is sent catapulting through the grass (ruining the carefully seeded, fertilized and limed area), but busts the tool while simultaneously shaving 1/8 of an inch of flesh off of his left shin.

Question:

Name four sure-fire ways for my three kids to send their father into orbit where he loses his normally cool demeanor.

CliffsNotes version:

Anything that moves from its appointed spot and goes to places where it doesn't belong and causes: a) A mess or b) Anything to be broken or people to be injured, makes my husband go nutty.

Answer:

1) Making me have to answer the same question 47 times in the span of 10 minutes when the answer has not and will not change. (As in, "No, you cannot have a snack now. I said you could have one at 3:30." Or, "No, you can't ride your skateboard over your brother's OR your sister's belly.")

2) Ignoring my repeated requests to please pick up your *fill in the blank* (Legos, marbles, K-Nex, Barbie shoes, colored pencils, soiled duds, books, etc.) from the middle of the family room and return it from whence it came. (*First request*: "Honey, could you please pick up your Legos and bring them upstairs?" *Second request*: "Those Legos are still there. Could you please pick them up?" *Third request*: "Hey! Get those Legos outta there!" *Fourth request*: *An unprintable word for a family-oriented publication, followed by the sights and sounds of my head exploding.*)

3) Fighting with me over what to wear for the day. (As in, "But you picked this sweatshirt out yourself at the store! You said you loved it. Now you won't wear it? . . . You're wearing this. We spent good money on this.")

4) A subset of item #3: Fighting with me over what I've made for dinner, even though you said you liked it last week. (As in, I serve dinner featuring the once beloved macaroni and cheese featuring images of licensed characters in pasta forms, and one of my children announces that she no longer eats "that stuff.")

Question:

Name four things that press my buttons and transform me from my natural demeanor (an over-caffeinated, sleep-deprived, hyphenated media-phile) into a stereotypical screaming mom. (Think Lois from "Malcolm in the Middle.")

CliffsNotes version:

To get me insane, just make me have to repeat myself, over and over and over and over, and give me the sense that I'm being ignored, or that the rules of the game keep shifting, and never in my favor.

Over-analysis:

Broken, messy stuff that dad has to clean up versus ignoring a mom like she's irrelevant. Could make for an interesting psychological study, comparing what makes moms and dads crazy. Think of the long, unwieldy scientific synopses: "Fathers feel personally attacked when their offspring are careless with things in their home, while mothers feel like they're about as effective as talking wallpaper: When they talk, no one listens."

Talking wallpaper? What a hideous idea. Could set off *both* mom and dad: Mom by repeatedly asking her the same questions, dad by intentionally peeling and falling to the floor, thereby making a mess. Better stick with paint in a muted color.

Random Ramblings

Little girl blue

I am the mother of a set of girl-boy twins, or, as I was informed by a complete stranger at the grocery store one day when my twins were but wee babies, I had a boy and a boy impersonator, like Hillary Swank in "Boys Don't Cry," only without the messy ending.

"Oh, so you have two boys, wow, you must be busy," said an older woman upon spying my kids in the shopping cart at the local supermarket one afternoon.

"No, actually, I have a boy and a girl," I replied as I casually placed my order at the deli counter.

The woman leaned over, squinted and scrutinized them. "So which one's which?" she asked, wrinkling her brow.

I looked at my then-baby girl, Abbey, who was wearing a white barrette and a green fleece jacket over a green floral shirt and blue jeans. My little baby Jonah was wearing a matching blue fleece jacket over some navy corduroys and a red shirt. I told the inquiring shopper who was who. My identification, however, did not satisfy her.

"Well, you can't really tell," she huffed, shaking her head. "She's not wearing pink." Not to be technical, but, neither was I, and I'm pretty sure she knew I wasn't of the male persuasion.

But the grocery store lady wasn't alone. She was a member of a rather large group of women – it was almost always older women — who thought it was scandalous that I put my baby daughter in jeans or in any shade of blue. What is the world coming to, they lamented, when you could no longer tell a tiny boy from a tiny girl?

And I didn't just hear about it from random strangers I encountered. At a friend's barbecue, I got an earful from my friend's aunt after she saw what Abbey was wearing: A shirt with dark blue, light blue and pink stripes and a scalloped edge around the scoop neck, along with blue stretch pants and black leather shoes with thin straps across the bridges of her slight feet. To me, she looked sweet. But to the aunt, she was an androgynous nightmare.

"Where's Abbey?" she asked after scanning the yard.

I pointed out that the 1-year-old girl was standing right in front of her.

"*That's* Abbey? Well how the heck am I supposed to know that *that's* Abbey? You've got her in blue for goodness sake. She looks like a boy."

I wasn't quite sure what was driving everyone's concern. Were they afraid that Abbey would somehow think she was a boy because she was wearing blue and would require years of expensive therapy to discern her true gender?

Many decades beforehand, I had dressed my younger brother up in girls' clothes and told him he was a girl when he was only 2 years old. (I always wanted a sister.) And, despite my attempts at brainwashing, Sean wasn't adversely affected. Sure, my dad was perturbed – particularly by my brother's persistent questions about why my parents hadn't told him he was female – but now, years later, Sean's a 6-foot-2-inch man's man babe magnet. No apparent lasting damage done, though he does have an affinity for hair gel . . .

When Abbey and Jonah were babies, people seemed compulsively compelled to learn their gender, and some actually got irritated when they couldn't tell at first glance. But when it comes to infants, aren't they kind of genderless anyway? I mean, many infants are hairless and have chubby faces that kind of blur their features so you can't really tell what they are. There are many adults who spend a lifetime trying to figure out just who they are, so what was the rush? I thought that, as a culture, we'd gotten past this. I thought that the days when girls only wore pink and boys only wore blue had faded away, like housecoats, avocado colored appliances, afternoon newspapers and Tab.

I was wrong. So very, very wrong.

It wasn't that I had anything against dressing girls in pink or boys in blue, but I definitely had a problem with people who thought that children shouldn't stray from a gender-color ghetto. I liked to dress my daughter in delicate duds as much as I liked to put my son in bold, primary colors. But they also had many pieces of clothing (jeans, T-shirts, sweaters and sweatshirts) that they wore interchangeably. This, to staunch die-hards who believe in exclusively owning girly-girl clothes OR boyish clothes, was juvenile fashion heresy.

But I came up with a way to mollify those pesky ladies. I decided I should write a letter to my congressman suggesting the creation of a new law so no one in a supermarket or at a family barbecue would ever be confused about a child's gender again. The law would require that children under age 12 wear gender-specified clothing, girls in pink, boys in blue. As an alternative to the color code, parents could choose the name tag option. Girls would wear government-issued pink stickers bearing bright, flowery script saying, "Hi! I'm a girl! Have a happy day!" (The exclamation points would have flowers and hearts beneath them.) Boys' stickers would have a blue background and block letters reading, "Hi! I'm a boy and I don't know why my parents are making me wear this stupid thing." (Pictures of bugs or trucks would appear randomly around the sticker.)

If parents failed to adhere to the federal gender codes, they would be sent to fashion education classes explaining the importance of making their children's gender crystal clear to all passersby. It was crucial that naive parents (I'm raising my hand here) who let their daughters don jeans and blue clothing understand that if crazy ladies at the deli counter can't tell what gender our kids are, we are contributing to the downfall of civilization as we know it.

God bless America.

Say cheese

I realized things had gotten out of hand when I wrestled my toddler son to the bathroom floor and pinned him down with my knees in order to make sure his haircut was even. Jonah began screaming and pushing my hands away halfway through the haircut, bobbing and weaving like a boxer to avoid being touched by the sinister scissors. I desperately tried to get him to stay still for fear I'd accidentally cut his ear. (Which I did. But it didn't bleed. Much.) I desperately gave him a plush Elmo to hold, a cartoon character toothbrush and a forbidden roll of toilet paper to unravel. When those didn't work, I vowed to give him unlimited car privileges when he gets his driver's license and all the candy he could ever want.

No luck.

I was in a panic. I *had* to complete his haircut. If I wanted his Official Portrait taken with his twin sister Abbey the following day, his hair had to be somewhere in the neighborhood of symmetrical.

The Official Portrait.

Two words that send chills down the spines of parents who have small children. The mere thought of trying to dress a kid in stiff, uncomfortable clothes and then coaxing a smile out of him seems like a doomed endeavor, never mind trying to do it with two uncooperative toddlers. But there's no avoiding it. Despite the multitude of snapshots taken of my kids and constantly disseminated to friends and family, no one's truly satisfied until they get that Official (re: professional) Portrait done. So you, the parent, shrug your shoulders and try to prepare for ordeal.

Abbey and Jonah had their first Portrait taken at a major department store when they were seven months old (much later than some other parents I know who go almost monthly when their kids are small). They had to be propped up by a box covered with a scratchy brown carpet that God knows how many other kids like mine had drooled, sneezed or urinated on.

Now I don't know about you, but I wouldn't exactly be inclined to smile if I were dumped onto an uncomfortable wooden platform, put under hot lights in a tiny 85 degree room while some strange man standing behind an ominously large, menacing looking contraption maniacally shakes a pathetic, worn bunny at my face. From a child's perspective, getting a Portrait done is akin to facing a relentless assault by lunatics. "Mommy's acting so weird, grinning wildly, waving her arms, snapping her fingers and calling for me to, 'Look up here,'" I imagined the kids thinking. Despite my ridiculous attempts to get them to smile – I was about as entertaining as a dial tone — I was still disappointed that we weren't able to get a shot of the babies smiling simultaneously. No wonder the babies in Anne Geddes pictures seem to be sleeping a lot.

After that first Portrait experience – the image we settled on had Abbey laughing and Jonah in that half-smile, half-about-to-cry look — I was determined never to be caught unprepared again. Planning for the next Portrait was not unlike preparing for war: A battle plan was drawn and ideal conditions to launch the offensive were identified. I had to decide in advance what they'd wear so I could have the items pressed and ready to go at any moment. But choosing the proper clothing was no small feat. It was fraught with potential disaster. Should I put them in the hip clothes Auntie Ellen bought them, or would the kids bemoan our fashion choices 20 years from now with a snide, "How could you dress us in *that*?" (Remember how you felt about those photos of you in orange Toughskins or plaid pants?) And would Grandma be upset if I didn't select the fancy outfits she recently got them?

After weighing the political implications of the clothes, you have to make sure your kid's hair is in decent condition, typically by getting a fresh cut. However getting a child's hair cut close to a Portrait session can be risky in the event the cut goes awry and your kid winds up looking like a practice mannequin at a hair dressing school. That's what I feared when I started trimming Jonah's hair myself, which had grown into a wild, Einsteinian curly mess. The initially peaceful effort quickly degenerated into a lame WWF match.

While I normally would have given up and attempted it again later, I was on a schedule. He was going to get his Official Portrait done the next day and couldn't do so looking like Einstein. I would never hear the end of it. At age 40, he'd still be reminding me of how demented his hair looked in that picture. I didn't even want to think about what my family would say.

The haircut incident notwithstanding (I'm sure it forever damaged Jonah's psyche, what with the pinning down on the floor business), I determined that we'd push ahead with the photo session plans. For the first time in what seemed like months, neither tot had a runny nose, facial bruises, scratches or fat lips courtesy of an errant run-in with a Tonka Truck. Grabbing the already ironed outfits, Scott and I got the kids ready with the swiftness and accuracy of an Army maneuver. We thought we had anticipated everything.

Then we arrived at the Alamo.

There was kicking, screaming, tears, an insistent hail of, "Nooooo!" and the angry throwing of cheesy props back at the photographer who cowered behind the giant camera. We shamelessly cajoled. We jumped up and down. We made sickeningly goofy noises. Essentially, Scott and I acted like we belonged in padded rooms. Then the whole sad episode came to a grinding halt when Abbey tried to take a chunk out of my left shoulder with her teeth.

The quality of the Official Portrait photographs steadily decreased throughout the session, going from images where the kids exhibited a look of quasi-amusement to stone-faced mug shots and finally arriving at the "Getmeouttahere!!" expression. When we selected an image from the rather paltry lot, the photographer looked relieved not to have to redo another session.

"I'll bet you want to have a nice cold drink after this," I said to the photographer, as I wiped the perspiration from my brow.

"Yeah, a cold drink all right, but not of water," she replied.

Say cheese.

I need a vacation

I went into this thing with low expectations. Really I did. I didn't delude myself into thinking that a weeklong Cape Cod vacation with twin toddlers would be relaxing. Banished were thoughts of romantic moonlit sunsets at the beach. Ditto for digging my tootsies in the sand and letting the sound of the ocean waves lull me into a sense of tranquility.

I expected the trip to be prominently marked by sand. A ton of it. In every bodily orifice. In every food container. In every sippy cup. I expected mere two-hour stints at the beach. Max. I expected at least an hour's worth of preparation to get two 22-month-olds into their beach gear, slather them with sunscreen and then complete subsequent clean-up after they peed through their swim diapers *before* we finished filling the beach cooler with juice boxes. I also expected some sleep disruption because the kids were in a new place. Above all, I kept in mind the wise adage uttered by my husband's experienced colleague, "When you have little kids, it's not a vacation. It's a change of venue."

But I did hope for maybe a nice dinner out and a shopping venture or two in picturesque towns. Forgeddaboutit. Scott and I quickly learned that when Abbey and Jonah didn't get their way when they were in an unfamiliar place, life was very unpleasant. We should've known better.

The first two "vacations" we had with our new babies were marked by sleepless infants. No naps. No night-night. The trip my friend Gayle and I took to her parents' Narragansett home with our three children — all 11 months old — brought me to my knees. (We were outnumbered by the band of three babies for most of the week while our husbands were hiding out, "working" they argued, in their quiet homes.) Gayle's son was a virtual angel while my two not only went on a seek-and-destroy mission around the unfamiliar environs, but refused to sleep. On one particularly steamy night, I wound up collapsing into a recliner at about 3:30 a.m., furiously rocking the twin furnaces who were sweating in my arms so they wouldn't cry and wake up Gayle's son Nolan who was peacefully slumbering. After a few nights of this, I was on the phone begging Scott to arrive early and relieve me.

Months earlier, Scott thought he was being sweet by surprising me for my very first Mother's Day as a mother. He whisked me and the kids to a New Hampshire bed and breakfast for a night. We're lucky the inn owners didn't banish us from the premises, as well as the entire state. For all of eternity. The babies squawked all night long, prompting us to immediately put them in our bed so they wouldn't wake the other guests in the old farmhouse. In the span of a few hours, I was peed, pooped, drooled and barfed on, not mention the fact that I, again, went sleepless.

Hap-py Freak-in' Mother's Day.

Who did we think we were, parents of twin babies, going on a vacation? We'd been lulled into thinking it was achievable upon hearing stories from parents whose trips with infants and young children had gone well, following reports that their kids never cried on airplanes or pooped on hotel rugs. Either they were all lying, or our kids were, shall we say, very "active."

So by the time we embarked on our summer vacation to Cape Cod with my family when our twins became toddlers, I must've come down with temporary amnesia, banishing the memories of the previous ill-fated trips from my brain. We should've known that there would be no such thing as a peaceful vacation after the first hour of our car ride in congested and oftentimes stop-and-go traffic. Envision an hour-plus of toddler screeching which prompted a parental debate over which would be worse: Jumping out of a moving car (albeit slowly moving), or withstanding another second of this endless verbal pediatric torrent. Instead of taking potentially life threatening measures, we opted to sing songs. Every children's song we knew. Scott and I were able to appease our little ones. Then, in the stop-and-go traffic, we pulled up alongside a Jeep filled with buff, young guys. You don't know how humblingly uncool it is to pull up alongside a vehicle whose occupants reek of hipness while you're singing a loud, off-key version of "The Wheels on the Bus."

The car trip foreshadowed our experiences with vacation dining. The moment we sat down in restaurants, Jonah would grab everything in sight and chuck it: Menus, forks, napkins, sugar packets, his toy truck, Daddy's food and Grandpa's scotch and water. This was typically followed by the telltale ominous, rumbling noise that warns of an impending Jonah meltdown. At this point, all the adults, including my parents and brother, would start giving Jonah private tours of the local landmarks outside. As soon as Abbey would get wise to the situation, she'd begin chanting, "Abbey too! Abbey out!" in increasing decibels. Thus began her personal tour of everything on the exterior of the restaurant.

Scott and I effectively ruled out going to restaurants until the kids were at least 25 after the last night we attempted (key word: *attempted*) to have dinner in Provincetown, a small town on the tip of the Cape. Jonah showed signs of another freak-out early after he refused all food and drink. When he began throwing things, yelling at the wait staff and spinning his head, we decided it was time for him to again inspect the restaurant's property. Abbey followed soon thereafter. Scott and I wound up eating dinner in the parking lot as the kids gleefully played in the car. It just didn't have the same ambiance though, eating a scallop and lobster casserole from a Styrofoam box with a fork stolen from the restaurant while sitting face-to-face with our car bumper.

Throw in the night when Jonah refused to go to sleep and stayed up until 11:30 p.m. watching "Bowfinger" with the grown-ups on the antique cottage VCR, along with his naked peeing escapades in bed and you had plenty to frighten my then-27-year-old bachelor brother into postponing having kids for years.

We resolved that it would indeed be quite a long time before we ventured out for another so-called family vacation with our little lovebugs . . . until the next summer.

The contents of my fridge

Two open cups of milk, of uncertain age, in those flimsy plastic cups you get from noisy, sticky family themed restaurants.

Several half-empty jars of Gerber baby food ranging from watery Stage 2 carrots to soupy Stage 3 apricots.

Sobe power drinks that purport to give you energy and pep.

A gargantuan jar of Welch's grape jelly (lid a bit sticky with congealed jelly), next to an even bigger plastic bottle of well loved (i.e. – also sticky) Heinz ketchup.

Squishy, blackened bananas (also of an uncertain age), propped up next to a bowl of leftover chili where the plastic wrap is only tenuously clinging to the sides of the bowl.

Forget that English proverb about the eyes being the windows of the soul. Take a peek in someone's fridge. Wanna know what's going on in the life and soul of a parent with young children? There it is, in black, white, yellow and some other indescribable colors and odors. In the fridge. All the hopes, dreams and nightmares of living with small people 24/7.

One can tell, just by looking at the contents of my refrigerator, that not only do I have kids, but they've taken over. Where there once were Styrofoam boxes containing exquisite meals from hot restaurants (ones that don't offer crayons and paper placemats with connect-the-dots puzzles), fresh ginger that would be grated over stir fries with a cornucopia of fresh vegetables and not allowed to sit unloved in the crisper to mold, fresh jalapenos, bunches of leeks, crisp chardonnays and bottles of Guinness, there are now Arthur juice boxes and Styrofoam containers harboring semi-hard grilled cheese sandwiches and slightly soggy tater tots.

Every item in the white, humming behemoth in my kitchen tells a story, the story of how my life has been transformed from that of a person who used to dine (meaning actually chewing one's food while it's hot and succulent), to a person who has two minutes to shovel everything down one's throat before my children make another, urgent request, or I need to stop them from chucking hot buttered peas at one another, or they need me to accompany them the bathroom for the 53rd time that day.

Take, for example, open milk cups.

At every meal – except breakfast – what my kids have to drink is almost always a test of wills. Regardless of what I set out in front of them, they can be counted on to demand something else. If I put out milk, they want juice. If I put out juice, they want water. If they get water, they demand the red cup, not the purple one. Should I be foolish enough to continue trying to please them by doling out milk, juice, water and then a second cup of water in a different colored cup, I can expect that they will again recoil at the new cup of water because it doesn't have a straw. Should I then be moronic enough to fetch a straw, it's inevitably the wrong color, which means that the kid will then become the embodiment of Mount Vesuvius and won't eat anything. At that point, I may as well just go to bed.

Scott and I have repeatedly told our offspring that we don't run a restaurant (not one we'd like to go to anyway). They have to drink the beverage that's served from the cup we give them. Whatever they don't drink winds up in the fridge. Sometimes it sits there for days, a testament to the fact that we have a house full of stubborn people. Neither Scott nor I can ever remember how long the half-consumed cups of liquid have been there since all the meals tend to blur together. Most of the time, the cups get dumped because we're afraid of giving them really old milk and the kids win out in the end.

Then there was the baby food.

When my youngest son Casey was just starting to eat solid food, he developed a boatload of eating preferences. At 10 months old, his entire diet consisted of pureed fruit, baby cereal, Cheerios and Mommy milk, along with pureed potatoes and peas. Carrots, squash, sweet potatoes, and basically anything else in the vegetable category, were unceremoniously dropped out of Casey's mouth via a slack, open mouth with his lower jaw just hanging there allowing the food to drip out onto the highchair like a slow, multi-colored shower.

For his entire babyhood, we adhered to the advice from the so-called baby experts who told beleaguered parents to continue to offer rejected foods, up to 15 times after the baby first curls his lips in revulsion, because eventually, we were told, the infant would eat it. Never happened, my friend. The half-empty baby food containers of all different brands and types began to pile up in our fridge, prompting local health officials to threaten us with hazardous waste violations if we didn't toss the stuff.

And ah, can't forget that infamous big bowl of uneaten chili.

One day, silly Mommy decided that she didn't want to have a kid-centered meal (chicken nuggets, hot dogs or mac-n-cheese) and had the audacity to make chili. Because she had a hankering. What on God's green earth was she thinking? Even though there were a plethora of side dishes the toddlers in the house *would* under normal circumstances eat — like plain pasta, sliced apples and grape tomatoes (the only fresh vegetable Abbey and Jonah would willingly consume) — it was insufficient.

My son Jonah burst into tears upon seeing the meal. "I hate chili! I want some otha food," he screamed, stomping his size 8-toddler feet.

"But you've never tasted chili," I tried to reason with him. "It's like the red sauce with meat you like to dip pasta in. It's like ketchup."

I was getting desperate. And he, the ruthless piranha he was, knew it. He and Abbey hunched over on their chairs, rear ends pointing toward the ceiling, and sobbed at their sad lot in life. They eventually acquiesced to eating slices of American cheese for supper and began whining a half-hour later that they were starving and that their wretched mother wouldn't feed them.

Maybe someday, in about a decade, the contents of my refrigerator will once again feature the likes of gourmet fare, exotic produce and fresh herbs. But my children will be teenagers by then, when everything — no matter what it is – will be consumed within 30 minutes of my returning from the grocery store. Too bad I can't save all the food I've been throwing away or letting rot inside my fridge until the kids reach their dreaded teenagerhood. But by then, I will have sunk in their eyes from not only being the most inadequate meal preparer they know, but also the most stupid person on the face of the earth.

Where's that Guinness?

Multiple madness

The smell of grated Parmesan cheese wafted through the air.

As soon as I detected the peculiar smell – peculiar given the fact that A) It was mid-morning and B) We hadn't eaten anything with Parmesan cheese recently — I followed it to the kitchen. There, I found my then 3-year-old twins Jonah and Abbey in T-shirts and Sesame Street and Blue's Clues underpants respectively crouched over something beneath the kitchen table.

"What are you doing?"

"Nothing," they said in unison.

"Come out of there now!" I demanded.

As they crawled out from their lair, I noticed that they'd dumped an entire plastic container of grated Parmesan cheese onto the dark red rug and spread it out in a 12-inch wide circle. (A pretty good circle by the way.)

Then I spied the fat-handled kid spoons lying atop a fluffy bed of cheese. "What were the spoons for?" I asked.

"We were eating the cheese with them," Jonah said cheerfully, as if the fact that he was using a utensil would somehow impress me.

Once I crawled under the table, I spotted slices of roast beef delicately fanned out across the seats of three newly re-covered dining room chairs. "What's with the roast beef?" I inquired, half dreading what preschooler rationale would emerge from their cheese-covered lips.

"In case we got hungry," Abbey chirped.

I used to worry. I worried that my kids were nuts. Well, nuts may be a bit too strong. Let's say, I worried that they were too energetically mischievous. It seemed like a majority of my friends – who only had one kid each at the time – had fewer problems with their children than I had with mine. Incidents like the Parmesan cheese caper and a seemingly endless list of their toddler antics had me very, very worried.

Among the worst incidents occurred during their "terrible two's" when my duo went through a phase where, instead of napping quietly each day, they repeatedly emptied their diapers of their contents and proceeded to pound their poop into the fibers of the light-colored rugs in their bedrooms with little plastic tools from Jonah's Fisher Price workbench. The piece de resistance was when they'd plunge Jonah's black plastic screwdriver upright in a mound of bodily waste in the center of the room.

These are children who had stripped a vacuum cleaner of its bag and dumped that bag's contents out as they walked down the hall. They'd written on one another with dark blue magic marker, paying extra attention to the bellybutton area. They'd found it amusing to slide pieces of wooden puzzles through the slats on the front of the dehumidifier in their play room. They devoured books, literally, like woodchucks and other mammals. One afternoon they emptied Scott's wallet and drew all over his credit cards and his driver's license with a blue pen, then moved on to his beloved Palm Pilot which was likewise covered in ink and had bizarre notations inputted into its memory.

Other parents who had just a single child at home didn't report this type of strange activity in their households. I began to worry that I'd soon be buying wholesale club-sized proportions of psychotropic medications. Then, after speaking with other moms who had twins, or had at least two children who were relatively close in age, I had an epiphany: Neither of my children was unitarily psychotic. It was the combination of my twins that made their behavior collectively insane. Sure, seems easy to figure out when you're not on your hands and knees, eight months pregnant, on a chest crushingly humid summer afternoon trying to remove mashed poop from a rug.

If either one of my kids had been born by him or herself, perhaps my home would've been relatively peaceful, like my friend Gayle's house when she only had her son Nolan, the portrait of a well-behaved child. Nolan didn't get into anything or destroy things like my offspring. But after one play date at Gayle's — where to my astonishment she still had picture frames on display, along with pretty decorative baskets containing seashells and a VCR within the kids' reach — I think she too began to question my kids' behavior, or at least the ability of their mother to control the duo of destruction. Jonah and Abbey taught Nolan, who was born just days after them, how to insert assorted hard plastic items into the VCR, how to play with the fireplace and how to knock picture frames over, things that never occurred to Nolan before.

While I was fretting to everyone who would listen, a couple of other moms of twins let me in on a little secret. I was not alone. One friend, Wendy, smiled and shook her head when I told her about the Parmesan cheese incident. That was nothing, she said. She had been war tested. Her twins were two years older than mine and, she said, I hadn't seen anything yet. When Wendy's boys were three, they would occasionally rebel against their mom when she'd reprimand them. Wendy's punishment for disciplining the boys? The two would urinate in various places around the house, like in potted plants or a trash can, where the pee would soak through the can's contents and then settle to the bottom so that the kitchen would smell like a Port-a-Potty the next morning. They once contaminated their basement dehumidifier by dumping poop inside the water bin. Wendy didn't find the offending material until days later when she was almost knocked over by the stench.

Michelle, another mom of twins, regaled me with a story about how her twins turned her living room coffee table into a scene from "Waterworld," sans a drippy-looking Kevin Costner. She awoke one morning to find one end of the living room coffee table propped up on the sofa. Her kindergarten-aged boy-girl twins were pouring water down the table and sliding onto the now slushy rug. She raged at them to not only clean it up but to promise never to do it again. The next day's feature attraction at Michelle's house? Waterworld II: If you liked the first version, you'd love the second one.

I began to sense a trend and stopped compiling family therapists' names and contact information.

When Gayle had her second child and could no longer have picture frames or VCRs at the kid-level, I realized that it wasn't a twin thing, it was a multiple kid thing. One kid, on his own, typically, is manageable. Throw in any more, and you're just askin' for trouble.

So what did I do after this life-altering realization? I had another kid. Guess who needs the corrective psychotropic meds now?

Drive-thrus rock

Drive-thrus rock. No doubt about it. In a kid-dominated universe, they rule.

When I had three kids under the age of 4 — two preschoolers and a baby – drive-thrus were my nirvana. If I wanted to attempt to get any more than two errands done in a day without risking a violent overthrow from the tyrants in the back seats of my minivan, I had to go the drive-thru route. Ever tried to take young kids in and out of car seats all day long? Not gonna happen. You're greeted with arched backs and camel-like spitting. And let's not forget about the howling. I'm talkin' children who howl like they're being mugged for their juice boxes, loudly, so that passersby will hear.

Parents faced with virulent car seat resistance must try to literally bend and force the kid into her car seat or else you ain't goin' nowhere. When my kids had fits like this, I felt like a fugitive from justice as I ducked down low and avoided making eye contact with anyone as I literally pressed the children's waists into the seats so I could buckle them in. (I was always worried that people think I was doing something sinister as they jotted down my license plate for the authorities, when all I was trying to do was make sure my kids were safely strapped in.)

I learned early on in my parenting that young kids will only tolerate going in and out of car seats for two, maybe three errands before staging a palace coup. So whenever I go out, I have to make it count. That's where the drive-thrus come in. I quickly began arranging my life around drive-thrus for everything. Drive-thru banking and ATMs. Drive-thru dry cleaners (not that I ever got a chance to wear anything that required dry cleaning when I had an infant who expelled bodily fluids from a variety of orifices all over Mommy on an hourly basis). Drive-thru pharmacies. Drive-thru doughnut shops which served my favorite uncontrolled substance (coffee).

With the baby and two toddlers on hand, I wanted the whole world to be drive-thru. I wanted a drive-thru video return and check out (for the mountain of movies – mostly unwatched because my endlessly cute infant would have a meltdown at 9 p.m. just when the older two went to sleep and I'd never get to watch the flick all the way through). Drive-thru delis which would still give you that free piece of cheese for each kid in your entourage.

And then there was the pinnacle of my drive-thru fantasies: The drive-thru convenience store. When you have more than one small child, getting something from a convenience store is ironically, inconvenient. It's not an easy feat to lug an infant carrier into a small convenient store while trying to hold onto one or more kids, praying they won't snag an errant bottle from a nearby display, prompting a cacophonous, dramatic crash of merchandise costing you $97.50 in warm, spilled Snapple.

Just for kicks, let's say you're brave enough to venture into such a store. While you're holding the infant seat and clutching a kid, try to grab a gallon of milk. Okay, let's make it a bit easier, a half-gallon of milk. And a loaf of bread. Or, how about trying some spring water and a dozen eggs? Can't do it, not without living dangerously by letting the older one walk unrestrained beside you while you lug the baby car seat and your merchandise to the counter, fumble through your purse, and then your wallet, for money. Then you need to get out to the car with all that stuff *and* the kids. You've got to pray that your little tykes don't see some cute squirrel scurrying around the parking lot that they chase after, putting them in the path of a careening car driven by a clueless driver who's got a cell phone pressed to his ear or who's furiously typing away on his Blackberry while turning into the parking area.

You've also got to hope that one of your tots doesn't shoplift anything. Remember, we're dealing with little kids with the common sense of a boiled potato. Ever patronize those stores with the candy displays that go from the ground up to an average adult's waist level at the checkout counters? Why do you think the candy's there in the first place? To put the sweet stuff at eye level with the rug rats so they'll bug the heck out of you to buy them some. Well with my kids, they firmly believe it is their personal mission to poke, prod and shake every piece of candy in front of them while I'm trying to pay for something else. I've witnessed them walk away with a box of Tic Tacs that I haven't paid for on many occasions. Luckily the Tic Tacs make noise so I knew something was awry and was able to grab the offending mint box and toss it back into the display, which was typically reduced to a heap courtesy of my children, the human wrecking balls.

You may as well skip the convenience store until you're sans children. It's just not worth the hassle.

Which brings me back to the lovely concept of drive-thru convenience stores. Think of the ease. Drive up to the window, collect that loaf of bread, milk, butter, and, if you're feeling spry, how about a copy of *The Wall Street Journal* so you can pretend you have the time to use more areas of your brain than the part that remembers that your son doesn't like to drink out of the red cups and your daughter prefers spoons, not forks, with her meals. I'd even be willing to tip these people because they'd make my life so much easier (and I'm frugal . . . okay cheap). I could get so much done in one day, without the in-and-out of car seats business.

A little while back, I read in my local newspaper that some communities were trying to cap or altogether eliminate drive-thru operations because they were viewed by some as tacky. A pox on all their houses. Don't these people realize who uses these things? Parents in fleets of minivans containing little people with peanut butter smeared across their chins in the backseats screaming for more Raffi songs, that's who.

I planned trips around where I could take advantage of drive-thru services so I could get the most out of my day without risking meltdowns. I didn't want fewer drive-thrus. I wanted more, more drive-thrus . . . and another 32-ounce coffee please, because when you're busy trucking kids around, you really need the caffeine.

The scrapbooking cult

Okay, so I "do" scrapbooking.

I'm one of the growing number of disturbed individuals who has taken a perfectly good noun ("scrapbook") and mutated it into a verb (as in "scrapbooking," a thing you do, not merely a resting place for the vestiges of one's youth like high school news clippings about your softball games and pressed senior prom corsages).

For those un-indoctrinated few who haven't heard of "scrap-booking," it's the latest fad to wash over American mothers. (Yes I'm talking exclusively about mothers, as I have yet to see a SINGLE father partaking of this insanity.) A simple explanation: You take family photos, cut them up in a variety of artistic shapes, maybe round the corners or use some fancy scissors to make the edges more edgy, and put them in sturdy, blank books with stickers and heavy stock, decorative paper.

You got it right, grown women, myself included, are going ga-ga over things like patterned paper and stickers. At times, I've had to fight my kids over my scrapbook stickers trying to explain why the oh-so-perfect ocean stickers would look much better in the family scrapbook rather than in their Dora the Explorer or Spider Man coloring books. And while I argued with them, the rational remnants of my mind would scream, "They are STICKERS for God's sake! How did it get to this?"

Did I happen to mention that scrapbooking is a glorified cult? No, I haven't had to blood-let or speak in tongues to become an official member of the order of "scrapbookers" (those who scrap, also known as "scrappers"), but I have accidentally swerved into a world I never dreamed I'd be seeing, never mind participating in, when I was taking some progressively minded classes in college.

It all started out innocently enough (says the intro to the made-for-TV movie, "Scrappers Gone Wild"). A friend, we'll call her "Kelly," was commencing a part-time gig as a consultant selling scrapbooking materials. Her first "party" (another word for a gathering where women sell stuff to other women and everyone's guilted into buying something lest they look cheap) was at a mutual friend's house. Although I'd never had anything to do with these grown-up scrapbooks before, I agreed to attend the party and support Kelly's new venture. Upon entering, I couldn't help but envision slightly chartreuse-hued images from home movies of early 1970s Tupperware parties. I felt as though I'd crossed a line and that once I attended a suburban home party, there was no turning back. There was a little wine, some light refreshments and a little friendly shame about how you, the mommy, could serve your family better by preserving memories and photographs, not yesterday's meatloaf in burping plastic ware. Kelly showed us how we could display and safeguard priceless moments in our young families by arranging and displaying our photographs with acid and lignen-free archival supplies. (I'm not quite sure what a lignen is, only that it's very, very bad. It eats cherished photographs apparently. And erases memories.)

Impressive presentation aside, it was Kelly's own personal scrapbooks that sealed the deal. When we caught a gander of her two-page spreads of her daughters' birthday parties, we were intrigued. Some of the photos were circular, while others were oval or even square. Some had jagged edges, or were wavy. There was beautiful paper surrounding the photos, sometimes cut into shapes, other times making little frames around the glowing, happy faces. Themed stickers complemented the photos along with Kelly's personal anecdotes of her family's life written by hand, a handcrafted family heirloom.

I was surprised to find myself imagining ways I could create "New Baby" pages with adorable baby bootie stickers and "It's a Boy"-themed, color coordinated papers. I could do a Christmas page. A Halloween page. A Cape Cod vacation page. The possibilities abounded. Wouldn't it be great to have a place to display the ticket stubs from my kids' first movie? And wouldn't my offspring like to know the stories behind the collection of images that would normally be lost in a regular photo album? So I did what any mother, and all the mothers in attendance did. I opened my checkbook and bought a bunch of stuff.

And then there was Gayle, my skeptical friend. A mother of

three, she attended a Kelly-led scrapbooking party, this time at my house. She called me the day after the gathering and denounced the whole enterprise as a twisted cult that made her feel like a bad mom for not documenting her family moments in multi-colored inks that were guaranteed not to smudge, but only if you bought their particular brand of pens. A few months after Gayle rebuffed the whole hobby — while I puttered around with my photo corner rounder — she became a scrapbooking addict. Not only did she start blowing huge wads of cash at craft stores for stickers, this former scrapbooking scoffer invested nearly $100 on eBay for a specialized bin for her scrapbooking materials. That's right. One hundred. Dead presidents. For a bin. (She'll tell you it's kick ass.) She got a special container for her pens and even a tool for carefully removing stickers when she mistakenly placed the precious, pricey gummy beauties in the wrong location on the page.

Gayle, who eventually became a scrapbooking consultant herself, hosted a party at her house run by a different consultant who should've been installed in the scrapbooking hall of fame. Or institutionalized. This woman informed us that she was simultaneously working on three scrapbooks, one for each of her three extremely young children. "When my kids get married, I plan to give them the collection of books, at least one for each year," she proclaimed.

It was at that point that I began to think that some members of the scrapping community were way beyond me. Sure, creating a scrapbook can be fun, when done in moderation, but not in triplicate and not in every waking moment when I wasn't changing diapers. Just don't lay your mitts on my stickers. It could get ugly.

Celebrating St. Patrick's Day with All-American mutts

Come the 17th of every March, I dust off my family's recipe for that good old corned beef and cabbage boiled dinner. I stock up on Irish soda bread and frothy Guinness. I buy shamrock paper plates and napkins and some cookies with green sprinkles. I drag the obligatory green clothing items out from the bottom of everyone's dresser drawers, put on Chieftains' or U2 CDs and fetch my claddaugh pin from my jewelry box so we can all get into the spirit of the day of the Irish.

My kids and I do some Irish-themed crafts, something with the obligatory shamrocks (Leprechauns just don't seem as politically correct as they used to be), while I keep an eye out for my youngest son to make sure he doesn't decide to eat any stray green crayons he can snag as he has in the past, resulting in his own personally tribute to the Emerald Isle.

Then I talk with the children about how they're Irish.

A teensy bit.

One-eighth to be exact. Despite having "O'Brien" in their names, only one-eighth of the blood coursing through their hyperactive veins can be in any way qualified as Hibernian. They're hardly the poster children for the typical Irish lads and lasses. Like me, they're mutts, all-American mutts, living testaments to that clichéd, gloppy, untidy but plenty hot melting pot. Their ancestors could cover the map of Europe: Ireland, England, Spain, Austria/Poland (no one's ever quite sure which), Russia and one woman from France who we think lived in a musty flat somewhere in Paris for the month of April something like a century ago and is purported to somehow be linked to royalty, however no one has seen nary a crown jewel or photo of anyone in any state of curtsy. Our children's extended family includes: Catholics, Jews, Episcopalians, Congregationalists, agnostics and those who have been worshipping at the altar of Fenway Park for generations.

If you include all of the folks who've married into our family and have (or could) contribute to my kids' cousins' gene pool, you'd have to add to the list Italy, Puerto Rico and the French part of Canada (maybe the relatives from this branch of the family traveled through Paris once during that one month in April, a century ago and met our lone French aunt and dined on cookies with royal icing).

How multicultural is our family? Consider one of our more unlikely family gatherings: Scott (who's Jewish) and I (raised Episcopalian) had my parents (one raised Congregationalist, one raised Catholic, both converted Episcopalians), my brother Sean and his then-fiancé Lisa Sanchez (Catholic) over for a Passover Seder dinner. None of them, except for my brother, had ever attended a Seder. And, since Scott and I celebrate Christian and Jewish holidays in our home, we wanted to share Judaism with the O'Brien half of the family, introduce them to new foods they'd never tried. Chief among the new culinary delights was something known as gefilte fish, that jelled fish loaf stuff which purports to be fish but, in reality, looks like stuff that you scrape off the bottom of your shoes and then plunge into a hearty vinegar soak to kill off any rogue, flesh eating bacteria. I had to choke that stuff down for years trying to score points with my mother-in-law. Then I had twins. After I had them, I no longer felt compelled to swallow any more gefilte fish whole, followed by a Manischewitz Concord Grape wine chaser.

It's rare these days when I come across a family that isn't some sort of unusual blend of cultures or faiths, because, at its root of this odd mixture was a mommy and a daddy who couldn't keep their hands off of one another regardless of whether one ate stuffed cabbage and the other ate fish mash. How many 100 percent "purebreds" do you see these days in, say, Hibernian clubs which have no doubt scheduled thousands of corned beef dinners throughout the month of March across the fruited plain? What about the participants of the countless St. Patrick's Day parades throughout the country, how many of those marching or watching can say with certainty that they are mostly or all Irish, or Catholic for that matter?

Scott and I have done our duty as a good parents of children who are 1/8 Irish and brought them down to South Boston – a part of the city well known for its overwhelmingly Irish population — to watch the annual St. Patty's Day parade amble by many years. Each year, my ankle-biters would wear green and put shamrock stickers on their cheeks. (The bottles of Guinness were obviously restricted to the adults, and only consumed once we retreated to my brother's apartment on West Broadway, the 50-yard line for the Southie parade, not too far from where Ben Affleck and Matt Damon visited the L Street Diner in "Good Will Hunting.")

To Abbey, Jonah and Casey, it didn't matter what percentage of their heritage was Irish, or whether or not those who are "more" Irish consider them legitimate claimants of the Gaelic heritage. They just are. They're just Irish, just like they're Spanish and Austrian/Polish and English and Russian and a wee tad bit o' French. They think everyone has a Christmas tree and a menorah in their houses in December. They think everyone's family makes paella with chicken and pork outdoors on a special grill in the summer and eats matzo for eight days in the spring.

It's all one big, glorious American hodgepodge.

Whenever I'm asked (it happened frequently when I worked as a newspaper reporter in Boston) what county my family's from – meaning what county in Ireland – I always feel compelled to announce that I'm not simply Irish, that I'm a mix of contradictory and oftentimes warring cultures, a heritage of people who both did some oppressing and were oppressed, which could of course explain my hot, fiery temper and ever so occasional stubbornness.

What in God's name does that mean for my all-over-the-map kids? It means shamrocks and corned beef on the 17th of March, pierogis and cabbage soup on Christmas Eve, Spanish hot peppers to add spice to life, matzo ball soup and potato kugel on the table, and "The Fiddler on the Roof" and "The Quiet Man" on the VCR.

I draw the line at the fish.

Cautionary tale

It's an unseasonably muggy, sunny, late spring afternoon in New England, which means it was muddy and crappy, but let's pretend for a moment that all you see is springtime splendor bursting with life. You, a conscientious, well informed parent, take one look at your 7-year-old son who you've just released into your Technicolor back yard to play, when it hits you. "Sunscreen! Forgot the sunscreen!" you mutter, in a Seinfeldian grumble.

Grabbing your kid by his freshly, naturally-scent-free laundered, cotton collar – voices of TV safety gurus about never leaving a child under 12 alone outside for fear he'll be abducted echoing in your head — you drag him back into the house. You dutifully slather his exposed body parts with sunscreen, which will serve as a superb dirt and muck magnet in your muddy yard. "Moooom, this is taking too long! Alex came over from next door and I wanna play with him!"

Nervously nibbling on the tips of your non-Purelled hands, you try to remember what you've forgotten. "Oh! Your hat," you yell as you run down the hall to fetch a baseball cap to shield your beloved, eldest offspring's eyes from the evil sun rays.

He heads outside, with you close behind. You start to wonder if, because of the unseasonably warm weather, the mosquitoes have come out yet. "In fact," you suddenly blurt out as you check your watch and see that it's 4 p.m., "now's the time of day when the mosquitoes are at their worst!"

Your brain flips through your mental flash cards, onto which you've recorded the dates of your kids' next pediatric appointments, your wedding anniversary, details the last episode of "24" and foggy memories of the days when you were free and unencumbered and didn't worry about sunscreen. After about 30 seconds, you arrive at the mental flash card you made last summer while reading a scary news article about West Nile Virus.

"Can't let ya outside without DEET bug spray," you tell your kid, who by now, feels as though he's aged three years waiting to go outside and play with Alex. "You wanna get West Nile Virus?" you snarl when he shoots you a disgusted look as you begin to spray the bug repellent on top of the layer of sunscreen.

Hearing the soft gurgling sounds emanating from the baby monitor clipped to the waistband of your jeans, you take a mental note that if your napping baby wakes up you can't take him outside without first grabbing the African safari-like netting to cover the baby seat because the experts say the bambino is too young for both sunscreen *and* DEET-related products. Your sweet infant, you think, would be better off in a hermetically sealed, germ-free but intellectually stimulating black, white and red striped environment where an endless loop of "Baby Mozart" DVDs are playing.

"Mooom?! Are you done with the spray?" your big kid asks, snapping you back into the present tense.

"Yeah," you reply, saying a silent prayer that your 5-month-old stays asleep.

As you stand up, you notice your son's clothes. Nothin' but a dark, short sleeved T-shirt and shorts. Not good, according to West Nile Virus (WNV) people. Gotta get him in light colors, long sleeves and long pants to protect him from the bugs. "Change your clothes. Can't wear that. The bugs'll get ya."

"But I'll be hot an' sweaty," he complains when he sees the pants, you just pulled out of the clean laundry pile on the sofa.

"You're right!" Your mental flash cards start whirring again, stopping when you come to the "heat stroke" card. "You *could* overheat with all these clothes on in weather like this."

Uncertain of what to do, you pause, trying to recall the health experts who prattled on and on while being interviewed for TV news segments, especially during the sweeps period when all the ominously menacing segments air on local newscasts warning that they have the answers to whether your child will live or die . . . only if you tune in at 11 for their special report. But if you don't let your kid go outside and play, he'll just get obese from a lack of exercise, you recall from another news report about the epidemic of childhood obesity. He needs to go outside (exercise good). You need to be with him (ward off abductors). He needs sunscreen (keep skin cancer at bay) and bug spray (ditto WNV), long sleeved shirt and long pants (keep cancer and WNV at bay, II) and a bottle of spring water (prevent heat stroke and dehydration, but not tap water unless it's been tested for contaminants by qualified environmental experts).

You finally decide to live on the wild side and let him stay outside for 15 minutes, maybe 20, until it's officially too buggy. You pat his head and march him out, keeping vigil from the deck.

Your frazzled brain is just starting to ratchet down from pediatric safety mania when it's time to go inside, have a snack and face another rash of seemingly contradictory pediatric expert advice. Once inside and everyone's washed his hands in anti-bacterial soap, you announce that the kids can only dine on certified organic fruit, but not too much fruit, because you don't want them to have too much sugar, even if it is natural.

The baby, who's just woken up, can eat as much of his organic baby crackers as he wants, you remind yourself, as long as the crackers don't contain hydrogenated fat which the nutritionists say is bad. "Do those crackers have hydrogenated fat or trans fat?" you wonder aloud, suddenly panicking, rushing to re-read the ingredients list on the box. "But wait, doesn't he need some fat for his brain development? But what kind of fat? I don't remember!"

Just then, your 7-year-old reaches for the whole milk and another organic, non-hydrogenated cookie. You scream, "NO!," snatch the cookie and the whole milk from him and instead hand a cup of organic 1% fat milk. "You're not supposed to have too much fat in the milk. And no more cookies. Need to save room for tonight's tofu-vegetable stir fry surprise."

He frowns. So do you. Deep down, you really don't want tofu surprise. What you do want is an all-American anything. Placing a single, unsanitized finger in front of your mouth, you motion to your grade schooler to be quiet as you extract two forbidden pieces of chocolate from your secret stash in the pantry.

"Just don't tell the other mommies," you whisper conspiratorially, while you and your son enjoy the moment, and, what's left of his so-called, carefree childhood.

Forgive us our parental sins

I'd be sitting on my bed reading, or talking with a friend on the telephone. My kid brother would stand in my bedroom doorway — with the door that would never completely click shut – and poke it open with the tap of a single index finger.

"Get outta my room!" I'd thunder in the direction of his smirking face.

"I'm not *in* your room," he'd reply. Out of the corner of my eye, I'd see him wave an arm over the threshold, clearly violating the room's air space. Then a foot. Wars have been started over such flagrant violations.

"Ha, ha, I'm in your room," he'd taunt as I'd slam the door shut, or, almost shut, as it bounced back open about an inch.

This routine would cycle in an endless loop until I'd do one of two things: 1) Spend the rest of the day with my back pressed against the door to keep it closed, or 2) The option any red-blooded, much tormented older sibling would pick — Slug him. Predictably, after his slugging, he'd cry and run to my parents who would summon and summarily punish me. "You know better than to hit your brother," a parental person would lecture me, as a wry smile would appear from beneath the torrent of my brother's crocodile tears.

When I was pregnant with my youngest child, I vowed that I'd never unfairly punish my older twins like I'd been punished for retaliating against my pain-in-the-butt kid brother. I was savvy to the taunting routines and would, before decreeing a punishment for striking one's younger brother, try to discern the context in which the blow was administered. I wouldn't melt into a puddle upon seeing my baby, who seemingly didn't know better, in tears. Wasn't I so superior, so much more rational than my parents?

Upon embarking on the journey that is parenthood, many of us righteously utter loads of promises about future parental conduct. We say we will *never* do the unfair things our parents did. We won't give our "baby" special treatment. We won't shoo our children away with the phrase, "Just go play." We won't serve food we hated as kids.

We won't use our children as go-betweens while we parents are having a spat. We most certainly won't embarrass them.

And then we actually *have* children and the truth comes round the corner to kick us in the fanny. So here, sadly, is a brief indictment of me, the parent who has unwittingly committed the same sins as my foremothers (and fathers):

Exhibit A: Though I am more cognizant of the circumstances surrounding altercations between my older kids and my younger child before meting out punishment, I find myself doing other things my parents did that I vowed not to do. For example, I sometimes (okay, a lot of the time) put the older ones in charge of the little one. ("Hey Jonah, can you help Casey put his coat on?" "Abbey, can you please help Casey buckle the seat belt?" "Will one of you please make sure Casey brushes his teeth?") I know I never liked being put in charge of my little brother, but, as a parent of multiple small children, I now realize that, sometimes a parent needs a little help. I also find myself imploring the older kids to "just go play with Casey," even though he's been bothering them and ransacking their Lego village or Barbie shopping mall. (As the older kid, I *hated* being made to play with my brother, particularly when he was being annoying.)

Exhibit B: After a long day of refereeing, overseeing and entertaining small children, I admit that I find myself shooing them into the family room to watch pediatric programming so I can make a meal that they won't eat. I've even used the verboten, "Can't you kids just go play?" phrase, anything other than having them roll around the kitchen floor whining that they hate the food I'm making, that they're bored and don't want to play with Casey "'cause he wrecks stuff." (Hardly how I pictured it would be when I was pregnant and thought they'd be well behaved children who'd sit quietly and color.)

Exhibit C: The promise about not serving my kids food that I found disgusting is now preposterous. Oh, how I lambasted my mother for serving me overcooked, crinkled peas that I simply chucked into our kitchen floor fan. And what is one of the primary vegetables I serve my kids? Crinkly peas, or at least they are crinkled by the time I get everything to the table. There's a 25 percent chance that my offspring will eat peas at any given meal. Typically, my children barely eat anything resembling any kind of vegetable (you name it, I've likely tried it) and I'm down to precious few options for my uber-finicky trio. So, the wretched peas I despised, it is. Either that or broccoli. Sometimes carrots.

Exhibit D: How about not embarrassing the kids? I have vivid memories of being made to repeatedly face a wall one evening while visiting my grandparents because "The Godfather" was playing on TV and my folks didn't want me to see some scenes. I grumbled loudly for years about how humiliating that was, questioning how my parents could have had that on TV while I was in the room, making me face the wall every five seconds (it was *"The Godfather"* after all). Decades later, I can't even turn on broadcast TV in my kids' presence without worrying about them getting a sudden peek at something like Janet Jackson's breast. During the notorious Super Bowl incident – before we got a glimpse of Jackson's odd solar nipple ring – we actually made our own kids face a wall while we scrambled for the remote control to turn off the sexually explicit and violent ads.

My name is Meredith. I am a parent. And I am guilty of parental sins. Case closed. (Sorry Mom. And Dad.)

What's in a nickname?

When I was a kid, my parents saddled me with this unwieldy moniker: Mere-Bear Sydney-Hood.

Why? Haven't got a clue. Don't even know what a Sydney-Hood is.

Perhaps they were in the throes of a 1960s flashback. Maybe they were sleep deprived. Maybe I'd thrown my wrinkled canned peas onto the floor or into the kitchen fan one too many times and they were exacting psychological distress on me as payback.

Granted, the "Mere-Bear" part of the nickname was cute, but the "Sydney-Hood" segment haunted me all the way through the halls of my high school. Boys on whom I had crushes would laugh, "Hey, it's Mere-Bear Sydney-Hood," as my face flooded with a rush of blood turning me into a blushing, bulbous, walking tomato head. Sure, when I was 3, calling me Mere-Bear Sydney-Hood might've been adorable, might've seemed harmless. But by the age of 15, when I'd transformed into an awkward girl with a mouthful of braces and a bad haircut, the nickname was an albatross.

Nicknames were common in my household growing up. My father loved pet names and assigned them to everyone and everything. Our dog Daphne was Daffy Doodles. A childhood friend of my brother's who resembled Whitey from "Leave it to Beaver" to this day is still called Whitey in some circles. When my dark-haired mother had, shall we say, *difficulty* with a particular home hair coloring kit, my father took to calling her Big Red. My dad, in fact, is the brain surgeon behind the Sydney-Hood fiasco.

He's not alone. Lots of parents and siblings — including yours truly — lob nicknames at kids and sometimes, much to the kids' chagrin, they stick.

When my kid brother was little, he oftentimes had multiple layers of dirt and various, unknown substances stuck to his body that he didn't want to wash off for all the candy bars at Duke's Corner Convenience store. You literally could tell how long it had been since his last washing by examining the color and tone of the different layers on his arms, not unlike checking the circles inside the core of a tree to determine its age. I, the affectionate, loving sister, responded to his lack of hygiene by calling him Scum's Rash. Now he's a perfectly-coiffed attorney whose hair smells like apples and whose fingernails are neat and clean. Scum's Rash he ain't. So did the nasty nickname, which he still despises, drive him to become a man who frequented upscale Boston salons?

Which brings me to this question: When parents and siblings tag someone in the family with a nickname – like when I, in the tradition of my father, casually referred to my then-2-year-old son Casey as The Thug, and to my then-5-year-old daughter Abbey as The Diva — does it create a self-fulfilling prophesy?

Toddler Casey did, in all truthfulness, act like a thug. It was not unusual to find Casey, with a mischievous twinkle in his eye, picking up hard objects – like wiffle ball bats and plastic hockey sticks – and swinging them in a menacing fashion to fend off his twin siblings. Once, after Casey punched his sister for some unknown, muddled toddler reason, his father put him on "the thinking chair" in a time out and admonished him, "You don't punch people."

Casey contemplated this directive while displaying an appropriate, albeit phony, exaggerated, sad face. He then turned toward my husband Scott and offered, "How 'bout kick?"

"No Casey, no punching and no kicking," his father told him.

Another pregnant pause. "How 'bout with a hockey stick?"

"No!" Scott exclaimed. (He really did exclaim. I heard him.) "You don't hit anyone at all!"

Now, just for the record, we don't watch boxing or wrestling. The kids didn't see violent programming when they were very young. (They now watch teen superhero "Kim Possible" on TV, but back when they were 6 and under, they didn't). We don't beat our crumb crunchers. Scott and I don't go around hitting one another with hockey sticks, nor do our eldest children, which is why we were quite shocked when our 2-year-old expressed his desire to strike his sister with a hockey stick. So by referring to Casey as The Thug — while simultaneously trying to convince him that he shouldn't hit people with his hands, feet or other objects – was I inadvertently helping to turn him into a thug?

Then there was The Diva, otherwise known as Abbey. The term "diva" befit her in every conceivable definition of the word, even though she didn't have a movie star staff of hundreds at the ready to fetch her favorite bottled water and give her pedicures on demand. (Secretly — actually, not so secretly — she viewed Scott and me as her personal hand servants and was apt to request foot massages with baby lotion after baths). Putting aside her sparkly, Pepto-Bismol hued wardrobe, and ignoring the fact that our presence was frequently commanded to watch her dance in the family room after which we were instructed to uproariously applaud, there are other little character clues that all pointed to one, irrefutable conclusion: Diva (either that or they pointed to Professor Plum in the study with a candlestick, I'm never quite sure).

Ask Abbey to do anything other than play – like clear her plate from the table, make her bed or put her coloring material away – she'll dramatically drop to the floor and feign abject exhaustion. "I'm too tired," she'll say as she hyperventilates like she's just completed the Boston Marathon. When the situation escalates and she's given a choice of picking up her toys or spending some time in her room, she'd rather sit on her bed for hours than do any manual labor.

If I have any hopes of Abbey dropping her diva routine and Casey acting civilized, perhaps it'd be wise to ditch the nicknames. As for my brother, however, I still plan on referring to him as Scum's Rash when the mood strikes me, even if his hair now smells like fruit instead of feet.

Daddy, rock star

He got a Standing O.

For making soup.

The kids literally stood on our kitchen chairs and applauded their father for making supper. (It was good matzo ball soup, I'll give him that, though not good enough for standing-on-top-of-the-chairs applause. Sorry, sweetie.)

Of course my brood rarely if ever eats the food I make for them, never mind applauds. In fact, I made that exact same matzo ball soup recipe weeks after the Standing O incident. And they scoffed. "This isn't like Daddy's," they said.

No Standing O.

No nothin'. (The pity Standing O prompted by the guilty feeling father who secretly revels in his elite status with his kids doesn't count.)

Yeah, I know I'm lucky, so *very* lucky to have a husband who cooks, on the occasion of a blue moon because he works so late that he's rarely home for dinner preparation . . . but that's another fish to fry.

I know that I'm so very lucky to have a husband who takes care of the kids (when he's home), who will bathe them, read to them, play with them, take them to Tae Kwon Do class and who kindly rearranged his work schedule for a few years so that I could teach a college class once a week.

Here . . . I'm pushing back my chair . . . Now I'm standing up . . . and applauding. See Scott, I appreciate you. (And I'm not even smirking. Not really.)

But, wanna know a dirty little secret, my dearest husband? (Not that you have a crush on Sandra Bullock, not that kinda secret.)

I'm jealous of you.

True, my timing was lousy when I first confided this little nugget of intel to you, which was during the month of June one year, during That Month when one shall celebrate one's father, as well as one's spouse who acteth as the patriarch of one's household.

Everyone raise your hands and clap for Scott's great acts of fatherhood.

Again.

I'm not trying to sound bitter. It's just that, in our household (and outside of it as well), Scott gets a massive amount of praise for being the good dad that he is. He gets accolades from his children, who mark his arrival home each day (if they're still awake when he gets back from a hard day of providing for his family) as though he were Bono just popping into town for a spontaneous U2 concert. I call it the Rock Star Greeting. (Think: Lots of screeching, jumping up and down, arms thrashing and his name echoing off the garage walls as he heads toward the kitchen door to collect his hugs and kisses.)

He gets accolades from people "on the outside" as well. Say we're at a family gathering and Scott takes one of our three children to the bathroom. Inevitably, a relative or family friend will comment, "Scott's such a good father. So involved." I take a kid to the bathroom, and no one notices, except of course, when one of their sneakers has accidentally snagged an errant piece of soiled toilet paper which I didn't notice until we were in front of the gathered assembly of relatives who then tsk and point.

Say we're at a child's birthday party in the midst of an assort-ment of moms and dads in our peer group, and Scott joins in with the kids in a game while I hang back and chat. Maybe he cuts up a piece of pizza for our daughter. Helps our littlest blow his nose. "And you say he'll watch the kids while you take a yoga class on Saturdays?" one person will inevitably incredulously ask.

Here's my beef: I *expect* my husband to be a great father. I *expect* that he will take the kids to the bathroom, that he will watch his off-spring in order to give their mother a break, that he will make meals when he's home and will take the kids to various activities when our schedule permits. He's a great dad and I have high expectations for him.

But what I don't get is how the outside world seems to only notice "great dads," while seemingly ignoring what mommies do. It's expected, you see — whether or not a woman is an at-home mom or a mom who works part-time or full-time outside of the house — that the mom will mother, that the mom will take the kids to the bathroom, that the mom will take the kids to ballet class. What's not expected is that a dad will do the same thing, or any one of these things.

To me, that's akin to putting dads down, to de-legitimizing their importance. Dads are important. Not only do kids need and crave their presence and involvement, but the moms do too. Many of the moms with whom I'm friendly frequently lament when their husbands have to go away on business or work past the kids' bedtimes. Not only are these women sad for their kids who miss their fathers, but they're sad for themselves because the moms need a break from mommying. Dads need to be daddying.

(By the way, to you at-home dads out there, you're likely the beneficiary of the "ain't-he-an-amazingly-involved-dad" sentiment, and therefore are NOT exempt from this screed, except, perhaps for the way your kids react to your spouse when the spouse comes back from working outside the home all day. You likely don't get the rock star treatment.)

Societally, I guess I have to just deal with the fact that dads get a bum rap. They are hurt by (to cop a phrase from President Bush) "the soft bigotry of low expectations," the expectation that dads don't really interact with their kids and that when they do something, ANYTHING, that that's cause for celebration.

As for the kids, I suppose the clichés, "the grass is always greener" or "absence makes the heart grow fonder," will have to suffice for now. I'll have to stuff those adages down my own throat whenever I feel jealous about the kids applauding Scott's cooking and sneering at mine, or when they're almost jumping out of their skin upon learning that Daddy has come home from work early. I just want you dads to know that all of you can be great fathers. I expect nothing less.

To yell, perchance to scream

My brother Sean and I were sitting at our round kitchen table eating lunch one sticky summer afternoon in the middle of my childhood, when my father opened the freezer to survey its contents and figure out what he'd make for supper that night. This freezer was always unreasonably disorganized and packed to the gills. Tin foil mysteries, hard as granite. Cans upon cans of frozen juice concentrate. Half gallons of sherbet and Friendly's coffee ice cream. It was like an unexploded mine, waiting to combust and assault you with frozen shrapnel the moment you opened its door.

And in this particular instance, it was a whole frozen chicken that got my dad. On his bare foot. So enraged that the chicken injured him, my dad shouted a blue streak as he grabbed the dead bird and dropkicked it through the doorway to our back porch with the uninjured foot, thus injuring a second appendage. Sean and I laughed because our dad looked ridiculous clutching his newly injured foot, hopping around like a foiled Homer Simpson, angrily muttering to himself.

My family has never been great at anger management. For people in my bloodline, moments of frustration and anger tend to approach quickly, like a freak storm dropping out of the sky, and just as rapidly blowing over when reason envelops us like a high pressure zone. We then take a deep breath, make sport of our own idiotic reaction, and issue the proper apologies to any witnesses for the behavior.

Since having my own children, I haven't dropkicked frozen food, but I have carried on this dubious family tradition. I shout and struggle to keep my emotional responses in check when faced with juvenile mischief or, even worse, potentially dangerous juvenile actions.

Just a point of clarification here, and given the current parenting climate where parents are judged and criticized mercilessly (and mostly out of context) for *everything* they do, I feel compelled to qualify myself: When it comes to my kids, I don't name call. I don't belittle. I, as a voracious consumer of parenting literature, always criticize the behavior, not the child. My shouting is the result of my gut reactions to situations, and is then quickly followed by me verbally employing my powers of reason.

Here's a sample of what may cross my lips during a moment of anger at my kids:

"What are you doing?" (Upon finding children who'd written ALL over themselves and the kitchen table with permanent marker.)

"Stop that now!" (After finding one child threatening another sibling with a hammer.)

"Everyone come down to the play room RIGHT NOW!" (After finding that not only had the jungle border print been torn off the play room walls, but the shreds of wallpaper border – along with dirty diapers, empty candy wrappers and soiled paper napkins — had been tossed into the bulkhead door area off the play room leading to the back yard, rendering my house unknowingly unlocked for an indeterminate amount of time.)

Once my initial rush of hot anger passes, I usually pull the offending kid (or kids as the case may be) aside, squat down and talk calmly with the child. I give him or her a chance to tell me, in the child's own words, what occurred and, if possible, why.

Despite my family's history of hair-trigger emotional outbursts, I'm doing my best not to blow my cool whenever I feel the compulsion to do so. I'm perpetually working on not becoming one of those ineffective, yapping parents to whom the children don't listen, whose yelling is simply tuned out like the sound of an annoying airplane flying over head.

I'm hardly alone in this constant internal struggle to not blow my stack because, as we all know, children can be infuriating. A November 2003 study in the *Journal of Marriage and Family* of 991 American parents found that almost every parent surveyed had shouted at their child in the past year. It didn't matter how much money the parents made, what kind of educational or cultural background from hence they came: Everybody yelled. But in today's parenting climate, we all feel like we're fugitives because we shout at our children behind closed doors, fearing retribution, scolding and scorn from the parenting gurus and their faithful disciples just waiting to chastise us for exhibiting our humanity.

You know who I'm talking about. I'm referring to that cadre of parenting experts out there who like to tell you and me that everything we know and do about parenting is wrong. An entire industry has been built around the concept of making us feel guilty about being *human*, about having real reactions to real situations, about using our guts when it comes to making decisions for our children and for our lives. Within the parenting industry, there's a core group out there trying to make me and 99 percent of the other parents out there feel like monsters because we shout at our children. A co-author of the aforementioned 2003 studying on shouting – the researchers called any form of yelling, regardless of its severity, "psychological aggression"— told a reporter that parents should *never* yell or scream. (That's NEVER. That's insane.) "It's harmful and it is not necessary," he told the Scripps Howard News Service in February 2004.

The creator of a mini-empire – known as ScreamFree living – has a book out entitled, cleverly enough, ScreamFree Parenting. While he offers some genuinely useful tips on handling some children's emotional outbursts, the author leaves virtually no wiggle room for real life parents who are not always perfect. Instead, the author and the researcher judge the likes of me, trying to shame me by saying that when I blow off steam on occasion, I'm putting pressure on my kids to make them feel as though they must calm *me* down. What a horrible, reckless mother I must be.

Both the researcher and the ScreamFree guy mean well. They want what's best for all children, I'm sure. But what they're doing in the meantime is demonizing a wide swath of parents, making us feel like we're fatally flawed, like we have no idea how badly we hurt our children on a daily basis simply by having natural, human reactions. (That's why we need their studies, their books and their products. Guilt can equal profits and national television exposure. Cha-Ching. And anything positive they may have to offer — like helpful suggestions on how to maintain one's cool — is drowned in a sea of guilt and judgment.)

When I finished reading these studies and other finger wagging parenting screeds, I felt like a big fat failure. Then I picked up a copy of <u>It Takes a Parent</u>, a book by nationally-syndicated columnist Betsy Hart. I felt the storm clouds part and my confidence return. Her book emphasized that these parenting experts insist that anything short of perfect parenting is unacceptable. I felt better after reading her book because I know in my own heart that I love my children and try my best to do right by them. There are times when I do still shout, but I know that they will survive and still love me.

My name is Meredith. And I'm a shouter, and still a good mom.

Quizzing the parents

Right around New Year's, I begin to think that I should be reflecting on something profound, significant, like my life, my family, my career goals, what those numbers in the TV show "Lost" really mean. It's a fresh new year, I should start eating right, cut back on the caffeine, take more yoga classes, breathe deeply, be nicer to my spouse, read more, show more patience with the kids.

You know the drill.

But sometimes I get tired of simply focusing on me. (And the pressure to eat right gets old quickly.) So instead of trying to reinvent myself, or craft an improved version, I decided that I wanted to know insightful things about my friends. More specifically, I wanted to know how my parenting peers lead their lives and whether I'm the only one who finds herself in weird situations, faced with constant parenting quandaries.

That's where the little quiz below comes into play. If you use e-mail – and who amongst us doesn't? – you've undoubtedly received at least one, okay, 47, "friendship" quizzes over the years, asking various questions like: Do you like kisses or hugs? Coke or Pepsi? What's under your bed right now?

I've monkeyed around with the typical friendship quiz and created a quiz designed for parents of small children. I struggle with my parenting choices almost daily, so it's helpful for me to know if, compared to others, I'm off the mark. So, instead of being introspective on New Year's ('cause sometimes being introspective can get kinda ugly, and who needs such judgment?), feel free to plague your parent friends and family with these 20 questions:

With what fictional character do you think your parenting style most resembles?

With what fictional character do you think your spouse's parenting style most resembles?

Do you let your kids watch TV, and if so, what do you let them watch? (Come on. No one will dime you out to the American Academy of Pediatrics if you say, "Yes" to this question. And don't give me that "only PBS" line. No one will believe you.)

Do you let your kids decide what music or programming is played when you're riding inside the family vehicle?

Say you're cut off in traffic by an idiotic driver. Your children are in the vehicle with you. Bad parent that you are, you let slip an angry curse word or two. One of the kids starts repeating the curse over and over. You respond how?

Your kids are fighting. Again. (You're seriously contemplating buying a whistle and a black and white striped referee's shirt.) This time the lil' darlin's are tussling over who gets to hold a dime store trinket they got from a Happy Meal (Shhh! Don't tell anyone they ate fast food.). They are screaming and making pounding noises in the other room. Someone starts crying. You hear at least one set of feet furiously pounding down the hall to your location. Do you intervene? Lay down the law about no physical fighting? Tell them to work it out? Or say, "Don't come to me unless someone is bleeding?"

Your youngest child appears in your bedroom at an unreasonably early morning hour. Your spouse starts moving in the bed so you know that your betrothed is awake. Do you let the spouse know that you're awake so you can both decide who will deal with the early riser or do you pretend that you're still sleeping?

What do you do or say when your child talks back to you? (Think of the precocious angel saying something like, "I don't have to listen to you!")

How many consecutive days would you let your child wear a particularly loved piece of clothing?

You have to leave your house NOW for an appointment or school. You've already made sure your children were dressed, that their hair was combed and teeth brushed. You put out their coats and shoes before you left the room for a brief moment. You come back to the door only to find that your daughter has unexpectedly changed into mismatched pajamas that not only don't fit her, but are a blinding combination of purple, Kelly green, fuchsia and canary yellow. Plus her shoes are missing. Do you take her out as is? Demand that she put on the original outfit and just be late? Physically put the clothes back on her? Just give up and go back to bed?

Dinner is on the kitchen table. One kid complains that he doesn't want milk, he wants juice. Another says he doesn't want the wheat bread on the table, he wants a roll from the pantry. The third says she needs a spoon, not a fork. Your reaction?

One of your child's school friends is visiting your home. The small visitor is an ill-behaved little heathen. Do you rat him out when his parent arrives to pick the kid up, keep your mouth shut or just silently vow not to invite the kid back?

You're cooking a whole chicken. (Yes, you're cooking and not having take-out, but let's not dwell on that.) One of your young kids comes over and examines the fowl as you prepare it in the roasting pan. He asks, "Where's its head?" followed by further inquiries like, "Where's its pee-pee? Where did the chicken come from? Where did it go poop? Did it hurt when the chicken was killed?" You say what?

You learn that a boy at school shoved your son onto the ground during recess while a group of other boys laughed at him as he cried. Do you call the school? The bully's parents? Teach your son how to fight back? Egg the kid's house?

Do you let your kids pick out their own clothes at the store or do you just buy their clothes?

You're arranging a play date at your house for your preschooler with another child and that kid's mom. The day before their scheduled funfest the kid's mom says on the telephone, "Don't forget. Susy and I only eat organic food, whole wheat, no refined sugar. That kind of stuff." You eat healthily, but not that healthily. What do you serve for a snack? Do you go out and stock up on organic stuff?

Your mother-in-law takes your son out for the afternoon for some grandma-grandson time. When they come back, you see that she's taken him to get his hair cut. A buzz cut. Where he previously had adorable little curls. What do you do?

What things do you let your kids do that you don't tell your spouse about?

What's the worst, most nutritionally-vacuous meal you've ever served your kids?

Have you ever been "caught" by your offspring while, uh, "wrestling" with your spouse?

Now, go harass friends and family with this quiz, but be sure to answer the questions yourself as well. No fudging the answers. Be honest. No one's a perfect parent, not even around New Year's when we're all expected to be working on new and improved selves.

Wanting what you've got

I found it in my then-7-year-old daughter's Disney Princesses lunch box after school: A fully intact peanut butter and jelly sandwich sitting in its plastic container, untouched, exactly where I put it earlier that morning.

"Why didn't you eat your peanut butter and jelly sandwich?" I asked.

"I don't like peanut butter and jelly any more," Abbey replied with blasé disregard. Her declaration came only a day after she announced that fruit punch juice boxes were distasteful, adding it to the "Reject List" alongside mac-and-cheese, yogurt, all forms of sliced luncheon meats (except roast beef, but it's got to be within a day or two of being freshly sliced or else it's out), ground meat and most forms of chicken.

This was in the same week when her brother Jonah — who's a better eater than his twin sister — labeled cheese flavored Goldfish crackers yucky, although he likes Cheese Nips and cannot explain the difference in taste between the two snacks. Additionally, Jonah recently told us that the Splash juice we buy (a vegetable-fruit juice mix we've been getting because our youngest son Casey won't willingly eat vegetables) is no longer to his liking.

All I could envision, as I looked at the container with the full sandwich and the giant container of Goldfish I'd purchased to dole out for school lunches, was the children I'd seen on the news at the beginning of September that year. You know the ones. The ones in New Orleans. At the Superdome. The children with no food. No drink. No sanitary facilities. The ones who lost everything in the aftermath of Hurricane Katrina on the American south coast, while my family argued over whether anyone would eat from any of the dozen side dishes I put on the kitchen table in an attempt to offer food that everyone liked.

Putting PB&J and Goldfish on the "Reject List" was the last straw. Part of me wanted to scream at my kids (just don't tell the ScreamFree guy), to tell them that they were being roundly ungrateful about everything. That they had no idea how great they had it. That they were spoiled. As I steamed, I almost let pass through my lips the latest incarnation of the old adage, "Eat your supper! There are starving children in (fill in the name of the starving country du jour)." But this time, I wanted to insert "New Orleans" into this parental chestnut of wisdom.

As the events in the Gulf Coast unfolded in September 2005, I explained to my kids what was happening to our countrymen. I showed them newspaper photos, told them stories about the families – especially the kids — who lost their homes and were very, very hungry and thirsty. And though they understood the gravity of the situation, they made little to no connection in their growing minds between their disregard for their abundance of food and life choices, and others' dearth of options.

Then, a few weeks later, we entered the season of giving — giving thanks, giving gifts — and I worried that, in some way, I failed to drive home the point to my kids that they should feel grateful, all the while fielding suggestions for their Christmas lists to send to Santa. It's hard to teach them not just about charity (we, as a family, discuss and make donations) but about being thankful in general, particularly when they get more presents for their birthdays and major holidays (largely from their relatives) than I ever did, when they are in a near-constant state of celebration in their schools (celebrating birthdays, a preponderance of holidays, special events, etc.) and when the number of birthday parties they attend has exploded in recent years, parties which send them home with generous goodie bags. Don't even get me started on the fact that every kid gets a trophy for just signing up to play a sport every season . . .

While many suburban kids are surrounded by such worldly bounty, by a multitude of choices (choices for what I wanted for dinner, you kiddin' me?), by the latitude children are given by their parents (if I declared scores of food categories off-limits my parents would've laughed), I am left to struggle with how to send my kids a different message, one of realizing what they truly have been graced with in their lives.

As the images from Hurricane Katrina have faded from public attention – the span of our collective memory is alarmingly very brief – and we prepared to gather with our families around beautiful tables for Thanksgiving dinner and then commence our frenzied must-have gift buying (How many "must-have" toy purchases of previous years are in a plastic shambles at the bottom of toy chests?), I wanted to remind my kids that they should scale back their expectations of gross quantities of everything, from food choices to Christmas gifts.

Not that I was going to take away from the magic of this season, mind you (I'm a sucker for sentimentality), but I wanted them to understand that everything they have is not a given: Not every kid has two parents sitting at a dinner table filled with nutritious, savory choices; not every kid opens dozens of presents at Christmas and Hanukkah; not every kid has a collection of soccer trophies by age 7.

There's a line from a Sheryl Crow song that puts things in perspective whenever I'm lamenting the state of things in my life: "It's not having what you want; it's wanting what you've got." Even though I'm sure, from my kids' point of view, I may, at times, sound like a Scrooge, a wet blanket ruining their fun, I want them to want what they've got. And to give thanks.

Pah-ty all the time

I approach my mailbox with trepidation. My hesitation isn't borne out of fear that I'll pull out envelope after envelope containing demands for my money, although I'm occasionally guilty of too much, um, exuberant book buying, or instances where I just couldn't resist that oh-so-swank top. What I fear is not the credit card bills. It is The Invitations, these are what fill my heart (and wallet) with fear.

Not Invitations for me, you understand, not to cocktail parties at which I could wear that oh-so-swank top and reference some pithy, puffy novels I got from Amazon.com. The Invitations I dread are for my kids. To attend birthday parties. No, let me be frank: To 447 zillion birthday parties. I sometimes wonder if my elementary school-aged children have secretly developed a web site to solicit these invitations from random kids in the area. Invitations to Tae Kwon Do parties. Gymnastics parties. Swimming parties. Bratz parties. Roller skating parties. Laser tag parties. Craft parties. Ice cream parties. They assure me that they know *all* of these children *very well* from their classes at school, from the baseball team, or from down the street somewhere. And, even if my kids aren't particularly buddy-buddy with the guest of honor, they insist that they *have* to attend the party as *everyone* will be there. They couldn't possibly be left out. And if I say, "No," I'm just a bad, mean mother.

Maybe it's a sign of my age – which my youngest child reminds me must date back to the Paleolithic era – but I don't recall gargantuan birthday celebrations when I was a kid. I don't remember parents shelling out mucho bucks for parties, being pressured to invite an entire class of 25 kids (and that doesn't even include the parents who oftentimes stick around), being pressured to provide cool goodie bags (instead of using that cash to buy Mama that cool top). As I combed my brain for my birthday memories, I remembered going to McDonald's (Junk food!) with a handful of friends one time, Mom with a homemade cake in tow (she worked really hard on making cakes of the popular characters), some balloons and inexpensive gifts from friends. There were sleepovers with three to four girls, pizza and ice cream. One time, a handful of girls accompanied my mom and I to see a taping of a locally televised kids' show. My brother, whose birthday is in July, typically opted for sleeping in the back yard in a tent with a few friends (my dad slept in the screened-in entryway to the tent as the guard). On the day of our actual birthdays, our four grandparents would come over to our house for cake and ice cream and modest presents. Today, those types of simple celebrations seem to have fallen out of favor. Now if you don't invite dozens of people and their parents to your child's birthday celebrations, you're a rude cheapo and everyone will say bad things about you behind your back.

My suspicions about how badly children's birthday celebrations have been warped in recent years were confirmed by newspaper articles on the topic. First, a local newspaper ran a story about the increasing parental pressure to have gala birthday events for their children, regardless of age. The story said birthday parties that cost $500 are not uncommon. One mom was quoted saying, "You don't want to keep up with the Joneses, but when you're in school and you owe an invitation, it's hard. There's no in-between." Another mother recounted how one particular party's goodie bag contents were mocked as sub-par.

The New York Times later painted an even pricier picture of today's pediatric birthday parties quoting from parents across the country, saying many shell out $1,000 or more. One soiree featured in the piece was for a 6-year-old whose mom paid $350 for a tea party where the girl's dad rented a tux and served the 18 attendees. A mom from an affluent town said of children's birthday parties, "It's almost competitive at this point."

We "owe" invitations. It's a competition. Are these birthday parties truly about celebrating the fact that you're grateful that your child was born, or are they about impressing the other parents? I had a great time as a kid going to small gatherings. There wasn't a lot of pressure to have loads of FUN!FUN!FUN! I didn't come home every other weekend with multiple, jam-packed goodie bags and fistfuls of candy from another piñata.

In fact, my grade-schoolers celebrate so many things these days – from marking birthdays of nearly all their classmates IN school, to marking every holiday, never mind special days for a wide variety of reasons – that my daughter came home from kindergarten one day and complained about having to commemorate yet another birthday in class. "It was bor-ing," she said.

That's what it has come to: We've taken a cherished childhood moment – the birthday party – and made it boring with our excess. We parents mean well, trying not to exclude anyone, trying to make everyone feel good. But we're vaporizing the truly special nature of celebration, cheapening birthdays if we celebrate 27 of them in grand style annually. Nothing will be special if *everything* is special.

When I have my kids' birthday parties in the summer (at least those dreadful summer gestations came in handy for something, even if it's just winnowed-down guest lists), I try to plan smaller scale gatherings, and don't have to worry about running into parents of kids who didn't get an invite in the school hallways. I don't go crazy with goodie bags or decorations. And I don't allow the kids to invite every single kid from their class. And I think they're relieved by that. It's my kids' birthdays and I'll be a party pooper if I want to.

School car line rage

Under normal circumstances, they'd seem like your garden variety, suburban American parents. Some are in jeans. Some are in work attire. They're in crumb-filled vehicles that likely have several packs of semi-melted or broken crayons (the kind you get from family-friendly restaurants) knocking around on the floor or wedged between the seats.

If you meet these people in a coffee shop, you'd probably have a pleasant conversation. Run into them at a cocktail party, and you could likely muse over the mysteries of ABC's "Lost" or the weird turns of "Desperate Housewives" over a bottle of beer or a Cosmopolitan in a cool-looking glass. But run into them in the school drop-off or pick-up lanes and you'd better don your flak jacket and flight goggles. It's gonna be a bumpy ride.

Welcome to the world of School Car Line Rage.

Parents – whether they're running late or not (everyone always seems late) – sometimes fall prey to the same sort of temporary insanity that overcomes normally rational people when they're stuck in rush hour traffic. One driver lets his kids off in the middle of the school drop off area, blocking all the other cars from leaving or advancing the queue; parents in the line of cars behind him and the building principal watching from inside her office go crazy. Drivers cut long lines of waiting vehicles or flout the car line system; other parents and the principal go crazy. School officials don't uniformly enforce the "system;" parents go crazy.

And go crazy in front of the kids.

After a bizarre encounter at my kids' school between two moms one winter, I decided to find out if this particular parental strain of road rage was something unique to my suburb, or more universal.

I plugged words like, "school, traffic, pick-up" into the Google search engine on the internet. Hits, oh the hits. Apparently what one woman dubbed "the beast that is the elementary school car line" is a plague to people nationwide, from Tennessee to Thousand Oaks, California, from Milton, Massachusetts to Anchorage, Alaska. I discovered school web sites plastered with car line policies, regulations and admonishments to parents to follow the rules.

I found an article about a mom in Australia who was arrested and taken into custody – while her 3-year-old was left alone in the backseat of the car – because she double-parked in front of the school in order to drop off two kids and then decided to argue with the police about it.

Then I happened upon a Chicago area mom's blog, "One Good Thing" (buggydoo.blogspot.com) where she detailed a horror of an experience when she picked up her 6-year-old from school for the first time. Leigh Anne, who normally walks her child to school, wrote that after she inadvertently failed to follow the car line rules — she says she was only following the lead of other parents — her school principal sent a policeman to her home to reprimand her.

"I get the feeling like I unwittingly blundered into a battle zone," blogger Leigh Anne wrote in an e-mail to me. ". . . I found it [the car line] more stressful than rush hour traffic, possibly because there are a thousand kids with questionable judgment skills rushing toward moving cars, and the school is the center of the circle with cars zooming in, then back out from all 360 degrees around it, and you just want to get out of there before you run over somebody and give the cops an actual, valid reason to come to your home during dinner time and freak out your kids."

My own incident of car line rage didn't reach to the level of local law enforcement, but it could have. During one bone-chilling afternoon, I went to pick up my twin first graders from school and sat in my running minivan, per the written directions of the school principal to all parents. I was in a long line of cars, all pulled over to the right next to the curb, waiting for a parking spot to become available. When I finally reached the front of the line, a mom in a large, white SUV came roaring past everyone on the left and pulled into an open spot just as it was being vacated by another parent.

This wasn't like what the Chicago mom experienced, where there was an honest mistake in following the car line procedure. This was a "To hell with you people, I'm more important!" line cutting.

Suddenly in the grips of what felt like irrational rage, I felt the urge to do something, anything, like yell at her, or at least give her the best nasty look I could muster. But my preschooler was in the car with me.

After I finally got a parking spot – about 30 seconds later – a different woman stopped me before I entered the school building. "Did you see that? Did you see that woman cut that line of people and just pull into that spot?" she asked, full of the heated, righteous indignation that I felt.

"Yeah," I said nodding. "I was next in line. I couldn't believe it."

"Well," said the mom, who I noticed had two wide-eyed children by her side, "I'm going to wait for her and give her a piece of my mind."

I didn't stick around to see what happened next, even though I admired the Vigilante Mom who was going to verbally rip the Cutting Mom a new one.

I'll be seeing these parents for the next dozen-plus years as my three kids make their way through the school system, I thought. Do I want to start a public argument with one of them now? Over a parking spot?

Many years ago, when I commuted through hellish Boston traffic to work, a good friend of mine bought me a bell on a thick ribbon to hang in my car. "It's a road rage bell," she told me. "Whenever you get ticked off, ring it and you'll feel better." So fellow slayers of the "beast" that is the school car line, when ya hear the bell ring, maybe somewhere an angel in a school drop off lane has gotten her wings, or at least acquired some patience.

Acknowledgments

This book has been years in the making. From the initial blossom of an idea for each column, through the research, the conversations and the writing, a great many people helped me along the way:

First, thanks to Erica Houskeeper, one of my first editors at *Parents & Kids*, with whom I discussed column ideas and who always handled the finished products with care.

Heather Kempskie, the current *Parents & Kids* editor, was likewise very gentle with my work, and for that, I thank her.

I'd like to thank Jana Christy, the illustrator who crafted amazingly, spot-on images to accompany my columns for so many years at *Parents & Kids*, was generous enough to give me permission to re-print her images in this book.

I also appreciated that the BabyZone.com editors agreed to let me re-publish many of the essays contained in this book.

While working on many of these pieces, I tapped my personal wealth of resources – fellow mothers and fathers – for advice, anecdotes and guidance. Thanks to all of those who helped point me in the right direction when I was trying to create essays capturing modern parenting, most especially my former college roommate, Gayle Long Carvalho, who helped me proof the manuscript and always gave me a reality check (and shoulder on which to cry) when I needed one.

Additionally, I want to extend my appreciation to members of my family – Mom, Dad, my brother Sean, my in-laws, my sisters- and brothers-in-law – for allowing me to write about all of your lives. And, while I'm on the subject of family, I pray that my three children will not read this book aloud in 10-15 years — while in their therapist's office — as evidence of how and why their mother has always been insane. Everything contained in these pages about my kids was written with love, and sometimes angst. Also, thanks to my husband Scott who allowed me to lift the veil of privacy on our everyday experiences and write about them for public consumption. That takes courage, my friend.

And, lastly, I want to thank Nancy Cleary for agreeing to publish *A Suburban Mom* and for being such a patient, patient woman with me.

Appendix

Complete list of previously published articles.

A Suburban Mom: Notes from the Asylum (*Parents & Kids*)

Hide and seek (posted on BabyZone.com as, "Peek-a-Boo! Where'd Mommy Go?")

My kid's better than your kid (posted on BabyZone.com as, "My Baby's Better Than Your Baby.")

Buh-bye (posted on BabyZone.com as, "Bye-Bye, Mama!")

Don't tell Daddy (posted on BabyZone.com as, "Shhh! Don't Tell Daddy…")

Play it again Sam (*Parents & Kids*)

Kid rock (*Parents & Kids*)

Passing down the pain (*Parents & Kids*)

Passing down the pain: Revisited (*Parents & Kids*)

Parental sex lives: An oxymoron? *Parents & Kids*)

Bowing to the Super Moms (Original)

Desperate for real desperation (posted on BabyZone.com under the same title)

Hot mommies (posted on BabyZone.com as, "Is It Hip to be Hot?")

Family drama (*Parents & Kids*)

Selling my feminist soul for Legos? (*Parents & Kids*)

Pregnancy, Birth & Other Bloody Things

Pregnancy jail (posted on BabyZone.com as, "Pregnant . . . and Grounded")

The stork patrol (posted on BabyZone.com under the same title)

Diapering Barney (Original)

Barney, reconsidered (posted on BabyZone.com as, "Barney: A Love-Hate Relationship")

Princess no more: No sympathy the second time around (posted on

BabyZone.com under same title)

To peek or not to peek? (posted on BabyZone.com under same title)

Great expectations (*Parents & Kids*, reprinted on BabyZone.com under, "Great expectations: Meredith's birth story")

Mother's Day for those who need it (*Parents & Kids*)

Sleeping thru the night? Yeah right! (*Parents & Kids*)

Newborn brain (*Parents & Kids*)

The maternity ward meets the Vegas strip (*Parents & Kids*)

Mum's the word (*Parents & Kids*, reprinted on BabyZone.com under the same title)

Mommy bodies (*Parents & Kids*)

Uh-oh (posted on BabyZone.com as, "Uh-oh!")

The boy next door (posted on BabyZone.com under same title)

Prison break (posted on BabyZone.com as, "From Crib to Bed: Taking the Plunge . . . Literally!")

The girlie-girl (*Parents & Kids*)

Baby no more (*Parents & Kids*)

Candy Land ain't so sweet (*Parents & Kids*)

Timeout travails (*Parents & Kids*, reprinted on BabyZone.com under the same title)

Twinkle toes (*Parents & Kids*)

Safe at first (*Parents & Kids*)

Tooth dismay (Original)

Whaddup Tooth Fairy? (*Parents & Kids*)

Fashion weak (*Parents & Kids*)

Dirty lemonade (*Parents & Kids*)

Going to the dark side (*Parents & Kids*)

The flood (*Parents & Kids*)

Not your mother's summer reading list (*Parents & Kids*)

Zone defense (posted on BabyZone.com as, "The Joys of Baby-Proofing")

Toy revenge (posted on BabyZone.com under the same title)

Don't play with your food (posted on BabyZone.com as, "Contradictions")

Pocket full of rye (posted on BabyZone.com as, "A Pocket Full of Rye")

A million pieces (*Parents & Kids*)

Adventures on the potty seat (posted on BabyZone.com under the same title)

Adventures on the potty seat: Part II (*Parents & Kids*)

Home sweet home (posted on BabyZone.com as, "Can You Keep a Clean House with Twin Toddlers?")

Handmade Halloween? Hah! (*Parents & Kids*, reprinted on BabyZone.com as, "Homemade Halloween: It's a Trick")

Holiday hangover (posted on BabyZone.com as, "After the Rush")

Lessons from "A Christmas Story" (*Parents & Kids*)

Poison Control's got my number (*Parents & Kids*, reprinted on BabyZone.com under the same title)

Homespun politics (*Parents & Kids*)

New beginnings (*Parents & Kids*)

Of spilled milk and talking wallpaper (FamilyManOnline.com)

Little girl blue (posted on BabyZone.com as, "Little Girl Blues")

Say cheese (posted on BabyZone.com as, "Say CHEESE . . . Please?!")

I need a vacation (posted on BabyZone.com as, "Vacationing With Kids: A Contradiction in Terms")

The contents of my fridge (*Parents & Kids*)

Multiple madness (*Parents & Kids*)

Drive-thrus rock (*Parents & Kids*)

The scrapbooking cult (*Parents & Kids*)

Celebrating St. Patrick's Day with All-American mutts (*Parents & Kids*)

Cautionary tale (*Parents & Kids*)

Forgive us our parental sins (posted on BabyZone.com under the same title)

What's in a nickname? (*Parents & Kids*, reprinted on BabyZone.com under the same title)

Daddy, rock star (*Parents & Kids*)

To yell, perchance to scream (*Parents & Kids*)

Quizzing the parents (*Parents & Kids*)

Wanting what you've got (*Parents & Kids*)

Pah-ty all the time (Original)

School car line rage (*Parents & Kids*)